Women and *Crack*-Cocaine

Macmillan Criminal Justice Series

Women and *Crack*-Cocaine

James A. Inciardi
Dorothy Lockwood
Anne E. Pottieger
UNIVERSITY OF DELAWARE

MACMILLAN PUBLISHING COMPANY
New York

MAXWELL MACMILLAN CANADA
Toronto

Editor: Christine Cardone
Production Supervisor: Sharon Lee
Production Manager: Roger Vergnes
Text Designer: Debra Fargo
Cover Designer: Curtis Tow
Cover Photo: The Stock Market

This book was set in Trump Mediaeval by Digitype, Inc. and was printed and bound by Book Press. The cover was printed by New England Book Components.

This text contains explicit material from actual interviews and research the authors conducted in crack houses in the United States.

Macmillan Publishing Company
866 Third Avenue, New York, New York 10022

Macmillan Publishing Company is part of
the Maxwell Communication Group of Companies.

Maxwell Macmillan Canada, Inc.
1200 Eglinton Avenue East
Suite 200
Don Mills, Ontario M3C 3N1

Library of Congress Cataloging-in-Publication Data

Inciardi, James A.
    Women and crack-cocaine / James A. Inciardi, Dorothy Lockwood, Anne E. Pottieger.
        p.   cm.
    Includes indexes.
    ISBN 0-02-359440-3
    1. Women — United States — Drug use.   2. Crack (Drug) — United States.   3. Cocaine habit — United States.   I. Lockwood, Dorothy.
II. Pottieger, Anne E.   III. Title.
HV5824.W6I53   1993
362.29'82'082 — dc20   92-31430
                                                                 CIP

Printing: 2 3 4 5 6 7   Year: 3 4 5 6 7 8 9

Dedication

To the memory of Brian R. Russe, who contributed much to the study of the Miami drug scene.

Acknowledgment

This research was supported, in part, by HHS Grant Nos. 1-RO1-DAO1827, 1-RO1-DAO-4862, and Contract No. 271888248, all from the National Institute on Drug Abuse.

Preface

Crack-cocaine was first discovered by the media during the closing weeks of 1985, and by the American people during the press and television reporting frenzy on the "the plague among us" and "the drug epidemic of our time" during the spring and summer of the following year. At that time, few observers could have anticipated, or even imagined, the havoc, degradation, and despair that the drug was to bequeath to many of its most chronic users. True, some of the early reports did mention that there were crack addicts who were selling "everything from their belongings to their bodies" to get a few more "hits" of this highly addictive form of cocaine base. But that was about all. Much of the coverage targeted other things — the inner-city drug dealers who manufactured and sold crack and purchased solid gold chains with the profits; the ghetto street kids who looked up to the success of the dealers and worked for pennies on the fringes of the crack economy; the open-air street markets where crack was hawked to passers-by in vehicles and on foot; the shootings and street violence among rival drug gangs that terrorized so many inner-city residents and neighborhoods; and eventually, the problems of the thousands of premature "crack babies" that were born to drug-addicted mothers.

Perhaps these topics were felt to be more newsworthy or more "polite" and "appropriate" subject matter for in-depth television coverage. For after all, the features, traits, and eccentricities of crack-house sex are certainly not "proper" material for *The CBS Evening News with Dan Rather*. But the media were not to be blamed. They were describing what they were seeing, what was being brought to their attention. Several of the more adventurous journalists were visiting crack houses in New York City, Los Angeles, and Miami. But they never stayed very long. That's the nature of the journalist's trade — get the facts and photos and put them together for the 4 P.M. deadline or the 6 o'clock broadcast. But again, the media can't be blamed. Crack houses are not particularly nice places to hang around. Most are dirty, dangerous, and depressing. Their tenants and customers are understandably suspicious and paranoid when it comes to strangers. Thus, even if a network television correspondent and camera crew were to visit a New York or Miami crack house, it is doubtful they would see much of what constitutes "business as usual." The result of all of these circumstances and contingencies is that the public at large, and even many people in the drug field, have seen only selected aspects of the crack epidemic. Generally hidden is the human suffering associated with crack addiction — among the users and their families, and particularly among crack-dependent women. Given this gap in the reporting and literature, this book attempts to fill in a few of the missing parts. A good bit of the material presented is verbatim quotes from more than four thousand pages of transcribed interviews with crack-addicted women. Much of it is unsettling and depressing, for it graphically describes the sexual activities, sexual exploitation, and sexual violence that many crack-dependent women encounter. If the narrative of the book seems slightly disjointed at times, it is because the material was drawn from three separate studies, and because there are many gaps that remain. There are certain limitations to doing research in crack houses, all of which can impact on the quality and depth of the information collected.* Yet despite the obstacles and complications, the message of the book should be clear: that crack-dependent women have likely suffered the most from this most recent of "drug epidemics," and that both social policies and treatment options generally fail to address the needs of this casualty population.

We would like to thank the following reviewers for their comments and suggestions: Phyllis D. Coontz, University of Pittsburgh; Karen McElrath, University of Miami; Sheila Murphy, University of California, San Francisco; and Jocelyn M. Pollock-Byrne, University of Houston. We would also like to thank Christine Cardone, senior editor at Macmillan, for her support during this project. Thanks are also due to Sharon Lee, production supervisor, John Sollami, managing editor, and Roger Vergnes, production manager.

---

*A discussion of the methods, dangers, and ethics of doing research in crack houses appears in Appendix A.

Contents

CHAPTER 1

Crack: The Discovery and Rediscovery of Rock Cocaine

"Cocaine is very scarce on the illicit drug market."
—*Harry J. Anslinger,*
U.S. Commissioner of Narcotics, 1953[1]

If anything has been learned from the history of drug use in America it is that "drug problems" are ever-shifting and changing phenomena. There are fads and fashions, rages and crazes, and alternative trends in drugs of choice and patterns of use. And if the media are to be believed, now and then there is even a "drug epidemic" or two.

Back in the early 1950s, as the United States reveled in its post–World War II optimism and economic prosperity, Americans began noticing that they had an emerging drug problem on their hands—in New York, Washington, D.C., Los Angeles, and elsewhere. Long since forgotten were the difficulties the nation had experienced during the 1880s and 1890s with the opium, morphine, and cocaine-based home remedies and patent medicines that were being sold over the counter in pharmacies, grocery stores, and through the mails. Overlooked, as well, was the notoriety in the early decades of the twentieth century given to apparently burgeoning populations of pickpockets, burglars, professional thieves, and other criminal addicts whose drugs of choice included heroin and morphine. Too, there were the "reefer madness" years of the 1930s when Harry J. Anslinger of the Federal Bureau of Narcotics crusaded against the dreaded marijuana—the evil weed of the fields, the seed of madness, the assassin of youth.[2]

"Drug abuse" in the 1950s meant heroin addiction in the American ghetto, primarily among minority youth. In *The Road to H,* a classic study of heroin use among New York City youth during the 1950s, New York University psychologist Isidor Chein described the addict as a casualty of

1

the daily struggle of the slum, and heroin as a means of escaping from it.[3] Sociologists Richard A. Cloward and Lloyd E. Ohlin viewed the matter somewhat differently. Addicts were "double failures"—ghetto youths who were unable to succeed in either gang subcultures or legitimate society. Thus, they embraced drugs as a way of finding a place for themselves in society.[4] And there were other explanations. Interestingly, cocaine was only a small part of the 1950s drug scene, and in the literature of the time it was only rarely mentioned. In 1956, for example, New York City Department of Health psychiatrist Marie E. Nyswander remarked in her pioneering work *The Drug Addict as a Patient*:

> With cocaine there seems to be scant evidence of any pharmacological dependence, but the unquestioned psychological dependence produces the same purposive behavior common to addicts of other narcotics: they will go to any lengths to obtain it. Cocaine users eagerly solicit the job of cleaning physicians' offices on the chance of picking up some applicators that have been used for cocaine. *Relatively unpopular in the addict world, cocaine is not a brisk black market item.*[5]

In retrospect, the reader may consider a few of Dr. Nyswander's comments a bit odd. First, although cocaine is a stimulant, it was often referred to as a narcotic years ago (as was marijuana). Second, the use of cocaine as local anesthetic in physicians' offices was not common. And third, although cocaine was *not* particularly popular in the inner-city heroin culture,* it *was* very much a part of the American jazz scene. In fact, cocaine, heroin, and addiction were characteristic features of the jazz world, and had been so for decades. "Chicago style" saxophonist Milton "Mezz" Mezzrow, who played on and off with such well-known jazz artists as Louis Armstrong, Eddie Condon, Ben Pollack, and Bud Freeman during much of the 1930s and 1940s, repeatedly mentioned in his *Really the Blues* how "jive" (music) and "jive" (heroin and cocaine) seemed to be so hopelessly woven into life on the bandstand.[6] In her autobiography *High Times Hard Times*, Anita O'Day, a jazz vocalist who was featured with the Gene Krupa, Benny Goodman, and other swing bands during the 1940s and 1950s described how so many musicians and singers, including herself, spent much of their careers "stoned" on cocaine, heroin, and speed.[7] And these were only a few from the jazz subculture caught up in drugs.[8]

Things seemed to change again in the 1960s. Researchers and clinicians in the drug field began observing that heroin users had multiple addictions, and that a black market in prescription amphetamines and barbiturates was flourishing. Then two Harvard University psychologists, Timothy Leary and Richard Alpert, began exploring the effects of a color-

---

*Cocaine was present in the inner-city heroin culture of the fifties as *speedball*, a cocaine/heroin mixture that is injected and extends the heroin "high."

less, odorless, and tasteless compound called *d-lysergic acid diethalamide,* or LSD.[9] They used it themselves, and experimented with the drug on colleagues, writers, artists, members of the clergy, and volunteer prisoners. They exhorted everyone — students, parents, politicians — to use the new consciousness-expanding "psychedelic" drug. Leary and Alpert were dismissed from Harvard in 1963, but by then LSD had a reputation. Taking a "trip" had come to suggest status on many college campuses.[10] LSD had become a household word. Even the country's recluses and others far removed from the psychedelic revolution understood what was meant by "tripping" and "blowing one's mind."

Later in the decade there was a new twist. In San Francisco's Haight-Ashbury district many young people had been living communally, dressing in flamboyant clothes, and generally having a good time of it. Living in relative poverty and chaos, sharing all they had with one another, and delving into new ways of defining themselves, they experimented with LSD, DMT, marijuana, and a host of other drugs. When these young "hippies" were finally discovered by the media and the rest of the country in 1967, the coverage was quizzically positive. Years later, social historian Ronald Fraser recalled:

> Hippies were good copy. They were young and attractive, colorful and outrageous. Magazines and television sent the images of pretty, long-haired teenagers speeding across the country. Drawn by such advertisements, thousands of runaway kids, curious tourists, and irresponsible thrill-seekers descended upon the Haight in the summer of 1967. The fragile hip community collapsed under the weight. But the culture it had modeled spread rapidly. Something vital had been touched in the younger generation. Long-haired hippies began appearing everywhere.[11]

In time, LSD, peyote, magic mushrooms, "tripping," and readings from *The Tibetan Book of the Dead*[12] had become hallmarks of the hippie youth culture. Curiously, however, with all of the drugs that were associated with the hippie counterculture of the 1960s, cocaine never seemed to be a part of it. Even in Haight-Ashbury where it all started, cocaine use was not particularly well known.[13] Moreover, in the task force reports of Lyndon B. Johnson's President's Commission on Law Enforcement and Administration of Justice, cocaine was excluded from the list of major drugs of abuse.[14] On the other hand, heroin in the ghetto, marijuana among the middle class, and drug-related crime were discussed in terms of new "epidemics" that needed to be addressed by the full resources of the federal government.

The Beginnings of the Cocaine Era

> Cocaine, though available for many years, is the new "in" drug, and the various new implements and rituals associated with the use of

cocaine have recently become subject to extensive commercial exploitation.
— *President's Domestic Council Drug Abuse Task Force, 1975*

At the beginning of the 1970s, in the midst of President Richard M. Nixon's "war on heroin" and at a time when the abuse of amphetamines and amphetamine-like drugs was widespread, the National Commission on Marihuana and Drug Abuse offered the following warning in its report to Congress:

> Laboratory experiments with animals have demonstrated beyond dispute that cocaine is the most powerful reinforcer of all psychoactive substances. . . . Little social cost has actually been verified in this country. . . . Although increasing, the incidence of use and the prevalence of chronic use remain relatively low. Prudent policy planning demands that the nature of cocaine-using behavior be kept under close scrutiny.[15]

The Commission was aware that its data — based on evidence drawn primarily from small-scale surveys and reports from treatment centers were limited, and that likely there were many "street" users of cocaine that it had failed to count. In the heroin culture, cocaine was still a luxury, and used almost exclusively as speedball. But importantly, systematic studies were beginning to find that speedballing had become quite common.[16] What most observers of the drug scene were unaware of, however, was the emergence of a West Coast cocaine "freebase" culture at the beginning of the 1970s.

Since the sniffing or "snorting" of cocaine was never the most efficient method of administering the drug, ardent users began looking for other ways. Smoking seemed like the logical alternative, but cocaine hydrochloride — that is, *powder*-cocaine, the typical form of "street cocaine" — has a high melting point and, thus, cannot be efficiently smoked. As a result, users sought to change the cocaine *salt* form to a *base* form, and they stumbled upon *freebase*. Freebase cocaine is a different chemical product from cocaine itself. In the process of preparing freebase, street cocaine — which is usually in the form of a hydrochloride salt — is treated with a liquid base (such as buffered ammonia) to remove the hydrochloric acid. The free cocaine (cocaine in the *base* state, *free* of the hydrochloride acid, and hence the name "freebase") is then dissolved in a solvent such as ether, from which the purified cocaine is crystallized. These crystals, having a lower melting point, are then crushed and smoked in a special heated glass pipe.

Smoking freebase cocaine provided a quicker and more potent "rush" (the intense flood of pleasure that is felt soon after drug intake), and a far more powerful "high" (feeling of euphoria) than regular cocaine. But freebasing tended to remain unnoticed. Even Lester Grinspoon and James B. Bakalar's comprehensive work *Cocaine: A Drug and Its Social Evolu-*

tion, published in 1976, made no mention of it.[17] However, as early as 1973, a few researchers in Miami had begun to come across the phenomenon. In the field notes of one observer it was reported:

> I came across something new today. On Tigertale Avenue at the edge of Coconut Grove, there's a garage that a few folk from the local "got any spare change" set use for tripping. Most of what they do is grass, LSD, PCP, and sometimes they sniff cocaine. This afternoon there was this couple smoking cocaine. They called it "base." I'll have to ask the Old Man about it.[18]

And several days later:

> I was back in the Tigertale garage this afternoon. The Old Man said he had heard of smoking coke, but didn't know much about it — only that it could be dangerous. I understand now what he meant. I got there early enough to watch them make their "base." They used ether and ammonia to make cocaine crystals. A couple of times I thought they were going to blow us all up.
>
> First they put a gram of cocaine into a test tube and mixed it with a little water (I don't know if the H_2O was hot or cold). Then they corked the test tube and shook it, until the cocaine was dissolved. The next thing they did was to add about 5 drops of ammonia to the test tube to separate the "hydrochloride" from the cocaine. With a different eye dropper (I guess they needed a clean one), they added a few drops of ether. It seemed to pick up the cocaine from the solution, because two layers formed, one at the bottom of the tube with the hydrochloride and whatever the cocaine was cut with. The top layer was the ether and cocaine base. With the eyedropper, they removed the top layer and put it on a dish to evaporate.
>
> The ether evaporated quickly, after about five minutes or so, and what was left was crystals of cocaine base. What was so dangerous about it all was that all while they were doing all this, mixing it up and fooling with ether, they were also lighting matches and smoking an earlier batch of base they had made, and they were stoned out of their heads. I could just see the matches igniting the ether and blowing us all to Miami Beach.
>
> What they did with the crystals was to crush them and put them in a glass pipe for smoking. I noticed that they got "high" a lot faster, but the high didn't last as long as when they snorted. *They* didn't feel that "basing" — as they called it — was all that dangerous. But they did say that it was expensive, that they used a lot at each smoking session.[19]

Although cocaine smoking had finally made its way into the literature in 1977,[20] it was not until 1980 that cocaine freebasing finally reached a national audience, epitomized by the near-death of comedian-actor Richard Pryor, from a small explosion presumably the result of freebasing.[21] By then, furthermore, cocaine had emerged as a major drug of abuse, and the violent struggles for control of growing markets in New York, Miami, and other cities were making national headlines.[22]

The Discovery of *Crack*-Cocaine

> It was just *garbage base*, just real garbage, you know, that rude garbage
> freebase cocaine you sometimes see on the street these days.
> —*Digger Dan, an early San Francisco "freebase man," 1974*

Among the innovations of the psychedelic era of the late 1960s were
the underground guides to illegal drug use. One of the first was Mary Jane
Superweed's *Marijuana Consumer's and Dealer's Guide* in 1968.[23] Sold
for $2 at local "head shops,"* this 16-page pamphlet provided instruc-
tions on how to extract hallucinogenic amides from morning glory seeds,
producing $2,000 worth of hashish from $85 worth of marijuana, and
converting inferior grade pot into connoisseur-quality "Super-Grass."
Other pamphlets offered tips on cannabis (marijuana) cultivation, preparing DMT (dimethyltryptamine, an LSD-like hallucinogen) at home, and
grafting marijuana to other plants.†

One of the early-1970s contributions to the genre was *The Gourmet
Cookbook*, a lengthy clothbound publication that seemed to touch upon
every aspect of cocaine—its history and legends, consumption and sale,
refinement and analysis, and effects and legal ramifications.[24] Curiously,
the *Cookbook* made passing mention of a rock-like variety of cocaine. Not
to be confused with "rock" cocaine or "Bolivian rock"—cocaine hydrochloride products for intranasal snorting—what the *Cookbook* was referencing was cocaine reconstituted into the base state in a rock form. That
was 1972, and few took notice of it.

In David Lee's *Cocaine Handbook*, published in 1981, the discussion
of what appeared to be the same commodity was a bit more explicit. In
detailing the freebase process, Lee offered the following brief footnote:

> A less pure base is sometimes made by dissolving the cocaine hydro-
> chloride in water, making the solution alkaline (sodium bicarbonate is
> the alkali most often used), and heating the mixture until all the water
> has evaporated. The waxy base which is produced contains the added
> alkali and the same adulterants and impurities as did the original
> cocaine.[25]

---

*Another innovation of the 1960s, the "head shop" sold the various accessories of the drug
and hippie cultures, including water pipes, cigarette papers, holders and clips for marijuana
cigarettes, incense, and psychedelic posters to name but a few. By the close of the 1970s the
shops had become quite widespread, selling any variety of equipment used for the cultivation of marijuana and the consumption of numerous drugs. State laws have since closed
most of these operations. See Kerry Murphy Healey, "Controlling Drug Paraphernalia," in
James A. Inciardi (ed.), *Handbook of Drug Control in the United States* (Westport, CT:
Greenwood Press, 1990), pp. 317–326.

†In addition to the Mary Jane Superweed series of pamphlets, there was the equally popular
Supermother's *Cooking With Grass*, a collection of recipes for marijuana-containing
brownies, soups, meatballs, muffins, and other "delicacies."

That was 1981. Few people took notice of the remark, but what both the *Gourmet Cokebook* and the *Cocaine Handbook* had been talking about was what a few years later became known as *crack*-cocaine. And it was dubbed "crack" in the mid-1980s because of the crackling sound that the sodium bicarbonate (baking soda) makes as it burns during the smoking process. Later commentaries offered explanations of why the "crack" of the early 1970s never caught on. In 1988, a former resident of Haight-Ashbury living in Miami recalled that it had been available for only a short period of time before it was discarded by freebase-cocaine aficionados as an inferior product:*

> In the Haight of the early seventies they called it "garbage freebase" because of all the impurities it contained. It was also considered in bad taste to offer that kind of crap. You never saw any of the real coke *diggers* doing garbage.†

The Rediscovery of Crack

Crack Kills!

—Miami graffiti, 1985

Although the "diggers" may have looked down on what later became known as "crack," cocaine users in many inner-city areas did not. It would appear that the drug arrived in the cocaine-infested neighborhoods of Los Angeles, Miami, and New York between 1981 and 1983.[26] The drug became immediately popular for a variety of reasons. *First*, it could be smoked rather than snorted. When cocaine is smoked, it is more rapidly absorbed by the body, crossing the blood–brain barrier within six seconds. Hence, an almost instantaneous "high." *Second*, it was cheap. While a gram of cocaine for snorting may cost $60 or more depending on its purity, the same gram can be transformed into anywhere from five to thirty "rocks." For the user, this meant that individual "rocks" could be purchased for as little as $2, $5 ("nickel rocks"), $10 ("dime rocks"), or $20. For the seller, $60 worth of cocaine hydrochloride (purchased wholesale for $30) could generate as much as $100 to $150 when sold as rocks. *Third*, it was easily hidden and transportable, and when hawked in small glass vials, glassine envelopes, or common plastic sandwich bags, it could be readily scrutinized by potential buyers. And as a South Miami narcotics detective described it during the summer of 1986:

---

*All undocumented quotations in this chapter are personal communications to the senior author during the course of field research in South Florida.

†The "diggers" was a Haight-Ashbury clan that had adopted the name of a group of seventeenth-century English radicals who appropriated common land and gave their surplus to the poor. In time, in the Haight and elsewhere, the term *digger* became synonymous with "hippie." See Allen J. Matusow, *The Unraveling of America: A History of Liberalism in the 1960s* (New York: Harper & Row, 1984), pp. 300–304.

Crack has been a real boon to both buyer and seller. It's cheap, real cheap. Anybody can come up with $5 or $10 for a trip to the stars. But most important, it's easy to get rid of in a pinch. Drop it on the ground and it's almost impossible to find; step on it and the damn thing is history. All of a sudden your evidence ceases to exist.

The discovery of crack by the media came later, and was unobtrusive at first. During the closing weeks of 1984, at a time when a single gram of reasonably good-quality cocaine cost $75 to $100 or more, the Los Angeles dailies began reporting on local "rock houses" where small pellets of cocaine could be had for as little as $25.[27] The following February, *Newsweek* gave half a page to the Los Angeles phenomenon, highlighting how "rock houses" had become a cottage industry in Los Angeles's South Central ghetto.[28] But still, the term "crack" was never used, and few seemed to notice. Then, on November 17, 1985, buried in the pages of the prestigious *New York Times*, a story about a local drug abuse treatment program identified "crack" for the first time in print media with the brief comment:

> Three teenagers have sought this treatment [program] already this year for cocaine dependence resulting from the use of a new form of the drug called "crack," or rock-like pieces of prepared "freebase cocaine."[29]

A few days later, crack reached the front page of the *Times*. "A New Purified Form of Cocaine Causes Alarm as Abuse Increases" the headline read in boldface.[30] Front-page news in the *New York Times* is rarely overlooked by the wire services, the network television news organizations, and the weekly news magazines. Coverage was intense. Writers, reporters, news anchors, and talk-show hosts began vaulting over one another for the latest story, the latest account, the latest interview. Coverage was feeding coverage, with stories of the "new deadly high" spreading across the land. A *Newsweek* commentary entitled "The Plague Among Us," which appeared on June 16, 1986 as a preface to the magazine's cover story on crack, seemed to capture the essence and direction of the national media storm. In its closing paragraph, editor-in-chief Richard M. Smith remarked:

> We are proud of our coverage thus far. But we realized, preparing this week's cover, that what we had been chronicling piecemeal over the years was in fact an authentic national crisis — an assault on the law and the peace, a waste of life and treasure, a test of the will and the character of a people. *We plan accordingly to cover it as a crisis, reporting it as aggressively and returning to it as regularly as we did the struggle for civil rights, the war in Vietnam and the fall of the Nixon presidency.* "In 1941 the Japanese bombed Pearl Harbor and we went to war," Joel Gilliam, a police inspector in Detroit, told us in the course of our inquest into crack. "Today, little white packets are being dropped on this country, and nobody seems to give a damn." We do,

and the story of crack and the law reflects our commitment to share
that concern with our readers.[31]

In the early reports, few could get it straight as to what, exactly, crack
was. It was called "purified" cocaine, "concentrated" cocaine, "extra
virgin" (as with olive oil) cocaine, "condensed" cocaine, and, most commonly, "freebase." But these terms were inaccurate — in a technical
sense, crack is neither "freebase cocaine" nor "purified cocaine." Part of
the confusion about what crack actually is comes from the different ways
the word "freebase" is used in the drug community. "Freebase" (the
noun) is a drug, a cocaine product converted to the base state from cocaine
hydrochloride *after* adulterants have been chemically removed. Crack is
converted to the base state *without* removing the adulterants. "Freebasing" (the act) means to inhale vapors of cocaine base, of which crack is but
one form. Finally, crack is not purified cocaine, for during its processing,
the baking soda remains as a salt, thus reducing its homogeneity somewhat. Informants in the Miami drug subculture indicate that the purity of
crack ranges as high as 80%, but generally contains much of the filler and
impurities found in the original cocaine hydrochloride, along with some
of the baking soda (sodium bicarbonate) and "cuts" (expanders, for increasing bulk) from the processing.

Not surprisingly, since freebasing had first appeared in the cocaine
subcultures of the avant-garde as opposed to those of street-drug users,
crack and freebase were understood to be one and the same drug to users
in the inner cities. As one Philadelphia user explained:

> What do you mean, do I know the difference between crack and
> freebase? Of course I know the difference between crack and freebase,
> because there's no fucking difference! Crack is freebase, and freebase is
> crack. It's the same fucking drug, same fucking drugs, crack and freebase!

The Growth of the Crack Problem

> Growth in Heroin Use Ending As City Users Turn to Crack!
> — New York Times *headline, September 13, 1986*

As crack moved across the country — north from Miami, west from
New York and Washington, D.C., and east from Los Angeles, the number
of crack users and crack dealers multiplied geometrically. Aside from its
low price and its rapid, potent high, crack became a popular fast-food
analog of cocaine because of the ease with which it could be concocted.
Unlike amphetamines and hallucinogenic drugs — which require a variety
of chemicals and equipment to produce — crack can be made at home
rather cheaply, quickly, and safely. In 1987, for example, a Miami crack
user/dealer/manufacturer described the process:

To make crack in "weight" (quantity) I use four kinds of common things. These are cocaine, baking soda, buttermilk, and plain tap water. Now, you put some cocaine into a test tube. Then you add the water and buttermilk and some of the baking soda, too. The formula calls for cocaine, baking soda, and cold water, but I prefer buttermilk because it makes the crack better.

Next, you hold the test tube in the pot of boiling water until everything in the test tube begins to melt and mix together. Next, you take the test tube out of the water and put into a holder on the table to cool it off. After it's a little cooler, you then put the test tube into the refrigerator. Then you take it out of the test tube and you have terrific rocks of crack. That's all it takes.

Crack's ease of production spawned competition and violence in many neighborhoods, primarily the result of some basic laws of consumer economics. Crack is a drug that lends itself to independent sales because customers make more frequent purchases of smaller amounts than they do with other drugs. Moreover, when a drug is in the hands of many sellers rather than a few major dealers, prices tend to be lower.* If making crack was uncomplicated, using it was even less so. Crack is "smoked" in a variety of ways—special glass pipes, or makeshift smoking devices fabricated from beer and soda cans, jars, bottles, and other containers and known as "stems," "straight shooters," "skillets," "tools," "ouzies," or more directly, the "devil's dick."† A "beam" (from "Beam me up, Scotty" of TV's original "Star Trek") is a hit of crack, as is a "bubb," "backs" (a single hit), and "back up" (a second hit). Crack is also smoked with marijuana in cigarettes, called "geek joints," "lace joints," and "pin joints." Some users get high from a "shotgun"—secondary smoke exhaled from one crack user into the mouth of another.

Users typically smoke for as long as they have crack or the means to purchase it—using money or sex, stolen goods, furniture, or other drugs. It is rare that smokers have but a single hit. More likely they spend $50 to $500 during a "mission"—a three- or four-day binge in which they smoke almost constantly—three to fifty rocks per day. During these cycles, crack users rarely eat or sleep. And once crack is tried, for many

---

*Curiously, crack missed Chicago during its sweep of urban America during the latter half of the 1980s. It was alleged that local street gangs had deliberately kept the drug out of the city, fearing that it would open the way for small dealers to challenge their control of the trade. Crack eventually appeared in Chicago in the early 1990s, spawning the same kind of turf wars that had been seen elsewhere. See *New York Times*, February 10, 1989, p. A14; *New York Times*, October 24, 1991, pp. A1, A22; *Drug Enforcement Report*, November 8, 1991, p. 8.

†Technically, crack is not really smoked. "Smoking" implies combustion, burning, and the inhalation of smoke. Tobacco is smoked. Marijuana is smoked. Hashish is smoked. Crack, on the other hand, is actually inhaled. The small pebbles or rocks, having a relatively low melting point, are placed on a screen covering a small hole in a special glass pipe or other smoking device and heated. Rather than burning, crack vaporizes and the fumes are inhaled.

users it is not long before it becomes a daily habit. For example, a recovering crack user indicated:

> I smoked it Thursday, Friday, Saturday, Monday, Tuesday, Wednesday, Thursday, Friday, Saturday — on that cycle. I was working at that time. I would spend my whole $300 check. Everyday was a crack day for me. My day was not made without a hit. I could smoke it before breakfast, don't even have breakfast, or I don't eat for three days.

And a current crack user/dealer reported:

> For the past five months I've been wearing the same pants. And the sneakers are new but with all the money you make in a day — at least $500 – $600 a day — you don't want to spend $100 in clothes. Everything is rocks, rocks, rocks, rocks, rocks. And to tell you the truth I don't even eat well for having all that money. You don't even want to have patience to sit down and have a good dinner. I could tell you rock is . . . I don't know what to say. I just feel sorry for anyone who falls into it.

And still a third declared:

> Every time I gets some money — $2, $10, or $1,000 — it all goes for the "base" (crack). When you have this base habit, that's all you do — base, base, and more base. I base all day, all week if I can.

This tendency to "binge" on crack for days at a time, neglecting food, sleep, and basic hygiene, severely compromises physical health. As such, crack users appear emaciated most of the time. They lose interest in their physical appearance. Many have scabs on their faces, arms, and legs — the result of burns and picking on the skin (to remove bugs and other insects believed to be crawling *under* the skin). Crack users tend to have burned facial hair from carelessly lighting their smoking paraphernalia; they have burned lips and tongues from the hot stems of their pipes; and they seem to cough constantly. And the tendency of both male and female crack users to engage in high-frequency, unprotected sex with numerous anonymous partners increases their risk for any variety of sexually transmitted diseases, including AIDS.

Postscript

According to national surveys, crack never caught on too well in the general population, and where it did, usage rates began to decline at the close of the 1980s.[32] But for reasons difficult to understand, crack's appeal in the majority of the nation's inner cities has endured, and may remain so for some time. Perhaps the best explanation of crack's appeal in the inner city came from anthropologist Philippe Bourgois towards the close of 1989:

> Substance abuse in general, and crack in particular, offers the equivalent of a born-again metamorphosis. Instantaneously, the user is transformed from an unemployed, depressed high school dropout, despised by the world—and secretly convinced that his failure is due to his own inherent stupidity and disorganization. There is a rush of heart-palpitating pleasure, followed by a jaw-gnashing crash and wide-eyed alertness that provides his life with concrete purpose: Get more crack—fast![33]

Evidence suggests that as the use of crack spread across America, it hit women especially hard, resulting in higher rates of dependence than were experienced by men, and correspondingly lower rates of treatment entry and retention in treatment.[34] Indications of the involvement of women in crack use are reflected in data from the Drug Use Forecasting (DUF) program. Established by the National Institute of Justice, DUF measures the prevalence of drug use among those arrested for serious crimes.[35] Since 1986, the program has used urinalysis to test a sample of arrestees in selected major cities across the United States to determine recent drug use. Urine specimens are collected from arrestees anonymously and voluntarily, and tested so as to detect the use of ten different drugs, including cocaine, marijuana, PCP, methamphetamine, and heroin. What the DUF data have consistently demonstrated is that drug use in general, and cocaine use in particular, is more pervasive among women coming to the attention of the criminal justice system. As indicated in Figure 1.1, for example, the proportions of women testing positive for *any drug* are higher than they are for men in 13 of 21 DUF cities. Similarly, the proportions of women testing positive *for cocaine* are higher in the majority of the DUF sites. Trend data indicate, furthermore, that this has been a consistent pattern over the past few years.[36] Moreover, it is held by most observers that most of the people testing positive for cocaine are, in fact, crack users.

Going further, there were reports of widespread child abuse and child neglect by crack-addicted mothers, and increasing numbers of crack-addicted newborns in pediatric wards of county hospitals.[37] And finally, accounts were indicating that crack was the "ultimate turn-on"; that crack users readily engaged in any variety of sexual activity—at any time, under any circumstances, and with a myriad of partners; that crack use had initiated a "new prostitution"; and that "hypersexual crack nympho-maniacs" would perform oral sex for a nickel [rock] and vaginal sex for a dime [rock] without any concern for modesty, morality, disease, or self-respect.[38] What became apparent, as well, was that women had become special victims of *crack*-cocaine, and that the levels of human suffering within the ranks of women drug users had surpassed those of any previous era or epidemic. *All* of these phenomena are examined in detail in the chapters that follow.

Figure 1.1
Drug Use Among Male and Female Arrestees*

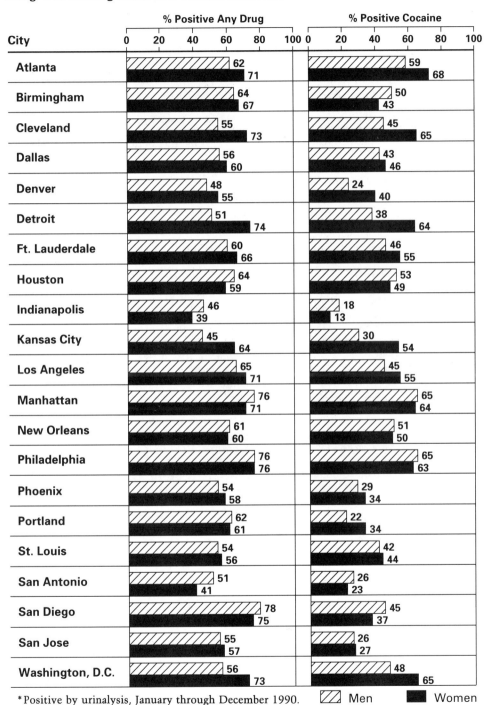

City	% Positive Any Drug	% Positive Cocaine
Atlanta	Men 62 / Women 71	Men 59 / Women 68
Birmingham	Men 64 / Women 67	Men 50 / Women 43
Cleveland	Men 55 / Women 73	Men 45 / Women 65
Dallas	Men 56 / Women 60	Men 43 / Women 46
Denver	Men 48 / Women 55	Men 24 / Women 40
Detroit	Men 51 / Women 74	Men 38 / Women 64
Ft. Lauderdale	Men 60 / Women 66	Men 46 / Women 55
Houston	Men 64 / Women 59	Men 53 / Women 49
Indianapolis	Men 46 / Women 39	Men 18 / Women 13
Kansas City	Men 45 / Women 64	Men 30 / Women 54
Los Angeles	Men 65 / Women 71	Men 45 / Women 55
Manhattan	Men 76 / Women 71	Men 65 / Women 64
New Orleans	Men 61 / Women 60	Men 51 / Women 50
Philadelphia	Men 76 / Women 76	Men 65 / Women 63
Phoenix	Men 54 / Women 58	Men 29 / Women 34
Portland	Men 62 / Women 61	Men 22 / Women 34
St. Louis	Men 54 / Women 56	Men 42 / Women 44
San Antonio	Men 51 / Women 41	Men 26 / Women 23
San Diego	Men 78 / Women 75	Men 45 / Women 37
San Jose	Men 55 / Women 57	Men 26 / Women 27
Washington, D.C.	Men 56 / Women 73	Men 48 / Women 65

*Positive by urinalysis, January through December 1990.   ⬜ Men   ⬛ Women

Source: National Institute of Justice, August 1991.

Endnotes

1. Harry J. Anslinger and William F. Tompkins, *The Traffic in Narcotics* (New York: Funk & Wagnalls, 1953), p. 17.

2. For a history of drug abuse in the United States, see James A. Inciardi, *The War on Drugs II: The Continuing Epic of Heroin, Cocaine, Crack, Crime, AIDS, and Public Policy* (Mountain View, CA: Mayfield Publishing Co., 1992), pp. 1–56; H. Wayne Morgan, *Yesterday's Addicts: American Society and Drug Abuse, 1865–1920* (Norman: University of Oklahoma Press, 1974); David T. Courtwright, *Dark Paradise: Opiate Addiction in America Before 1940* (Cambridge: Harvard University Press, 1982); David F. Musto, *The American Disease: Origins of Narcotic Control* (New Haven: Yale University Press, 1973).

3. Isidor Chein, Donald L. Gerard, Robert S. Lee, and Eva Rosenfeld, *The Road to H: Narcotics, Delinquency, and Social Policy* (New York: Basic Books, 1964).

4. Richard A. Cloward and Lloyd E. Ohlin, *Delinquency and Opportunity* (New York: Free Press, 1960).

5. Marie Nyswander, *The Drug Addict as a Patient* (New York: Grune & Stratton, 1956), p. 28, emphasis added.

6. Milton "Mezz" Mezzrow and Bernard Wolfe, *Really the Blues* (New York: Random House, 1946).

7. Anita O'Day, *High Times Hard Times* (New York: Limelight Editions, 1989).

8. See the comments in Mel Torme, *Traps the Drug Wonder: The Life of Buddy Rich* (New York: Oxford University Press, 1991).

9. For a thorough discussion of LSD, see Albert Hofmann, *LSD: My Problem Child* (Los Angeles: J.P Tarcher, 1983).

10. Richard Goldstein, *1 in 7: Drugs on Campus* (New York: Walker and Co., 1966).

11. Ronald Fraser, *1968: A Student Generation in Revolt* (New York: Pantheon Books, 1988), p. 112.

12. See Timothy Leary, Ralph Metzner, and Richard Alpert, *The Psychedelic Experience: A Manual Based on the Tibetan Book of the Dead* (New Hyde Park, NY: University Books, 1964).

13. Charles Perry, *The Haight-Ashbury: A History* (New York: Random House, 1984).

14. President's Commission on Law Enforcement and Administration of Justice, *Task Force Report: Narcotics and Drug Abuse* (Washington, DC: U.S. Government Printing Office, 1967), p. 3.

15. National Commission on Marihuana and Drug Abuse, *Drug Use in America: Problem in Perspective* (Washington, DC: U.S. Government Printing Office, 1973), p. 146.

16. John Langrod, "Multiple Drug Use Among Heroin Users," in Leon Brill and Ernest Harms, eds., *The Yearbook of Drug Abuse* (New York: Behavioral Publications, 1973), pp. 303–332.

17. Lester Grinspoon and James B. Bakalar, *Cocaine: A Drug and Its Social Evolution* (New York: Basic Books, 1976).

18. James A. Inciardi, unpublished field notes, July 16, 1973.

19. James A. Inciardi, unpublished field notes, July 21, 1973.

20. See Ronald K. Siegel, "Cocaine: Recreational Use and Intoxication," in Robert C. Petersen and Richard C. Stillman, eds., *Cocaine: 1977* (Rockville, MD: National Institute on Drug Abuse, 1977), pp. 119–199.

21. *Time*, July 6, 1981, p. 63.

22. See Paul Eddy, Hugo Sabogal, and Sara Walden, *The Cocaine Wars* (New York: W.W. Norton, 1988).

23. Mary Jane Superweed, *The Marijuana Consumer's and Dealer's Guide* (San Francisco: Chthon Press, 1968).

24. *The Gourmet Cokebook: A Complete Guide to Cocaine* (San Francisco: White Mountain Press, 1972).

25. David Lee, *Cocaine Handbook: An Essential Reference* (San Rafael, CA: What If?, 1981), p. 52.

26. For a discussion of the entry of crack into inner-city areas during these years, see Gordon Witkin, "The Men Who Created Crack," *U.S. News & World Report*, August 29, 1991, pp. 44–53; Inciardi, *The War on Drugs II*, pp. 108–113.

27. For example, see *Los Angeles Times*, November 25, 1984, pp. CC1, CC8.

28. *Newsweek*, February 11, 1985, p. 33.

29. *New York Times*, November 17, 1985, p. B12.

30. *New York Times*, November 29, 1985, pp. A1, B6.

31. *Newsweek*, June 16, 1986, p. 15.

32. Edgar H. Adams, Ann J. Blanken, Lorraine D. Ferguson, and Andrea Kopstein, *Overview of Selected Drug Trends* (Rockville, MD: National Institute on Drug Abuse, Division of Epidemiology and Prevention Research, 1990). Also, see Chapter 2 of this book.

33. Philippe Bourgois, "Just Another Night on Crack Street," *New York Times Magazine*, November 12, 1989, pp. 52–53, 60–65, 94.

34. See Arnold M. Washton and Mark S. Gold, *Cocaine: A Clinician's Handbook* (New York: Guilford Press, 1987); Barbara C. Wallace, *Crack Cocaine: A Practical Treatment Approach for the Chemically Dependent* (New York: Brunner/Mazel, 1991).

35. *Leading Drug Indicators* (Washington, DC: Office of National Drug Control Policy, 1990); National Institute of Justice, *Drug Use Forecasting* (Washington, DC: National Institute of Justice, 1988); Eric D. Wish and Bernard A. Gropper, "Drug Testing by the Criminal Justice System: Methods, Research, and Applications," in Michael Tonry and James Q. Wilson, eds., *Drugs and Crime* (Chicago: University of Chicago Press, 1990), pp. 321–391; Eric D. Wish, "Drug Testing and the Identification of Drug-Abusing Criminals," in James A. Inciardi, ed., *Handbook of Drug Control in the United States* (Westport, CT: Greenwood Press, 1990), pp. 230–244; Bernard R. Gropper, "Drug Detection: Developing New Approaches for Criminal Justice Questions," paper presented at the annual meeting of the Academy of Criminal Justice Sciences, San Francisco, April 1988; Eric D. Wish, "Identifying Drug-Abusing Criminals," in Carl G. Leukefeld and Frank M. Tims, eds., *Compulsory Treatment of Drug Abuse: Research and Clinical Practice* (Rockville, MD: National Institute on Drug Abuse, 1988), pp. 139–159.

36. For trend data, see National Institute of Justice, *DUF: 1989 Drug Use Forecasting Annual Report* (Washington, DC: National Institute of Justice, 1990).

37. *New York Times*, August 25, 1986, pp. B1, B2; David A. Bateman and Margaret C. Heagarty, "Passive Freebase Cocaine (Crack) Inhalation by Infants and Toddlers, *American Journal of Diseases of Children* 143 (January 1989), pp. 25–27; Damian McNamara, "New York City's Crack Babies," *The New York Doctor* 2 (April 10, 1989), pp. 1, 22; *USA Today*, June 6, 1989, p. 3A; *Miami Herald*, August 20, 1989, p. 21A; *New York Times*, September 17, 1989, pp. 1, 26; *New York Times*, October 18, 1989, pp. B1, B2; Wendy Cravkin, "Drug Addiction and Pregnancy: Policy Crossroads," *American Journal of Public Health* 80 (April 1990), pp. 483–487; *Miami Herald*, April 16, 1990, pp. 1A, 6A; *Miami Herald*, August 19, 1991, p. 13A.

38. *Substance Abuse Report*, November 15, 1988: 1–4; *Substance Abuse Report*, June 1, 1989: 1–2; Mary Ann Chiasson, Rand L. Stoneburner, Deborah S. Hildebrandt, William E. Ewing, Edward E. Telsak, and Harold W. Jaffe, "Heterosexual Transmission of HIV-1 Associated with the Use of Smokable Freebase Cocaine (Crack)," *AIDS* 5 (1991), pp. 1121–1126; Mindy Thompson Fullilove and Robert E. Fullilove, "Intersecting Epidemics: Black Teen Crack Use and Sexually Transmitted Disease," *Journal of the American Women's Medical Association* 44: 146–153; *Miami Herald*, May 31, 1988, pp. 1B, 2B; *Miami Herald*, October 22, 1989, pp. 1G, 6G; *New York Times*, May 1, 1990, pp. C1, C12; James A. Inciardi, "Trading Sex for Crack Among Juvenile Drug Users: A Research Note," *Contemporary Drug Problems* 16 (1989), pp. 689–700; Patrick T. Macdonald, Dan Waldorf, Craig Reinarman, and Sheigla Murphy, "Heavy Cocaine Use and Sexual Behavior," *Journal of Drug Issues* 18 (1988), pp. 437–455.

CHAPTER 2

Women and Drugs: Reviewing the Issues

"Chemically dependent women are among the most wounded and needy members of our society, yet their special problems have long gone underrecognized and undertreated."
—*Josette Mondanaro, M.D.*[1]

Although intensive research on substance abuse can be traced back at least sixty years, the great bulk of existing work is concerned with either male alcoholism or male heroin addiction. This presents several difficulties for purposes of understanding *crack*-cocaine use among women. One is that research on cocaine use is very limited. This may not appear surprising given the recency of cocaine use on the scale seen in the contemporary United States, as discussed in Chapter 1. However, cocaine has been used in medical practice for almost a century, it has been used illegally for almost as long, and yet even its pharmacology is not well understood.[2]

A second aspect of the concentration on alcohol or heroin is more difficult to understand: this preponderance of studies focused on only one drug suggests that research has lagged well behind reality in acknowledging that socially problematic drug use tends to entail *polydrug* use.[3] That is, for at least twenty years — ever since the explosion in drug availability, types, and popularity in the 1960s discussed in Chapter 1 — most people with drug problems have been involved with multiple substances, in dosages or time schedules that have the effect of simultaneous usage. Several implications of polydrug use are discussed later in this chapter, but for now the point is that continuation of single-drug studies far into the era of polydrug problems, plus the intensive focus on alcoholism and heroin addiction, has been a detriment to understanding *crack*-cocaine use among women.

A third problem with the concentration on male alcoholism or heroin addiction is that variations in usage patterns have been ignored. Research on alcohol use other than alcoholism, or heroin use other than addiction, is surprisingly limited — and yet alcoholism and heroin addiction are often not even defined in studies of them. This is problematic because sufficient evidence exists to make it very clear that both antecedents and consequences of socially problematic substance use — be they biological, psychological, or sociocultural — vary substantially by such drug usage characteristics as quantity and frequency of use, route of administration, and duration of use.[4] These topics are especially important in studying cocaine, because — unlike alcohol and heroin — it permits an enormous potential range of usage quantity and frequency. That is, cocaine can be self-administered several times an hour for days on end — a pattern that is physiologically impossible with heroin or alcohol because it would rapidly result in stupor or death. The existing substance abuse literature thus provides relatively little guidance on working with a factor that is both very important and highly variable in the case of cocaine. Further, there is some evidence that due to physiological factors — e.g., female hormones in the case of alcohol, a higher percentage of body fat for women in the case of marijuana — female drug use patterns may show more variability than those typical of males.[5]

However, the most important gap in the substance abuse literature for purposes of understanding women's use of crack is the long tradition of ignoring gender as a drug use variable. As recently as 1975 a group of women researchers at the Addiction Research Foundation questioned whether enough was known about women's substance abuse to justify attempting to publish an entire book on the subject.[6] Thus, intensive research on socially problematic drug use among women is only a few years older than the crack problem itself. While this field of study has made enormous strides in the past twenty years, its limited history continues to restrict the amount of available information required to understand and deal with women's crack use. Further, the inclination to ignore women in drug research still persists today. This makes a brief look at the history of research on women's drug problems a useful starting point for looking at the problems themselves.

Research on Women's Drug Problems

Not only did the great majority of early research on drug and alcohol problems simply ignore women, but a surprisingly large percentage of the work that was done with women focused not on women's lives but rather on the impact of a pregnant woman's addiction on the health of the fetus.[7] The recent hysteria surrounding "crack babies" suggests that this topic remains a strong focus of public attention, and a very large share of research funding continues to be devoted to the drug/pregnancy connection rather than drug treatment and prevention issues among women who are not pregnant.[8]

The other major category of research on women and drug use prior to the early 1970s was the clinical analysis of female heroin addicts and alcoholics as self-destructive, unstable, sexually maladjusted, insecure, socially immature, and other variations on a diagnosis of "inadequate personality."[9] Similar diagnoses were made of male heroin addicts and alcoholics, but such analyses constituted a markedly smaller percentage of all research on these subjects and the literature as a whole was in fairly strong agreement that while chemically dependent males are sick, their female counterparts are even sicker.[10] As Barbara G. Lex of Harvard Medical School points out in the specific case of alcohol, these allegations of greater psychological disturbance among women were being made at the same time that other researchers were presuming that gender distributions were not important enough to report because chemical dependence was similar in men and women. At the same time, still other researchers assumed that substance abuse was essentially a male problem because sociocultural factors protected women from involvement in highly deviant behavior.[11]

By the 1970s, research on women's drug problems began to change because of two revolutions during the late 1960s: the American drug crisis and the women's movement. The explosion of drug use among large numbers of high school and college students in the 1960s provoked a major change in how illicit drug use was explained. The emphasis shifted from psychopathology to peer groups and subcultures, making strictly psychiatric explanations of any illicit drug use — even heroin use — suspect. Several now-classic ethnographic studies showed (male) heroin users as being not the passive, socially inadequate escapists of psychoanalytic theory, but alert, resourceful, purposive "hustlers" — "ripping and running," "taking care of business," engaged in that multitude of activities required to secure heroin and avoid arrest.[12] These studies of male street culture set the stage for later research on how female heroin users viewed their own lives.

The drug crisis also led to the funding of the first large-scale epidemiological studies of illicit drug use. The results confirmed that many adolescents and young adults in the conventional household population were in fact using illegal drugs. Rates for marijuana use among female students, in particular, turned out to be surprisingly high — lower than rates for males, but much higher than would be predicted given the assumption that girls are very unlikely to engage in illegal activities. Further, most rates of increase for illicit drug use by young women outstripped those for young men in the 1967 – 1972 period.[13] This trend toward convergence of male/female rates apparently did not continue past the mid 1970s, but gender ratios for all types of drugs remain much lower for youth than for older Americans.[14]

The other aspect of the 1960s drug crisis of particular consequence for research on women was heroin use. It now seems clear that the general increase in illicit drug use during this time was also specifically a time of increase in heroin use, with a major heroin epidemic peaking around 1968–69 in big cities, and later in smaller cities.[15] Further, heroin appears to be one of the illicit drugs for which usage rates for females grew faster than did those for males. This is indicated by national statistics — arrest rates for narcotic offenses and gender distributions of addicts appearing for treatment — as well as studies of individual cities and observations concerning the number of pregnant addicts admitted to hospitals.[16] By the mid-1970s women were accounting for 25% or more of the heroin addicts appearing for treatment. Since this represented a 33% increase from figures generally being reported only ten years before, it became increasingly apparent to some clinicians that women's particular treatment needs would have to be given more attention.

The other major influence on the study of women's drug use during the late 1960s was modern feminism. Fairly simultaneously with the drug crisis, a revived women's movement began to apply pressure for change on virtually every American institution from the federal government to the Miss America Pageant.[17] In the social sciences, the movement sparked a surge of feminist critiques of existing research, theory, and policy, and it stimulated new interest in all aspects of women's behaviors and experiences, including drug use.

An initial focus of feminist attention was the perfectly licit medical use of prescribed sedatives and tranquilizers by middle-class women and its relationship to the gender-role stereotypes expressed in physician prescribing patterns and pharmaceutical company advertising.[18] The resulting publicity helped to educate both physicians and at least their middle-class female patients. However, it should be noted that this problem persists — physicians still write more prescriptions for psychoactive drugs for women than they do for men, more women than men are seen in emergency rooms suffering from overdoses of prescription drugs, and it has been reported that the formerly middle-class problem of prescription drug misuse is now being seen in low-income women as a result of prescriptions written for women on Medicaid.[19] Further, cynical manipulation of women's fears and desires still provide advertisers and manufacturers with huge profits from sales directly to women of over-the-counter stimulants and depressants, alcohol, and cigarettes.[20]

A second kind of early feminist critique of drug studies was concern about the needs of women being treated for drug use problems — including what was by then the growing number of female heroin addicts appearing in treatment centers, as noted above. These were some of the first studies in which women who used heroin were interviewed about how they viewed their own lives. The findings were basically a series of horror stories about treatment programs: sexual exploitation, humiliation, sexual voyeurism by both male staff and male clients, being used as an aid in the treatment of male addicts (e.g., by role-playing problem situations), or being excluded from aspects of the program deemed unnecessary for women — such as employment training.[21] Partially as a result of such studies, several major research projects were begun — with guidance and funding from the National Institute on Drug Abuse (NIDA) and the National Institute on Alcohol Abuse and Alcoholism (NIAAA) — to study ways in which women could be given more meaningful help in drug treatment programs.[22]

The 1975–1985 time period also saw several other new kinds of research on women and substance abuse. One kind of research included studies of female heroin users who were *not* in treatment or prison — intensive interviews with prostitutes by Paul J. Goldstein and Jennifer James, a notable ethnography of women heroin users on the street by Marsha Rosenbaum (which remains the sole such work, in contrast to the half dozen completed on men), and several large studies entailing street interviews with female heroin users as well as other female criminal offenders in the same communities.[23] A second kind of research was concerned with the empirical investigation — and repudiation — of the often reported but never documented increase in women's alcohol problems alleged to have resulted from their increasing participation in the work force, generally taken to mean their increased participation in the world that used to belong solely to men.[24]

These various kinds of new research led to significant progress in understanding the social psychology of women's drug and alcohol involvement, differences between male and female substance use patterns, and contrasts between women involved in problematic types or levels of substance use and women from similar backgrounds who were not drug-involved. At the same time, however, traditional research limitations have continued. Pregnancy and psychopathology appear to remain primary foci for studies of women's drug use, and reports continue to appear with all male samples or, more commonly now, analyses that ignore gender.[25] It is particularly unfortunate for understanding *crack*-cocaine use among women that such analyses are used in major new studies that focus on cocaine use and treatment effectiveness.[26]

Major Findings on Women and Socially Problematic Drug Use

Drug researchers today are finally at the stage of recognizing that useful research requires comparative analysis rather than single sex-single drug studies, as well as attention to linkages between drug use and other socially problematic behaviors.[27] Even looking at existing single-drug research from a cross-drug comparative perspective can be useful. In the case of women's drug use, this perspective leads to the conclusion that women's experiences with socially problematic substance use are strikingly similar regardless of the drug's legal status or psychopharmacological properties. Suburban women with drinking problems and inner-city women using heroin or crack are highly likely to undergo the same initial drug use situations, have similar motives for taking drugs, and experience many of the same kinds of problems as they go from experimentation to problem use. The difference introduced by the use specifically of street drugs, and especially expensive street drugs, is simply additional layers of life problems as consequences for the user. Before examining the particulars of these similarities and differences, however, it is helpful to recognize the context within which they occur: the psychological, social, and cultural experience of stigmatization associated with socially problematic drug use of any type by a woman. Such behavior violates female role expectations so seriously that it can result in social isolation, cultural denigration, and feelings of shame that help to perpetuate the very behavior at issue.

Deviance, Gender-Role Deviance, and Stigma

By definition, "socially problematic drug use" — the disapproved use of licit substances or any use of illicit drugs — is deviant behavior for men as well as women. But there are many ways in which such drug use is actually *compatible* with role expectations for *males* — which is exactly what makes it an especially strong violation of role expectations for females. Many common social situations — a night out with friends, business lunches, attending ball games, working-class tavern life, teenage parties — virtually require males to use alcohol and encourage them to drink at high volumes. Females in the same situations are generally expected to drink, but they are not expected, let alone encouraged, to be in such situations as often or to drink at the same rate.[28] In fact, it has been suggested that even light or moderate drinking is still slightly suspect behavior in women — tolerated, but not totally approved due to lingering associations with immorality.[29]

A related factor is that among preteens and adolescents, both street drug use and heavy drinking often represent risktaking, a behavior expected of males, but not expected — and often not valued when it does occur — for females. Similarly, such activity is not uncommonly regarded as a normal "boys will be boys" flirtation with the boundaries of acceptable behavior; it is not a "kids will be kids" situation because part of what boys are thereby defining themselves as is "not girls" — i.e., not persons who routinely obey the rules and control their public behavior. Males whose behavior is seen as controlled and inhibited are subject to name calling (names such as "wimp," "wuss," and "pussy") and other social reprimands, while intoxicated or otherwise disinhibited behavior in a female is commonly seen as a sign of sexual promiscuity with possible implications of emotional disturbance.

The most basic mechanism operating here appears to be that deviance —behavior that violates sociocultural expectations — is highly likely to be perceived as specifically gender-role deviance for women. Women are expected, as women, to be sensitive to other people's feelings, opinions, wishes, and criticisms; men, on the other hand, are not even expected to notice such things as intently, let alone be as affected by them. One consequence of this deviance/gender-role deviance connection for women is that any deviant behavior — such as socially disapproved drug use — raises questions about a woman's overall gender role performance. In particular, it implies the possibility that a woman is deviating from even the most fundamental female gender-role expectation: essentially, moral and psychological suitability for motherhood, of which the archetypal opposites are sexual promiscuity and emotional instability.

It is important to recognize that "gender-role expectations" are not just rules imposed by other people, but also rules ordinarily internalized by the people to whom they apply. As such, these expectations form part of the basis for ordinary attitudes and behaviors, and are thereby reflected in behavioral rates. This is confirmed in a study that compared the relative legality of drugs to the relative gender ratios for their use (number of males using per every one female using), based on ten large studies of drug use prevalence.[30] The investigators found an extremely high negative correlation (−.92) between the rank order of these two factors — the more illegal a drug is, the less likely a user is to be female. Another way of phrasing the same finding is that illegal drug use is even more deviant for females than it is for males, and the greater the illegality, the greater the deviance from expected — and typically enacted — behaviors.

One consequence of male-role compatibility and female-role incompatibility is that socially problematic drug use can result in dramatically different outcomes for males and females. For males, drug use can actually certify proper gender-role performance; a limited number of episodes are in any case generally seen as excusable, so that discarding such behavior is generally an open option. Even after extended drug involvement, men not uncommonly receive support for quitting from conventional persons worried about their behavior, especially spouses and parents.[31] For females, the same kind of drug use not only violates gender-role expectations in and of itself, but it is often interpreted as implying the existence of still other violations — particularly those of sexual misbehavior and emotional instability. Consequently, even a limited number of problematic drug use episodes can spoil a woman's entire social identity, stigmatizing her as wild, promiscuous, unstable. Thus, for example, even though men in the general population generally experience more adverse social effects from substance use — be it alcohol, marijuana, or cocaine — women are significantly more likely to experience the specific adverse social effect of having more arguments and fights with family and friends.[32]

Deeper drug involvement may make the stigma and conflict nearly permanent, so that a female addict is much more likely than her male counterpart to be completely isolated from conventional society. Rates of divorce and separation are much higher for chemically dependent women —and if they are still married, their spouses are likelier to be chemically dependent themselves.[33] Similarly, female adolescents are likelier to become disconnected from their families due to drug use. In a sample of youths seriously involved in drug use and crime, for example, a surprising 76% of the 50 females age 16 and 17 had left home, compared to only 18% of the 206 males the same age.[34] Or, if — as is quite likely — a chemically dependent woman has children, she may lose them to family members or the court since most people see drug involvement as indicating an "unfit mother." A study of 126 women in a methadone clinic, for example, found that 91% were mothers and 63% of these 115 mothers had lost custody of at least one of their children.[35] Even if women want to stop their drug involvement, they may have less social support for their effort than men do. When asked about friends or family members who would help them quit, a study of 100 crack users in treatment found that 50% more women than men reported that no one would provide such support; in fact, this was the most common response for the female patients.[36]

The stigma associated with socially problematic drug use by women is both the most consistent and most consequential similarity in the experience of drug-involved women. As will be apparent in the discussion below, it is therefore a recurring aspect of the other characteristics and behaviors common to chemically dependent women, regardless of the substances involved.

Starting and Continuing Drug Use

For girls as well as boys, initiation of substance use of any type usually occurs among peers during adolescence — although it may begin later, in young adulthood. Chances are good, however, that the younger a drug user is now, the younger she or he was at initial drug use. This is because historically, typical age at initiation has decreased continually over the last fifty years — a trend found across all drug types, in many different kinds of user populations, and for both males and females.[37]

A further similarity across drug types is that family as well as friends have commonly been found to influence the timing and degree of adolescent drug involvement.[38.] On the whole, it is not clear from this research whether there are meaningful gender differences in the degree to which family controls influence youthful misbehavior. However, one particular impact of family on drug use that does show marked gender differences is the greater incidence of problem families in the background of chemically dependent women compared to their male counterparts — i.e., families with histories of violence, child abuse, alcoholism and drug addiction, suicide, and mental illness.[39]

A gender difference of even greater magnitude is the importance of opposite-sex friends in drug initiation and at least the first stages of continued use. For both alcohol and illicit drugs, boyfriends and husbands are much more likely to introduce a young woman to substance use than girlfriends and wives are to introduce young men to it; for illicit drugs, a commonly reported means of access for women is reliance on a man — most often a dealer — to supply drugs in exchange for companionship and sexual favors.[40] These arrangements, however, tend to be temporary ones that occur only in the early stages of a woman's drug involvement. The drug use that brought a couple together tends to tear them apart as well, for several reasons. Marsha Rosenbaum of the Institute for Scientific Analysis in San Francisco summarizes the problems for heroin use by saying that:

> . . . heroin becomes the focal point of the relationship and erodes other aspects of affection or mutuality; the heroin life disrupts traditional sex role delineation to the dissatisfaction of the couple; and unscrupulousness and money problems cause nearly constant bickering.[41]

The same problems appear even more likely when the drug being used is, unlike heroin, one highly likely to cause personality changes — notably, increased aggressiveness in users of alcohol (especially males) and cocaine (regardless of gender).[42]

Women's motivations for drug use are another area of similarity across drug types. First drug use may occur for a variety of reasons having to do with curiosity and experimentation with new behaviors, motives common among both male and female adolescents.[43] But motivation for continued use — a requirement for developing drug dependency — differs by gender. Females are much less likely than males to use illegal drugs for thrills or pleasure, or to drink or use illegal drugs in response to peer pressure, and instead much more likely to use any and all drug types for self-medication — i.e., as a coping mechanism for dealing with situational factors, life events, or general psychological distress.[44] Depression is a particularly common problem among chemically dependent women, and —unlike men who are both clinically depressed and chemically dependent — women are highly likely to have been depressed before, rather than only after, the development of a drug problem.[45]

Some of the problems motivating women's drug use for self-medication can be traced to the problems of women as devalued citizens. As the psychiatrist Josette Mondanaro has commented:

> The legacy of growing up female in a society that undervalues and denigrates the role of women is a low sense of self-esteem, high levels of depression and anxiety, and a sense of powerlessness. Learned helplessness is another result of the daily confrontation with the dominant culture. Women learn, through repeated negative reinforcement, that they are helpless to change their situation and thus see no alternative but to continue on their present path. All these characteristics act in concert to immobilize many chemically dependent women.[46]

The importance of such factors is also shown by the repeated finding that counseling to foster self-esteem and a sense of personal competence are critical elements in the successful treatment of drug dependence in women.[47]

Still other problems motivating self-medication may stem from traumas of personal history — particularly rape, incest, and other sexual abuse. Such histories are much more common among women than men, and have been found to be extremely frequent — 60% is a not an uncommon estimate — among women with drug problems, including dependence on both licit and illegal drugs.[48] A recent study of 572 women in treatment also found that sexual and physical abuse is increasingly common in the histories of younger women compared to earlier cohorts: while only slightly likelier to undergo childhood sexual abuse, younger women were much likelier to have been involved with men who abused them both sexually and physically.[49]

Women are also more likely than men to undergo serious economic pressures, since they are less likely than men to have adequate job income and, in addition, the majority have children to support.[50] Most descriptions of women entering treatment describe them as having inadequate levels of education and job training and extremely high rates of unemployment.[51]

Many of these inspirations for self-medication may be magnified for a woman who is from a socioeconomically disadvantaged background or a member of an ethnic minority. These characteristics increase the chance that a woman will undergo additional problems of both devaluation by the majority culture and severe economic pressures. The connection of poverty and minority-group ethnicity to substance abuse may be even further exaggerated by either the main culture — such as the alcohol industry's recent inundation of black neighborhoods with pro-drinking advertising — or the community itself — such as the special shame and guilt associated with substance abuse for Mexican-American women because they have violated strong cultural traditions about the behavior of a "good" woman.[52] Finally, minority women in inner-city communities have the additional stress of worrying about the impact of this crime and drug-ridden environment on their children.

Experiencing Problems and Terminating Use

Women involved in all kinds of drug use also have some striking similarities in the experiences they undergo once they have begun heavy use. One they share with men is that, as previously discussed, any problem drug use today tends to be polydrug use.[53] Alcohol/prescription drug combinations appear particularly often among women;[54] heroin users commonly prefer "speedballs" — combinations of heroin and speed or heroin and cocaine, plus marijuana and often pills; cocaine users almost always use considerable amounts of some kind of depressant — alcohol or pills or sometimes heroin — as well as marijuana. Polydrug use is problematic because it complicates and exacerbates the user's addiction pattern and the effect of drugs on the user's body, both of which make treatment efforts even more difficult.

Another common problem for chemically dependent men and women is impaired sexual functioning.[55] This includes physiological damage, disruption of reproductive functioning, and diminished sexual interest. The latter is of particular interest in that many recreational drugs — including alcohol, marijuana, inhalants, heroin, and cocaine — have been reputed to be aphrodisiacs (see Chapter 5), and chemically dependent women in particular are commonly labelled sexually promiscuous. While the aphrodisiac claim may have some psychopharmacological basis for low to moderate dosages taken only occasionally, heavy use is almost always associated with impaired functioning and a devotion to drug use that permits little interest in any other activity.[56] Impaired sexual functioning for chemically dependent women, in particular, may also be related to their male partners' sexual dysfunctions resulting from drug use; for both alcohol and cocaine, these dysfunctions include impotence and lack of sexual interest.[57]

The female promiscuity label is more difficult to analyze. In some cases it is merely an erroneous generalization based on the "female deviance = gender-role deviance" assumption discussed earlier. In other cases, claims have been made based on the prostitution activities of female drug users, when prostitution may have considerably less to do with expression of sexuality than it does with the need for income to support drug use.[58] In still other cases, promiscuity may be a joint outcome with chemical dependency — both traceable to trauma experienced as an abused or neglected child, and especially prevalent among incest victims.[59] And in still other cases it is difficult for clinicians to evaluate their female patients' self-descriptions as promiscuous because these kinds of statements are so intertwined with generalized shame and guilt about their chemical dependency.[60] In any case, identification and self-identification as promiscuous is an aspect of impaired sexual functioning that is common among women and rarely if ever seen among men.

A chemical dependency problem necessarily unique to women is complications in pregnancy and childbirth. Both have been found to be associated with alcohol, cocaine, heroin and other opiates, marijuana, PCP, and prescription sedatives and tranquilizers.[61] Because these drugs cross the placental barrier to affect the fetus, children born to chemically dependent women are subject to problems that increase the risk of both neonatal mortality (premature birth, low birth weight even if not premature, incomplete development, withdrawal symptoms) and significant long-term developmental disabilities (brain injury, growth impairment, decreased psychomotor performance, learning disabilities). Alcohol, as the most commonly used substance, is responsible for more of these problems than is any other drug; fetal alcohol effects are seen even with moderate levels of alcohol intake.[62] However, during the 1980s, hospitals reported large increases in cocaine-related problems, particularly as cheap cocaine — crack — became more widely available.[63] It should be noted that identification of specific drug effects is difficult because of the tendency of drug users to use multiple drugs, and this polydrug phenomenon appears to be especially common among cocaine users.[64]

The subject of pregnancy complications, fetal damage, and child impairment is also one that illustrates particularly well the gaps in existing knowledge about both women's drug use and linkages between substance abuse and other socially problematic behaviors. That is, although many of the physiological effects discussed above have been seen in animal studies, indicating a direct drug effect, others have not. One reason is the long neglect of females in drug research, since "in the experimental areas of the field, the subjects of choice have most frequently been males, ranging from rats to college students."[65] But a second reason is that drug involvement is almost never a woman's sole life problem, and it can be very hard to separate the effects of drug use from those resulting from other difficulties. In the case of pregnancy and childbirth, especially pertinent complications often seen among drug users include poverty, sexually transmitted disease, cigarette smoking, poor nutritional status and general health, and little or no prenatal care.[66] The effects of cocaine are particularly difficult to identify for at least three reasons: (1) the drug is so rapidly metabolized that urine tests even a few hours after last use may not show its presence, (2) the particularly high probability that, as previously noted, a cocaine user also uses multiple other drugs, and (3) a strikingly high correlation for pregnant women between cocaine use and total lack of prenatal care.[67]

Substance abuse of all types also has a more general deleterious effect on health, and many such problems appear to be more substantial for women than men.[68] Part of the explanation is simple body composition differences: compared to men, women have a smaller average body weight, less body water per pound, and more body fat per pound. Thus, a water-soluble drug such as alcohol or cocaine will result in higher blood or plasma levels for women than men even if dosage and body size are the same, and for fat-soluble drugs such as marijuana and minor tranquilizers, fatty tissue will store and gradually release a drug into a woman's system over a longer period of time than will occur for a man.[69] Further, the liver is the organ which breaks down poisons — such as alcohol and other drugs — taken into the body, and the female sex hormone estrogen apparently has an adverse effect on liver functioning.[70] At high levels of drug intake, women thus develop physiological problems after fewer years. Female alcoholics have a more rapid development of cardiovascular, gastrointestinal, and — especially — liver diseases; and while mortality rates for male alcoholics are two or three times those of men of similar ages in the general population, the equivalent factor for women is 2.7 to 7 times as many deaths.[71] Similarly, drug dependence itself appears to occur more rapidly among women — a finding reported for alcohol, heroin, and cocaine.[72]

There are also markedly fewer intervention points for women with drug problems than there are for their male counterparts. Men are often subject to intervention on the job, but women have higher rates of unemployment; when they do work they are likelier to work for businesses too small to have organized employee assistance programs.[73] Similarly, male addicts are often subject to pressure to quit from a spouse, but a female addict's spouse is more likely either to have left the marriage or to be an addict himself.[74] Even the greater expectation for males to drink in common social contexts leads to greater chances of intervention for them: men are three to ten times more likely than women to be caught driving under the influence — a legal event that can serve to pressure a user into treatment.[75] Further, when women do come in contact with police and courts because of their drug and alcohol use, they are less likely than men to be arrested or convicted because the behaviors officially defined as problematic — such as violent behavior or traffic accidents — tend to be behaviors less common among women than men.[76]

Even when they do enter treatment, women are likely to enter a program that does not meet their needs because it was originally designed for men. One problem is the subject matter included in therapy. An obvious example is that chemically dependent men often have a problem with controlling their behavioral expressions of anger, while women are much more likely to be troubled by not having ever learned to express anger in the first place. Or the type of therapy may need to be quite different. Successful group therapy for chemically dependent men, for example, often involves confrontations by peers in order to help them recognize and admit their underlying problems, while women tend to react badly to confrontational techniques and instead benefit from intensive mutual support from peers.[77] Women also require a broader range of ancillary services for successful treatment — notably, a broader range of medical and psychological services, help with childcare (possibly to even enter treatment in the first place), and services aimed at reducing the extreme isolation typical of women drug users, such as mutual support groups and family therapy.[78] Since these additional services require additional financing, they are not as common as one might wish. In addition, problems still persist with sexist assumptions in both staff attitudes and service planning (e.g., the idea that women do not need vocational training). Even the language traditionally used by therapists and support groups such as AA can be a problem for women. A male psychiatrist with extensive experience treating cocaine users has stated:

> . . . I feel I'm reasonably sensitive to the times we live in, and I know that women tend to feel more disempowered and disenfranchised. But

once when I told a woman she was not surrendering to her healing
process, she correctly admonished me that women have been advised
all of their lives to stay humble and surrender, and it's gotten them
nothing but more victimization and subjugation.[79]

Great progress has been made over the last fifteen years in designing
programs more suitable for women, but treatment oriented to the male
gender remains a problem shared by chemically dependent women regardless of the drugs they use.

Nonetheless, women appear to be involved in chemical dependence
for shorter durations than men. This has been found for heavy drinking in
the general population, as well as for alcohol, heroin, and cocaine use
prior to treatment entry.[80] One factor may be that women are often
motivated to discontinue drug use out of concern for their children, a
consideration that is much less compelling for men.[81] Ironically, children
can also be a particular impediment to women's treatment entry, since
many programs continue to ignore the childcare needs of their female
clients.[82] Pregnancy can likewise motivate a woman to seek treatment,
but again, this can represent a problem because there has always been a
shortage of drug treatment programs that will accept pregnant women.
The new efforts to have pregnant addicts prosecuted for "child abuse" or
"delivering drugs in utero" will, if successful, necessarily serve to push
more women away from treatment — since requesting treatment could
lead to arrest for this new offense.[83]

A second factor is that women are also generally more willing than
men to seek help for a problem, although — probably because they see
substance use as an attempted answer to depression or anxiety — they are
likely to seek medical assistance or counseling rather than drug treatment.[84] One implication of women's willingness to seek help is that the
previously noted tendency of chemically dependent women to display
high levels of anxiety and low levels of self-esteem may in fact be helpful
rather than destructive. As Beth Glover Reed points out:

> . . . one could argue that the presence of depression and anxiety indi-
> cates that denial defenses are not preventing the acknowledgment of
> psychic pain; such pain can be a powerful motivator if the woman can
> correctly label the source of the pain and determine where to seek help
> with it.[85]

Chemically dependent men, on the other hand, are likelier to deny the
pain that may lie behind their own drug use.[86]

Unfortunately, however, a woman's determination of where to get
help is often problematic. Women still living in relatively stable socioeconomic circumstances are especially likely to consult a physician, but a
woman seeking help for depression or anxiety is not uncommonly treated
with prescribed tranquilizers, which can easily make her drug problem
even worse, and in any case does nothing to treat it or its underlying
causes.[87] As the psychiatrist Sheila Blume has noted:

Physicians do not think of alcoholism or drug dependence when they evaluate a well-dressed, poised, employed, accomplished middle-class female patient. Even when the patient's complaints and physical condition are suggestive, the matter is often not pursued. Guided by the stereotype of the fallen woman, health professionals in general miss early-stage dependence in women. . . . Education of health professionals about women and chemical dependency is one of the most critical needs in our present system of care.[88]

Chemically dependent women living in poverty, on the other hand, are particularly likely to have no idea at all of where to turn for help.[89] This lack of information can also be linked to the failure of medical professionals to recognize the symptoms of chemical dependency, since many women using hospital emergency room services have drug problems but are not in treatment; in addition, school personnel and other people working with the children of chemically dependent women are often in a position to recognize the existence of a problem, yet they only rarely use their potential influence to help get a woman into treatment.[90]

Street Drugs in Particular

Street drugs in particular introduce additional problems. Because these drugs can be purchased only on the illegal market, their use is even more deviant and hence subject to additional stigmatization. A woman dependent on alcohol or prescription drugs may be "protected" from definition as an addict by denial of the problem on the part of family, friends, and even physicians. This only extends the damage done by her addiction, of course, but the stigma remains only a potential. Women strongly involved with street drugs, however, are much more likely to experience criticism, denigration, and loss of relationships.[91]

Yet street drugs are used even by women in the conventional household population — i.e., not counting such high drug-use rate locales as youth/young-adult residences (boarding schools, college dormitories, etc.) or the temporary residences associated with street life (cheap hotels, rooming houses, homeless shelters, a night with one relative and the next night with another, and so forth). As indicated in Table 2.1, young women in the household population are almost as likely as young men to use marijuana, and among young adults a surprisingly large number — one in five women — used marijuana in the past year. Frequent marijuana use and any use of cocaine is much less common, and use of inhalants or hallucinogens is largely confined to small percentages of teenagers and young adults. Nonetheless, the past-year prevalence rate for cocaine use among young women — 6.0% of those age 18–25 — is markedly higher than the rate ever seen for heroin use in the household population, even among young men. For example, in a large household survey of men age 20–30 (a high heroin-use age group), during 1974–75 (a relatively high heroin-use time period), investigators found a current heroin-use rate of

Table 2.1

Street-Drug Use in the American Household Population by Age Group and Gender, 1991 (Percentage)

	12–17		18–25		25–34		35+	
	M	**F**	**M**	**F**	**M**	**F**	**M**	**F**
Any Past-Year Use								
Marijuana	11.5	8.6	27.7	21.6	18.5	10.6	5.7	3.0
Cocaine	1.6	1.5	9.5	6.0	7.0	3.3	2.3	1.1
Inhalants	4.2	3.9	4.6	2.4	1.3	0.6	0.7	0.6
Hallucinogens	2.1	2.2	6.2	3.4	1.7	0.6	0.5	0.5
Use Weekly or More								
Marijuana	2.9	2.0	9.6	4.2	5.9	2.5	1.7	0.5
Cocaine	0.3	0.4	0.9	0.7	0.8	0.6	0.3	0.2

Source: National Institute on Drug Abuse: *National Household Survey on Drug Abuse: Population Estimates 1991*. Rockville, MD: NIDA, 1992.

only 1.8%.[92] The lifetime prevalence rate for cocaine use in women is similarly impressive — at 9.2%, it indicates that almost one in every ten American women has tried cocaine.[93] Further, as noted in Chapter 1, these generally uncommon drug-use forms are actually the norm among persons taken into police custody, and they tend to be more prevalent among female than male arrestees.

However striking these household usage rates may be, it is significant that they are lower than those reported only a few years ago, particularly for cocaine. The 1980s saw dramatic increases in not only cocaine use but cocaine problems, as the 1-800-COCAINE hotline received an average of over 1400 calls per day between 1983 and 1985, totalling some 1.5 million calls for help in the three-year time period.[94] Further, research conducted with random samples of callers showed that a surprisingly high percentage of people experiencing enough trouble with cocaine to call the hotline were women — 33% in the 1983 survey, and 42% in the 1985 study. Since women tend to ask for help more readily than do men, as previously discussed, these figures do not necessarily reflect the actual gender proportions of all cocaine users or even all cocaine users with problems. But they do reflect a significant female involvement in problem-level use of a highly illegal drug.

In 1988, the household survey found the most female cocaine use among women in the 18–25 age category, with 9.2% of this group having used cocaine during the prior year — markedly higher than the 6.0% reported for 1991.[95] Comparison of the 1988 and 1991 surveys shows even more of a drop in past-year cocaine use among adolescent females — from

2.9% in 1988 (3.0% for males) to 1.5% in 1991 (1.6% for males). The decrease is further documented by the national surveys of high school seniors and college students conducted annually by the University of Michigan's Institute for Social Research as part of the "Monitoring the Future" study. The latest results indicate that student cocaine use dropped between 1990 and 1991, reflecting further decreases since the peak years of 1985 for high school seniors and 1986 for college students.[96] Use of most other illicit substances also fell during this period, in most cases continuing what appears to be a longer-term decline.

The Monitoring the Future researchers attribute these declines not to decreased availability but rather to increased peer disapproval of illicit drug use, probably linked to increased perception of it as harmful. Disapproval is at especially high levels among high school seniors. What this disapproval means for the people who do use illicit drugs anyway— especially if such use is rare among their age and gender peers — is the risk of a broader disapproval of the users themselves, as people. That is, indicators of disapproval are also measures of potential stigmatization. The increase in such indicators through the late 1980s into the 1990s suggests an increasing trend toward a separation of the American population into two drug-use worlds: (1) the conventional household population, in which illegal drug use is rare and disapproved of — and becoming rarer and more disapproved of, and (2) street subcultures, in which such behavior is not decreasing, and is perhaps even increasing.[97] It should also be noted that these surveys indicate that cocaine use in the general population is unlikely to be crack use. This puts crack in the position traditionally held only by heroin — a drug regarded as exclusively associated with street life.

Another aspect of street-drug use is the high probability that a street drug is a second or third drug being used, which may help make it more stigmatizing than alcohol use. Numerous studies of a variety of populations — students, the adolescent household population, and young adults — have documented that drugs tend to be used in a very clear sequence of drug types.[98] Alcohol use almost always comes first; a certain percentage of alcohol users then begin marijuana use, although they still continue to use alcohol as well. Then a certain percentage of marijuana/alcohol users begin use of still other drugs — most commonly pills but sometimes hallucinogens or inhalants, and sometimes cocaine or heroin.

The mechanism through which this sequence operates is, simply, the nature of the illegal drug market.[99] Extremely occasional social use of marijuana may be conducted entirely with marijuana secured by other people and shared. But use at any level beyond this obliges one to reciprocate, which necessitates buying marijuana. Buying is easily shifted up one step into buying a little extra and selling "just to friends" — and this level of course can readily evolve into selling more broadly. At least by then, if not before, relationships must be established with people who can sell large enough quantities for resale — and such people are highly likely to at least use if not also sell additional street drugs. This social contact through the illegal drug market is what makes marijuana a "gateway" drug to further and possibly more dangerous drug involvement.

For small-town and suburban teenagers, the initial drug market contacts are most likely to be school-related — fellow students who may sell "just to friends" or who may be the primary local dealers for students. Such contacts are not difficult to find; the 1991 Monitoring the Future study found that 83% of high school seniors considered marijuana "fairly easy" or "very easy" for them to get.[100] Over half the seniors (51%) even considered cocaine to be this available. This is a legacy of the 1960s, when street drugs for the very first time became widely available to virtually any adolescent — not just those in inner-city areas with traditional established drug markets. Suburban teens who want larger quantities of street drugs, however, have to find a connection to the traditional inner-city drug markets.

Those markets have been active since before the end of the nineteenth century, even prior to the passage of the Harrison Act in 1914 which, in effect, officially criminalized opiate use in the United States for the first time.[101] Since inner-city drug markets are extremely common — and sometimes blatantly open to public view — young people who grow up in the neighborhoods in which they operate are highly likely to know people who patronize them or even operate them. If these people are friends or family members, drug use may be a particular temptation — or even an encouraged behavior. The environmental and social proximity of street drugs probably explains why girls as well as boys growing up in inner-city neighborhoods tend to begin use of any given street drug a year or two earlier than their suburban or small-town counterparts.[102] For the same reasons, these youngsters are most in danger of making the transition from marijuana, and perhaps pills or hallucinogens, to expensive street drugs.

Expensive Street Drugs

Although street drugs are illegal by definition, only the use of expensive street drugs — heroin and cocaine — is associated with criminality more serious than minor delinquency.[103] The term "expensive" in this context refers not to a per dose cost, which in the case of crack can be quite small, but rather to the cost of supporting an addictive use pattern. For heroin, this means a required three, or more typically four, doses every day, without fail, on penalty of withdrawal. For crack, a single dose may cost only one-fourth, perhaps only one-tenth, the price of a single dose of heroin — but because crack addicts tend to use continuously until their supply is gone, the number of doses used per day can be phenomenal. Dozens are not unusual, hundreds are possible.

Obviously then, the most basic problem brought about by specifically expensive street drug use is that of finances. There are essentially three ways of financing cocaine or heroin use. One is to vigorously control one's habit and have a good enough job income to pay for it. It is unclear how commonly, or for how long a time, this strategy can succeed, but three apparent requirements are (1) relatively good initial mental health, so that drug use is not used as a coping mechanism; (2) a personally satisfying lifestyle, so that drug use is of clearly less importance than work and family; and (3) routines and rituals that impose limits on drug use.[104] This strategy is probably easier for men than women, since men are more likely to have the required job income. In a sample of hospitalized cocaine users, for example, 78% of men compared to 50% of women had been employed when admitted — and 61% of men but only 20% of women had professional, executive, or sales jobs.[105] However, the fact that even most *employed* cocaine users seen in treatment programs report financial difficulties indicates that because the level of cocaine usage is difficult to control, financing can be a problem even for relatively affluent users.[106]

A second financing method is some kind of personal relationship with a more involved user, so that this other person supports both habits. As previously noted, this kind of support is much more commonly received by women than men — but it generally occurs early in a woman's drug-use career and the drug use itself tends to have a negative impact on the relationship. Consequently, most women using expensive drugs for very long end up, eventually, having to support their own drug-use — that is, later, even if not sooner, a woman using an expensive drug will have a financing problem. Further, it may well be a worse financing problem than if she had never received the drug for free, because her dependency can grow all the more rapidly if there are no financial consequences to be suffered. It is also important to recall that, just as in the conventional household population, women drug users tend to have fewer economic resources than their male counterparts. This means that a woman's expensive drug use may well reach the stage of financial crisis earlier than occurs for a man, and losing male financial support for an expensive drug habit may be one factor encouraging treatment entry. The same hospital study cited above, for example, found that while males and females used similar amounts of cocaine, men spent three times as much money on it in the last six months — means of $9,375 versus $3,050.[107]

The third financing method is crime. Among people with little or no employment income, this is probably the most common method, for both men and women. Crime to support heroin or cocaine use, however, is not generally a user's introduction to crime. On the contrary, most studies of heroin users indicate that criminal activities were initiated well prior to heroin use, most typically theft or drug sales before or around the same time as regular marijuana use. However, other studies also show that the *amount* of crime committed by heroin and cocaine users depends on whether and how much they are using these drugs.[108] The *type* of crime committed may also change as users spend more time with other of-fenders and become more familiar with street life. For women, a particu-larly likely shift is from drug sales to prostitution. Such a change typically first occurs because something interrupts the supply of drugs for sale, but then women generally continue this type of behavior even after a drug supply is again available because prostitution brings in more income than street-level drug sales.[109]

In addition to finances, the other problem added by specifically ex-pensive street-drug use is that of not just stigma but severe stigma. Most notably, a female heroin user is considered not just probably promiscuous but doubtless a prostitute — and this presumption is made by not just conventional citizens but by other users on the street.[110] This label, of course, has some self-fulfilling prophecy aspects, encouraging a woman who "has the name" to "play the game" as well. Indications are that this process, which is well documented for female heroin users, also happens to female cocaine users, but even faster because of cocaine's reputation as an aphrodisiac.

The presumption of prostitution is just the most obvious aspect of the lower-than-low status accorded to women who use expensive street drugs. As Jennifer James pointed out some time ago, every complimentary term traditional on the street for a heroin user — "stand-up cat," "righteous dope fiend" — applies only to men and never women, and every tradi-tional term on the street for a female heroin user — "junkie broad," "junkie chick," "bag bride" — is an insult.[111] Thus, women using heroin, and presumably cocaine, are isolated by stigma from not only the life they had before but even from the kind of subcultural support received by men using the same drugs. With increased time as a heroin or cocaine street-addict, furthermore, comes an increased probability that even still-exist-ing personal relationships will be terminated — marriages end in large part due to fighting about drug use, and children are taken away by courts or conventional relatives. In short, a woman's participation in the ulti-mate drug involvement of the heroin/cocaine street-addict lifestyle very often leads to a situation which is the ultimate in social isolation.

Women and Cocaine

Cocaine has been portrayed in both the scientific and popular literature as a drug with particular appeal to women.[112] The reasons presented cover a wide spectrum of attractions:

1. Cocaine imparts a feeling of self-confidence and empowerment — and women are particularly prone to impaired self-esteem and feelings of powerlessness. This appeal of cocaine may be especially strong for women with a childhood history of abuse and neglect, which describes

a larger percentage of chemically dependent females than it does their male counterparts.

2. Cocaine, as a central nervous system stimulant, makes users feel energetic, competent, productive, and enthusiastic — and women are particularly subject to depression. Further, women's dual work force and home obligations mean that they are especially likely to have both physically and emotionally exhausting daily schedules.

3. Cocaine increases libido, at least for less-than-heavy, less-than-long-term users, which women may find helpful given modern expectations of women's "sexual liberation" in the face of a still generally ambivalent socialization for women about the permissibility of sexual expression.

4. Cocaine suppresses interest in food, and women are particularly likely to be concerned about body size and on a diet. Weight loss is generally only a discovered side-effect rather than an initial reason for use, but women are likely to see it as a positive reason to continue using cocaine.

5. Snorting cocaine and smoking crack permit self-administration of a powerful drug without resorting to needle use, a drug-use technique that women are more reluctant than men to initiate.

6. Cocaine use avoids two disadvantages of depressants that tend to be worse for women than men. One is that depressants cause a user to speak and move in ways often regarded as comical in a man's behavior but repellant in a woman's — slurring words, lack of coordination, nodding off. The other is that intoxication with a depressant can be sufficiently incapacitating to put female users at increased risk for victimization, especially sexual assault.

This list is impressively varied, but it has several flaws in logic. Given the women/drugs literature just reviewed, perhaps the most obvious flaw is that none of the cited appeals are unique to cocaine. Stimulant effects —self-confidence, energy, anorexia, a high without drowsiness— are available with prescription drugs; many different drugs relieve depression and anxiety, including sexual anxiety; most drugs of abuse do not involve needle use.

A second logical flaw is that, on the face of it, cocaine seems obviously more appealing to men than women since its primary effect is to make the user feel powerful, competent, in total command — certainly a more stereotypically male than female concern. Third and relatedly, one can easily argue that the drug effects that should appeal to women more than any other are those of heroin. As one of Marsha Rosenbaum's informants told her:

> It's just a good feeling. At that particular time, shit, you don't have a problem in the world. Nothin.' I heard a doctor say right here in this

> jail that heroin preserves people. You are not sick. You don't feel pain.
> Fuck the rent, fuck the food, fuck the phone, fuck the kids, fuck how
> you look. Really, it's just an "aw, fuck it" attitude. At the time you
> are loaded, nothing bothers you.[113]

Women, after all, have always been the gender most charged with being responsible, not the one expected to sow wild oats. They are particularly supposed to be the ones taking care of other people — their children, their husbands, their bosses, the sick people in their families, the clients they deal with in their service and teaching jobs. But not, one might note, themselves. Further, the greater experience of physical ills among female as opposed to male drug users, and their greater rates of anxiety-related psychological conditions, also argue that what they need, want, and would truly be attracted to is relief. The most seductive drug for women is arguably not one that energizes them to get more work done, but one that gives them relief from tension, responsibility, pain, and anxiety — relief so thorough that it constitutes its own nirvana.

So why has no one argued that heroin is "the perfect trap for women"? Most likely because it is too exclusively associated with street life to be a meaningful option to most women. Cocaine, on the other hand, can be given such a label,[114] because it also has associations with Hollywood, Wall Street, and the lives of the rich and famous. But such lifestyles bear no more relationship to the lives of average American women than do the demiworlds of street addicts. This suggests another flaw in the logic of seeing cocaine as the ultimately attractive drug for women — it isn't any more real to most women than is heroin. What is a real option, and consequently a significant potential attraction to women, is alcohol and, especially, pills — drugs they can easily and legally obtain, drugs that will give relief from anxiety or pain *and* drugs that give them energy and enthusiasm. And, unlike the cocaine and heroin attraction arguments, this hypothesis is supported by the epidemiological data — most chemically dependent women are addicted to alcohol or alcohol and pills, and women's rates of pill use, misuse, and dependency have always been markedly higher than men's rates.

Patricia G. Erickson and Glenn F. Murray also disagree with the claim of cocaine's special appeal to women, calling it greatly overstated since (1) more males than females use cocaine, (2) there is no evidence that female rates of use are growing faster than those of males, and (3) there is likewise no evidence that (among typical users not in treatment or jail) women are more susceptible to cocaine's effects.[115] These researchers conclude that the primary reason for the greater publicity given to women's cocaine involvement is that, in one more life area, a sexual double standard is being applied. Women's cocaine use is seen as more alarming than men's because it is connected to both old ideas about women's drug use (but not men's) being a source of sexual corruption and newer ideas about women's work-force participation leading to new pressures and temptations for women — including drug use — because they are taking on male role characteristics. In short, women who use cocaine "are subject to considerably more negative stereotyping and social repercussions than are men who engage in the same behavior."[116]

Postscript

Much of the rest of this book suggests that there is one way in which cocaine, compared to other drugs, does have a truly unique impact on women. This impact appears to be particular to *crack*-cocaine, and further, particular to heavy use of *crack*-cocaine, and further still, particular to heavy use of *crack*-cocaine in inner-city street-life settings. Specifically, the sex-for-crack phenomenon and the incredible degradation of women surrounding much of its routine enactment is like nothing ever seen in the annals of drug use, street life, prostitution, or domestic woman-battering. A number of recent ethnographic reports document that crack dependence, especially among the patrons of crack houses, often entails a variety of hypersexual behaviors — high-frequency sex, numerous anonymous partners, public as well as private sex, groups as well as couples, heterosexual or homosexual or both simultaneously.[117] The women involved are often treated abusively, some of them living as virtual slaves of the crack house owner, providing sexual services on demand in return for "room and board" — typically, a mattress, junk food, and ready access to crack.

Earlier studies of cocaine effects gave no hint that "crack house whores" might be the next development in street life. In fact, at least three kinds of research findings might lead one to doubt it could happen. First, as discussed earlier, the cocaine/sexuality link is not a new kind of drug connection in general or for women. Cocaine is just one of the multitude of drugs alleged to have an aphrodisiac effect, and female users of all kinds of drugs have been suspected of sexual promiscuity. The alcohol/sexuality linkage is so old, in fact, it can be traced back to the Old Testament.[118]

Second, studies of low-frequency cocaine users find that sexual arousal is among the acute effects commonly reported by both men and women, but it is neither invariable nor necessarily important to users. A study of "typical" cocaine users, for example, found that sexual arousal "always" was reported by only 17% of women and 18% of men; no sexual arousal even "sometimes" was reported by 28% of women and 22% of men; and in an open-ended question concerning the major appeal of cocaine, only one or two respondents specified sexual enhancement.[119] These findings in general do not predict hypersexual behavior in crack addicts, and the lack of gender differences in particular implies no special hypersexual effect of crack on women.

Third, other studies actually contradict the cocaine/sexuality linkage, especially for women. For example, in contrast to the study noted above of "typical" cocaine users, a study of sexual behavior among *heavy* cocaine users states that "Perhaps the most relevant variable in determining one's sexual experience while on cocaine is that of gender."[120] None of the 139 males and 89 females interviewed in this study were in treatment or jail, and heavy users of other drugs were excluded from the study so as not confound the results. An exclusively positive effect of cocaine on sex was reported by 40% of the men but only 22% of the women, while an exclusively negative effect was reported by 48% of the women compared to 29% of men. Some 23.5% of women even said cocaine had no effect at all on their sex lives (even in itself, less evidence of a cocaine/sexuality linkage than represented by the 12.5% of men who reported no effect). Further, longer heavy use of cocaine was significantly associated with greater perceived negative effects on sex, greater probability of sexual insensitivity/numbness, and more likelihood for males of erectile dysfunction. These findings strongly suggest that heavy crack users would likely become either sexually dysfunctional or at least sexually disinterested, particularly the women.

How, then, to explain the apparent "hypersexual" behavior observed in crack houses? The answer apparently has less to do with crack's psychopharmacology per se than with the interaction of that psychopharmacology with the new cultural and economic expectations and arrangements surrounding crack use today. Those new phenomena require new research, some of which is reported in the rest of this book. Because of the special importance of crack-house arrangements, this topic is examined first. The following chapter describes the various kinds of crack-house setups and compares them to their many historical antecedents.

Endnotes

1. Josette Mondanaro, *Chemically Dependent Women: Assessment and Treatment* (Lexington, MA: Lexington Books, 1989), p. 1.

2. Reese T. Jones, "Psychopharmacology of Cocaine," in Arnold M. Washton and Mark S. Gold, eds., *Cocaine: A Clinician's Handbook* (New York: Guilford, 1987), pp. 55–72.

3. See, e.g., David D. Celentano and David V. McQueen, "Multiple Substance Abuse among Women with Alcohol-Related Problems," in Sharon C. Wilsnack and Linda J. Beckman, eds., *Alcohol Problems in Women* (New York: Guilford, 1984), pp. 97–116; Richard R. Clayton, Harwin L. Voss, Cynthia Robbins, and William F. Skinner, "Gender Differences in Drug Use: An Epidemiological Perspective," in Barbara A. Ray and Monique C. Braude, eds., *Women and Drugs: A New Era for Research* (Rockville, MD: National Institute on Drug Abuse, 1986), pp. 80–99; Stephen E. Gardner, ed., *National Drug/Alcohol Collaborative Project: Issues in Multiple Substance Abuse* (Rockville, MD: National Institute on Drug Abuse, 1980); Dooley Worth, "American Women and Polydrug Abuse," in Paula Roth, ed., *Alcohol and Drugs are Women's Issues, Vol. I, A Review of the Issues* (Metuchen, NJ: Women's Action Alliance and The Scarecrow Press, 1991), pp. 1–9.

4. See, e.g., Clayton, Voss, Robbins, and Skinner, "Gender Differences"; Jones, "Psychopharmacology"; Shirley Y. Hill, "Vulnerability to the Biomedical Consequences of

Alcoholism and Alcohol-Related Problems Among Women," in Sharon C. Wilsnack and Linda J. Beckman, eds., *Alcohol Problems in Women* (New York: Guilford, 1984), pp. 121–154.

5. See, e.g., Barbara W. Lex, "Some Gender Differences in Alcohol and Polysubstance Users," *Health Psychology* 10 (1991), pp. 121–132.

6. Oriana Josseau Kalant, "Sex Differences in Alcohol and Drug Problems — Some Highlights," in Oriana Josseau Kalant, ed., *Research Advances in Alcohol and Drug Problems, Vol. 5: Alcohol and Drug Problems in Women* (New York: Plenum Press, 1980), pp. 1–24.

7. Debra L. Ashbrook and Linda C. Solley, *Women and Heroin Abuse: A Survey of Sexism in Drug Abuse Administration* (Palo Alto, CA: R & E Research Associates, 1979), p. 27; Thomas J. Glynn, Helen Wallenstein Pearson, and Mollie Sayers, eds., *Women and Drugs* (Rockville, MD: National Institute on Drug Abuse, 1983); Denise F. Polit, Ronald L. Nuttall, and Joan B. Hunter, "Women and Drugs: A Look at Some of the Issues," *Urban and Social Change Review* 9 (1976) pp. 9–16.

8. Sandie Johnson, "Recent Research: Alcohol and Women's Bodies," in Paula Roth, ed., *Alcohol and Drugs Are Women's Issues, Vol. I. A Review of the Issues* (Metuchen, NJ: Women's Action Alliance and The Scarecrow Press, 1991), pp. 32–42.

9. For summaries, see Ashbrook and Solley, *Women and Heroin Abuse*; Polit, Nuttall, and Hunter, "Women and Drugs"; Marvin R. Burt, Thomas J. Glynn, and Barbara J. Sowder, *Psychosocial Characteristics of Drug-Abusing Women* (Rockville, MD: National Institute on Drug Abuse, 1979); Mary Ellen Colten, "A Descriptive and Comparative Analysis of Self-Perceptions and Attitudes of Heroin-Addicted Women," in *Addicted Women: Family Dynamics, Self Perceptions, and Support Systems* (Rockville, MD: National Institute on Drug Abuse, 1979), pp. 7–36.

10. See Gregory A. Austin, Mary A. Macari, Patricia Sutker, and Dan J. Lettieri, eds., *Drugs and Psychopathology* (Rockville, MD: National Institute on Drug Abuse, 1977).

11. See note 5 above.

12. See, e.g., Michael Agar, *Ripping and Running: A Formal Ethnography of Urban Heroin Addicts* (New York: Seminar Press, 1973); Harvey W. Feldman, "Ideological Supports to Becoming and Remaining a Heroin Addict," *Journal of Health and Social Behavior* 9 (1968), pp. 131–139; Edward Preble and John J. Casey Jr., "Taking Care of Business: The Heroin User's Life on the Street," *International Journal of the Addictions* 4 (1969), pp. 1–24; Alan G. Sutter, "The World of the Righteous Dope Friend," *Issues in Criminology* 2 (1966), pp. 177–222.

13. Ira Cisin, Judith D. Miller, and Adele V. Harrell, *Highlights From the National Survey on Drug Abuse: 1977* (Rockville, MD: National Institute on Drug Abuse, 1978).

14. Mary Ellen Colten and Jeanne C. Marsh, "A Sex-Roles Perspective on Drug and Alcohol Use by Women," in Cathy Spatz Widom, ed., *Sex Roles and Psychopathology* (New York: Plenum Press, 1984), pp. 219–248; Roberta G. Ferrence and Paul C. Whitehead, "Sex Differences in Psychoactive Drug Use: Recent Epidemiology," in Oriana Josseau Kalant, ed., *Research Advances in Alcohol and Drug Problems, Vol. 5: Alcohol and Drug Problems in Women* (New York: Plenum Press, 1980), pp. 125–201.

15. Mark H. Greene, "An Epidemiologic Assessment of Heroin Use," *American Journal of Public Health* 64 Supplement (1974), pp. 1–10; Leon Gibson Hunt and Carl D. Chambers, *The Heroin Epidemics* (New York: Spectrum Publications, 1976).

16. Colten and Marsh, "A Sex-Roles Perspective"; Jane E. Prather and Linda S. Fidell, "Drug Use and Abuse Among Women: An Overview," *International Journal of the Addictions* 13 (1978), pp. 863–885; David N. Nurco, Norma Wegner, Howell Baum, and Abraham Makotsky, *A Case Study: Narcotic Addiction Over a Quarter of a Century in a Major American City 1950–1977* (Rockville, MD: National Institute on Drug Abuse, 1979); Barry S. Ramer, David E. Smith, and George R. Gay, "Adolescent Heroin Abuse in San Francisco," *International Journal of the Addictions* 7 (1972), pp. 461–465; Walter R. Cuskey, Arthur H. Richardson, and Lisa H. Berger, *Specialized Therapeutic Community Program for Female Addicts* (Rockville, MD: National Institute on Drug Abuse, 1979).

17. See, e.g., Barbara Sinclair Deckard, *The Women's Movement: Political, Socioeconomic, and Psychological Issues* (New York: Harper & Row, 1975), pp. 322–375.

18. For summaries, see, e.g., Sara E. Gutierres, Deanna S. Patton, Jonathan S. Raymond, and Deborah L. Rhoads, "Women and Drugs: The Heroin Abuser and the Prescription Drug Abuser," *Psychology of Women Quarterly* 8 (Summer 1984), pp. 354–369; Richard Hughes and Robert Brewin, *The Tranquilizing of America: Pill Popping and the American Way of Life* (New York: Warner Books, 1979), pp. 70–95.

19. Susan Galbraith, "Women and Legal Drugs," in Paula Roth, ed., *Alcohol and Drugs Are Women's Issues, Vol. I, A Review of the Issues* (Metuchen, NJ: Women's Action Alliance and The Scarecrow Press, 1991), pp. 150–154.

20. See, e.g., Jean Kilbourne, "The Spirit of the Czar: Selling Addictions to Women," in Paula Roth, ed., *Alcohol and Drugs Are Women's Issues, Vol. I, A Review of the Issues* (Metuchen, NJ: Women's Action Alliance and The Scarecrow Press, 1991), pp. 10–22.

21. See Ashbrook and Solley, *Women and Heroin Abuse*; Polit, Nuttall, and Hunter, "Women and Drugs"; Carolyn A. Eldred and Mabel N. Washington, "Female Heroin Addicts in a City Treatment Program: The Forgotten Minority," *Psychiatry* 38 (1975), pp. 75–85; Stephan J. Levy and Kathleen M. Doyle, "Attitudes Toward Women in a Drug Abuse Treatment Program," *Journal of Drug Issues* 4 (1974), pp. 428–434.

22. See George M. Beschner and Peggy Thompson, *Women and Drug Abuse Treatment: Needs and Services* (Rockville, MD: National Institute on Drug Abuse, 1981); Beth Glover Reed, "Intervention Strategies for Drug Dependent Women," in George M. Beschner, Beth Glover Reed, and Josette Mondanaro, eds., *Treatment Services for Drug Dependent Women, Vol. 1* (Rockville, MD: National Institute on Drug Abuse, 1981), pp. 1–24.

23. Paul J. Goldstein, *Prostitution and Drugs* (Lexington, MA: Lexington Books, 1979); James A. Inciardi and Anne E. Pottieger, "Drug Use and Crime Among Two Cohorts of Women Narcotics Users: An Empirical Assessment," *Journal of Drug Issues* 16 (1986), pp. 91–106; James A. Inciardi, Anne E. Pottieger, and Charles E. Faupel, "Black Women, Heroin and Crime: Some Empirical Notes," *Journal of Drug Issues* 12 (1982), pp. 241–250; Jennifer James, "Prostitution and Addiction: An Interdisciplinary Approach," *Addictive Diseases* 2 (1976), pp. 601–618; Jennifer James, Cathleen T. Gosho, and Robbin Watson, "The Relationship Between Female Criminality and Drug Use," in Research Triangle Institute, *Report of the Panel on Drug Use and Criminal Behavior* (Springfield, VA: National Technical Information Service, 1976), pp. 441–455; Marsha Rosenbaum, *Women on Heroin* (New Brunswick, NJ: Rutgers University Press, 1981).

24. See Roberta G. Ferrence, "Sex Differences in Prevalence of Problem Drinking," in Oriana Josseau Kalant, ed., *Research Advances in Alcohol and Drug Problems, Vol. 5: Alcohol and Drug Problems in Women* (New York: Plenum Press, 1980), pp. 69–124; Kaye Middleton Fillmore, "'When Angels Fall': Women's Drinking as Cultural Preoccupation and as Reality," in Sharon C. Wilsnack and Linda J. Beckman, eds., *Alcohol Problems in Women* (New York: Guilford, 1984), pp. 7–36.

25. See Sandie Johnson, "Recent Research"; Glynn, Pearson, and Sayers, *Women and Drugs*; Lex, "Some Gender Differences."

26. Dan Waldorf, Craig Reinarman, and Sheigla Murphy, *Cocaine Changes: The Experience of Using and Quitting* (Philadelphia: Temple University Press, 1991); Robert L. Hubbard, Mary Ellen Marsden, J. Valley Rachal, Henrick J. Harwood, Elizabeth R. Cavanaugh, and Harold M. Ginzburg, *Drug Abuse Treatment: A National Study of Effectiveness* (Chapel Hill: University of North Carolina Press, 1989).

27. Celentano and McQueen, "Multiple Substance Abuse"; Clayton, Voss, Robbins, and Skinner, "Gender Differences"; Lex, "Some Gender Differences"; Beth Glover Reed, "Linkages: Battering, Sexual Assault, Incest, Child Sexual Abuse, Teen Pregnancy, Dropping Out of School and the Alcohol and Drug Connection," in Paula Roth, ed., *Alcohol and Drugs Are Women's Issues, Vol. I, A Review of the Issues* (Metuchen, NJ: Women's Action Alliance and The Scarecrow Press, 1991), pp. 130–149.

28. See, e.g., Lex, "Gender Differences"; Kaye Middleton Fillmore, "Women's Drinking Across the Adult Life Course as Compared to Men's," *British Journal of Addiction* 82 (1987), pp. 801–811.

29. Fillmore, "'When Angels Fall.'"

30. Ferrence and Whitehead, pp. 171–173.

31. See, e.g.,. Carol J. Boyd and Thomas Mieczkowski, "Drug Use, Health, Family and Social Support in 'Crack' Cocaine Users," *Addictive Behaviors* 15 (1990), pp. 481–485; Carolyn A. Eldred and Mabel N. Washington, "Interpersonal Relationships in Heroin Use by Men and Women and Their Role in Treatment Outcome," *International Journal of the Addictions* 11 (1976), pp. 117–30.

32. Cynthia Robbins, "Sex Differences in Psychosocial Consequences of Alcohol and Drug Abuse," *Journal of Health and Social Behavior* 30 (March 1989), pp. 117–130.

33. Lex, "Some Gender Differences"; Jeanne C. Marsh and Nancy A. Miller, "Female Clients in Substance Abuse Treatment," *International Journal of the Addictions* 20 (1985), pp. 995–1019; Beth Glover Reed, "Drug Misuse and Dependency in Women: The Meaning and Implications of Being Considered a Special Population or Minority Group," *International Journal of the Addictions* 20 (1985), pp. 13–62; Patricia B. Sutker, "Drug Dependent Women: An Overview of the Literature," in George M. Beschner, Beth Glover Reed, and Josette Mondanaro, eds., *Treatment Services for Drug Dependent Women*, Vol. 1 (Rockville, MD: National Institute on Drug Abuse, 1981), pp. 25–51.

34. James A. Inciardi, Ruth Horowitz, and Anne E. Pottieger, *Street Kids, Street Drugs, Street Crime* (Belmont, CA: Wadsworth, 1993), p. 119.

35. Anitra Pivnick, Michael Mulvihill, Audrey Jacomson, Ming Ann Hsu, Kathleen Eric, and Ernest Drucker, "Reproductive Decisions Among HIV-Infected, Drug-Using Women: The Importance of Mother-Child Coresidence," *Medical Anthropology Quarterly* 5 (June 1991), pp. 153–169.

36. Boyd and Mieczkowski, "Drug Use, Health, Family."

37. See, e.g., Robert P. Gandossy, Jay R. Williams, Jo Cohen, and Henrick J. Harwood, *Drugs and Crime: A Survey and Analysis of the Literature* (Washington, DC: National Institute of Justice, 1980); Judith Green, "Overview of Adolescent Drug Use," in George M. Beschner and Alfred S. Friedman, eds., *Youth Drug Abuse: Problems, Issues, and Treatment* (Lexington, MA: Lexington Books, 1979), pp. 17–44; Denise B. Kandel, "Drug Abuse by Youth: An Overview," in Dan J. Lettieri and Jaqueline P. Ludford, eds., *Drug Abuse and the American Adolescent* (Rockville, MD: National Institute on Drug Abuse, 1981), pp. 1–24; Arnold M. Washton, "Cocaine: Drug Epidemic of the '80's," in David F. Allen, ed., *The Cocaine Crisis* (New York: Plenum, 1987), pp. 45–63.

38. See, e.g., Inciardi, Horowitz, and Pottieger, *Street Kids*, pp. 117–171; Ruth Seydlitz, "The Effects of Age and Gender on Parental Control and Delinquency," *Youth & Society* 23 (December 1991), pp. 175–201.

39. See Gutierres, Patton, Rayond, and Rhoads, "Women and Drugs"; Lex, "Some Gender Differences"; Reed, "Linkages . . .".

40. See, e.g., Gutierres, Patton, Raymond, and Rhoads, "Women and Drugs"; M. Douglas Anglin, Yih-Ing Hser, and W. H. McGlothlin, "Sex Differences in Addict Careers. 2. Becoming Addicted," *Americal Journal of Drug and Alcohol Abuse* 13 (1987), pp. 59–71; Karen N. File, "Sex Roles and Street Roles," *International Journal of the Addictions* 11 (1976), pp. 263–268; Yih-Ing Hser, M. Douglas Anglin, and William McGlothlin, "Sex Differences in Addict Careers. 1. Initiation of Use," *American Journal of Drug and Alcohol Abuse* 13 (1987), pp. 33–57; Patricia J. Morningstar and Dale D. Chitwood, "How Women and Men Get Cocaine: Sex-Role Stereotypes and Acquisition Patterns," *Journal of Psychoactive Drugs* 19 (1987), pp. 135–142; Nathan Smithberg and Joseph Westermeyer, "White Dragon Pearl Syndrome: A Female Pattern of Drug Dependence," *American Journal of Drug and Alcohol Abuse* 11 (1985), pp. 199–207; Arnold M. Washton and Mark S. Gold, "Recent Trends in Cocaine Abuse as Seen from the "800-Cocaine Hotline," in Arnold M. Washton and Mark S. Gold, eds., *Cocaine: A Clinician's Handbook* (New York: Guilford, 1987), pp. 10–22.

41. Rosenbaum, *Women on Heroin*, pp. 88–89.

42. See, e.g., Irene Hanson Frieze and Patricia Cooney Schafer, "Alcohol Use and Marital Violence: Female and Male Differences in Reactions to Alcohol," in Sharon C. Wilsnack and Linda J. Beckman, eds., *Alcohol Problems in Women* (New York: Guilford, 1984), pp. 260–279; Barry J. Spunt, Paul J. Goldstein, Patricia A. Bellucci, and Thomas Miller, "Race/Ethnicity and Gender Differences in the Drugs-Violence Relationship," *Journal of Psychoactive Drugs* 22 (July–September 1990), pp. 293–303.

43. See Sutker, "Drug Dependent Women," pp. 30–31.

44. Reed, "Linkages . . ."; Yih-Ing Hser, M. Douglas Anglin, and Mary W. Booth, "Sex Differences in Addict Careers. 3. Addiction," *American Journal of Drug and Alcohol Abuse* 13 (1987), pp. 231–251; Margaret L. Griffin, Roger D. Weiss, Steven M. Mirin, and Ulrike Lange, "A Comparison of Male and Female Cocaine Abusers," *Archives of General Psychiatry* 46 (February 1989), pp. 122–126; Jill Novacek, Robert Raskin, and Robert Hogan, "Why Do Adolescents Use Drugs? Age, Sex, and User Differences," *Journal of Youth and Adolescence* 20 (1991), pp. 475–492; Frederic Suffet and Richard Brotman, "Female Drug Use: Some Observations," *International Journal of the Addictions* 11 (1976), pp. 19–33.

45. See Sheila B. Blume, "Chemical Dependency in Women: Important Issues," *American Journal of Drug and Alcohol Abuse* 16 (1990), pp. 297–307.

46. Mondanaro, *Chemically Dependent Women*, pp. 2–3; also see Reed, "Drug Misuse and Dependency."

47. Marsh and Miller, "Female Clients,"; Reed, "Drug Misuse and Dependency."

48. See, e.g., Mondanaro, *Chemically Dependent Women*; Reed, "Drug Misuse and Dependency", "Linkages . . ."; Sally Stevens, Naya Arbiter, and Peggy Glider, "Women Residents: Expanding Their Role to Increase Treatment Effectiveness in Substance Abuse Programs," *International Journal of the Addictions* 24 (1989), pp. 425–434; Maria Vandor, Patti Juliana, and Rose Leone, "Women and Illegal Drugs," in Paula Roth, ed., *Alcohol and Drugs are Women's Issues, Vol. I, A Review of the Issues* (Metuchen, NJ: Women's Action Alliance and The Scarecrow Press, 1991), pp. 155–160; Sharon C. Wilsnack, "Drinking, Sexuality, and Sexual Dysfunction in Women," in Sharon C. Wilsnack and Linda J. Beckman, eds., *Alcohol Problems in Women* (New York: Guilford, 1984), pp. 189–227.

49. Patricia Ann Harrison, "Women in Treatment: Changing Over Time," *International Journal of the Addictions* 24 (1989), pp. 655–673.

50. Gutierres, Patton, Raymond, and Rhoads, "Women and Drugs"; Mondanaro, *Chemically Dependent Women*; Sutker, "Drug Dependent Women."

51. See Reed, "Drug Misuse and Dependency."

52. Juana Mora and M. Jean Gilbert, "Issues for Latinas: Mexican American Women," in Paula Roth, eds., *Alcohol and Drugs Are Women's Issues, Vol. I, A Review of the Issues* (Metuchen, NJ: Women's Action Alliance and The Scarecrow Press, 1991), pp. 43–47; Ashaki H. Taha-Ciss, "Issues for African American Women," in Paula Roth, ed., *Alcohol and Drugs are Women's Issues, Vol. I, A Review of the Issues* (Metuchen, NJ: Women's Action Alliance and The Scarecrow Press, 1991), pp. 54–60.

53. It has also been argued that polydrug use has had a long history for women; see Worth.

54. Lex, "Gender Differences."

55. See Lex, "Gender Differences."

56. Patrick T. Macdonald, Dan Waldorf, Craig Reinarman, and Sheigla Murphy, "Heavy Cocaine Use and Sexual Behavior," *Journal of Drug Issues* 18 (1988), pp. 437–455; Mondanaro, *Chemically Dependent Women*, pp. 143–146.

57. Macdonald, Waldorf, Reinarman, and Murphy, "Heavy Cocaine Use"; Wilsnack, "Drinking, Sexuality, and Sexual Dysfunction."

58. See Wilsnack, "Drinking, Sexuality, and Sexual Dysfunction." p. 212.

59. See Reed, "Linkages . . . ."

60. See Wilsnack, "Drinking, Sexuality, and Sexual Dysfunction."

61. Mondanaro, pp. 33–51; Sutker, "Drug Dependent Women."

62. See Ruth E. Little and Cynthia H. Ervin, "Alcohol Use and Reproduction," in Sharon C. Wilsnack and Linda J. Beckman, eds., *Alcohol Problems in Women* (New York: Guilford, 1984), pp. 155–188.

63. See, e.g., Ira J. Chasnoff and Sidney H. Schnoll, "Consequences of Cocaine and Other Drug Use in Pregnancy," in Arnold M. Washton and Mark S. Gold, eds., *Cocaine: A Clinician's Handbook* (New York: Guilford, 1987), pp. 241–251; Leo Habel, Katherine Kaye, and Jean Lee, "Trends in Reporting of Maternal Drug Abuse and Infant Mortality Among Drug-Exposed Infants in New York City," *Women & Health* 16

(1990), pp. 41–58; Beatrix Lutiger, Karen Graham, Thomas R. Einarson, and Gideon Koren, "The Relationship Between Gestational Cocaine Use and Pregnancy Outcome: A Meta-Analysis," *Teratology* 44 (1991), pp. 405–414; Sandra McCalla, Howard L. Minkoff, Joseph Feldman, Isaac Delke, Martin Salwin, Gloria Valencia, and Leonard Glass, "The Biologic and Social Consequences of Perinatal Cocaine Use in an Inner-City Population: Results of an Anonymous Cross-Sectional Study," *American Journal of Obstetrics and Gynecology* 164 (February 1991), pp. 625–630; Mondanaro, p. 36; Diana B. Petitti and Charlotte Coleman, "Cocaine and the Risk of Low Birth Weight," *American Journal of Public Health* 80 (January 1990), pp. 25–28.

64. See Jones, pp. 67–68; Todd Wilk Estroff, "Medical and Biological Consequences of Cocaine Abuse," in Arnold M. Washton and Mark S. Gold, eds., *Cocaine: A Clinician's Handbook* (New York: Guilford, 1987), pp. 23–32; Reginald G. Smart, "Crack Cocaine Use: A Review of Prevalence and Adverse Effects," *American Journal of Drug and Alcohol Abuse* 17 (1991), pp. 13–26.

65. Kalant, p. 1.

66. Lutiger, Graham, Einarson, and Koren, "Cocaine Use and Pregnancy."

67. On metabolism, see Estroff, "Medical and Biological Consequences"; on prenatal care, see McCalla, Minkoff, Feldman, Delke, Salwin, Valencia, and Glass, "Biologic and Social Consequences."

68. See Lex.

69. See Blume; Lex.

70. See Hill.

71. For reviews, see Shirley; Lex.

72. See Anglin, Hser, and McGlothlin; Griffin, Weiss, Mirin, and Lange; Lex.

73. Mondanaro; Reed, "Drug Misuse and Dependency."

74. Lex; Marsh and Miller; Reed, "Drug Misuse and Dependency"; Sutker.

75. Lex; Mondanaro, p. 2.

76. Blume; Lex; Reed, "Drug Misuse and Dependency."

77. See Reed, "Drug Misuse and Dependency."

78. See Anglin, Hser, and Booth; Beschner and Thompson; Marsh and Miller; Reed, "Drug Misuse and Dependency"; Reed, "Linkages . . ."; Stevens, Arbiter, and Glider; Linda J. Beckman and Hortensia Amaro, "Patterns of Women's Use of Alcohol Treatment Agencies," in Sharon C. Wilsnack and Linda J. Beckman, eds., *Alcohol Problems in Women* (New York: Guilford, 1984), pp. 319–348.

79. Edward Khantzian, in an interview with Vicki D. Greenleaf, *Women and Cocaine: Personal Stories of Addiction and Recovery* (Los Angeles: Lowell House, 1989), pp. 24–25.

80. See Beckman and Amaro; Griffin, Weiss, Mirin, and Lange; Fillmore "Women's Drinking Across the Adult Life Course"; M. Douglas Anglin, Yih-Ing Hser, and Mary W. Booth, "Sex Differences in Addict Careers. 4. Treatment," *American Journal of Drug and Alcohol Abuse* 13 (1987), pp. 253–280.

81. See Anglin, Hser, and Booth; Rosenbaum, pp. 102–103; Beckman and Amaro.

82. Margaret Blasinsky, "Childcare Support Services for Female Clients in Treatment," in George M. Beschner, Beth Glover Reed, and Josette Mondanaro, eds., *Treatment Services for Drug Dependent Women*, Vol. 1 (Rockville, MD: National Institute on Drug Abuse, 1981), pp. 408–454.

83. See Blume; Ann Geller, "The Effects of Drug Use During Pregnancy," in Paula Roth, ed., *Alcohol and Drugs are Women's Issues, Vol. I, A Review of the Issues* (Metuchen, NJ: Women's Action Alliance and The Scarecrow Press, 1991), pp. 101–106.

84. See Reed, "Drug Misuse and Dependency."

85. Ibid., 35.

86. Ibid.

87. Mondanaro; Reed, "Drug Misuse and Dependency."

88. Blume, p. 299.

89. See Marsh and Miller, pp. 1001–1003.

90. Reed, "Drug Misuse and Dependency."

91. See Vandor, Juliana, and Leone; Patricia G. Erickson and Glenn F. Murray, "Sex Differences in Cocaine Use and Experiences: A Double Standard Revived?" *American Journal of Drug and Alcohol Abuse* 15 (1989), pp. 135–152.

92. John A. O'Donnell, Harwin L. Voss, Richard R. Clayton, Gerald T. Slatin, and Robin G. W. Room, *Young Men and Drugs—A Nationwide Survey* (Rockville, MD: National Institute on Drug Abuse, 1976).

93. National Institute on Drug Abuse, *National Household Survey on Drug Abuse: Population Estimates 1991* (Rockville, MD: National Institute on Drug Abuse, 1992), p. 31.

94. See Washton; Washton and Gold.

95. National Institute on Drug Abuse, *National Household Survey on Drug Abuse: Population Estimates 1988* (Rockville, MD: National Institute on Drug Abuse, 1989), p. 29.

96. University of Michigan News and Information Services press release, January 27, 1992.

97. See James A. Inciardi and Duane C. McBride, "Legalization: A High Risk Alternative in the War on Drugs," *American Behavioral Scientist* 32 (January/February 1989), pp. 259–289; Eric D. Wish, "U.S. Drug Policy in the 1990s: Insights from New Data from Arrestees," *International Journal of the Addictions* 25 (1990–1991), pp. 377–409.

98. See Denise B. Kandel, "Drug and Drinking Behavior Among Youth," in Alex Inkeles, Neil J. Smelser, and Ralph H. Turner, eds., *Annual Review of Sociology*, Vol. 6 (Palo Alto, CA: Annual Reviews, 1980), pp. 235–85.

99. See, e.g., Bruce D. Johnson, *Marihuana Users and Drug Subcultures* (New York: Wiley, 1973); Marcia R. Chaiken and Bruce D. Johnson, "Characteristics of Different Types of Drug-Involved Offenders," *National Institute of Justice Issues and Practices* (February 1988; NCJ 108560); Richard R. Clayton and Harwin L. Voss, *Young Men and Drugs in Manhattan: A Casual Analysis* (Rockville, MD: National Institute on Drug Abuse, 1981).

100. University of Michigan, Table 7.

101. See, e.g., H. Wayne Morgan, *Yesterday's Addicts: American Society and Drug Abuse, 1865–1920* (Norman: University of Oklahoma Press, 1974; H. Wayne Morgan, *Drugs in America: A Social History, 1800–1980* (Syracuse, NY: Syracuse University Press, 1981); David T. Courtwright, *Dark Paradise: Opiate Addiction in America Before 1940* (Cambridge: Harvard University Press, 1982); David F. Musto, *The American Disease: Origins of Narcotic Control* (New Haven: Yale University Press, 1973).

102. See Inciardi, Horowitz, and Pottieger, *Street Kids*, p. 78.

103. James J. Collins, Robert L. Hubbard, and J. Valley Rachal, "Expensive Drug Use and Illegal Income: A Test of Explanatory Hypotheses," *Criminology* 23 (1985), pp. 743–764; Lloyd D. Johnston, Patrick M. O'Malley, and Leslie K. Eveland, "Drugs and Delinquency: A Search for Casual Connections," in Denise B. Kandel, ed., *Longitudinal Research on Drug Use* (Washington, D.C.: Hemisphere Publishing, 1978), pp. 137–156.

104. Waldorf, Reinarman, and Murphy, pp. 140–156; also see Norman E. Zinberg, *Drug, Set, and Setting: The Basis for Controlled Intoxicant Use* (New Haven, CT: Yale University Press, 1984).

105. Griffin, Weiss, Mirin, and Lange.

106. See, e.g., Waldorf, Reinarman, and Murphy, pp. 168–171.

107. Griffin, Weiss, Mirin, and Lange.

108. For a review, see David N. Nurco, Thomas Hanlon, and Timothy W. Kinlock, "Recent Research on the Relationship between Illicit Drug Use and Crime," *Behavioral Sciences and the Law* 9 (1991), pp. 221–242.

109. See James A. Inciardi, *The War on Drugs: Heroin, Cocaine, Crime, and Public Policy* (Mountain View, CA: Mayfield, 1986), pp. 163–167.

110. Arthur Maglin, "Sex Role Differences in Heroin Addiction," *Social Casework* 55 (1974), pp. 160–167.

111. James, p. 612.

112. See, e.g., Erickson and Murray; Mondanaro, pp. 135–149; Greenleaf, pp. 5–15.
113. p. 44.
114. For example, it is the title of Mondanaro's chapter on women and cocaine.
115. Erickson and Murray, "Sex Differences."
116. Erickson and Murray, p. 150.
117. See, e.g., Robert G. Carlson and Harvey A. Siegal, "The Crack Life: An Ethnographic Overview of Crack Use and Sexual Behavior Among African-Americans in a Midwest Metropolitan City," *Journal of Psychoactive Drugs* 23 (January–March 1991), pp. 11–20; Mitchell S. Ratner, ed., *Crack Pipe as Pimp: An Eight-City Ethnographic Study of the Sex-for-Crack Phenomenon* (Lexington, MA: Lexington Press, 1993).
118. See, e.g., Blume, pp. 297–298.
119. Erickson and Murray, p. 147.
120. Macdonald, Waldorf, Reinarman, and Murphy, p. 442.

CHAPTER 3

Crack Houses and Other Drug Dens

"Crack is not a black thing, not a white thing. It's a death thing, and death doesn't give a shit about color."

—*New Jack City, 1991*

As the volley of media reports of crack addiction and despair spread across the nation during the spring and summer of 1986, many of those in the Miami street scene thought wistfully about what they were hearing. They had definite feelings of *deja vu*. Crack had been a part of the street scene in Miami by the early 1980s, and according to several informants, the drug could be purchased at several inner-city *get-off houses** as early as mid-1981. One of the elder statesmen of Miami's remnant "beat generation" poets musingly commented in 1992:

. . . I was sitting there watching the television in this place in the Grove [Miami's fashionable Coconut Grove area], and on comes Dan Rather. He's got this real serious look on his face, as if he's about to tell us that the President was assassinated or that we're about to get nuked by the fucking Martians. Then he starts talking about a new killer drug up there in New York City. And they flash a picture of these pasty little drug rocks. And I said to myself: "Oh shit, Dan, I've been here before. I've seen those little fuckers before!" And then I said something like: "Oh shit, Dan, you stupid, dick-headed, mongoloid, blind-sighted, myopic, simpleton, mother-fucked, ass-fucked dip-shit. That shit-killer drug is *base*, you dumb fart! It's the early eighties Miami base, that was early seventies Hashbury [Haight-Ashbury] base. It's goddamn fucking base, an' you're telling the world a goddamn outrageous, preposterous, fatuous, inane, fucking untruth!"

Get-off houses, also know as *shooting galleries*, are places where drugs are injected, and are described later in this chapter.

In a somewhat less animated fashion, a long-time heroin user and resident of the Miami's Overtown community recalled:

> I remember it clear like it was yesterday, 'cause I remember my brother Freddie and me were out celebrating. He had just finished doin' eighteen months for a B & E [breaking and entering] and this was the first I had seen him since he was out. That was the last time he done any hard time, and he got out in May of '81.
>
> Anyway, there was this place on 17th Street, near a little park. It was a get-off house, you know, a shooting gallery. Freddie wanted some white boy [heroin], so since he was just out an' all that I told him it was on me. So we go to this place on 17th. After we're there a few minutes the house man [shooting gallery owner] shows me these small cocaine rocks. I forget exactly what he called them, but later on we know'd it as crack. Said they were comin' down every day from Little Haiti [Miami's Haitian community] and he'd been dealin' them out of his place for three months for the smokin' cokeys [cocaine users]. I remember Freddie laughin' about it, that with there bein' coke there and the kind of people it attracted the place wouldn't be respectable much longer.

Other drug users encountered on the streets of Miami during the course of various studies remembered the first appearance of crack early in the decade. As indicated in Table 3.1, for example, of 254 seriously crime-involved adolescents questioned about their crack use as part of a larger mid-1980s study, many were aware of crack as early as November 1983.*

The use of crack and the existence of crack houses proliferated in Miami throughout the 1980s.[1] Crack quickly became a major drug problem, particularly in the criminal justice sector. Early in 1987 a Miami prosecutor emphasized this point:

> All we ever seem to hear about any more is crack — crack dealers, crack wholesalers, crack manufacturers, crack users, crack houses, crack cases. The police are all jammed up, spending all of their time chasing the dealers; they've clogged the courts, and they've got the jails and prisons overloaded.

And in the local jail, a custodial officer sarcastically noted:

> The jail just isn't the respectable place that it once was. There was a time when we got a pretty decent crowd — crooks yelling about how they were set up and put upon by the cops, hookers uttering obscenities at the jailers and public defenders, junkies with the shakes, and drunks scratching their balls and pissing on the floors and puking on themselves. Now all there is is the crackheads, the scum of the streets. They're all crazy and unpredictable and you can't control most of them.

---

*This adolescent sample is described in somewhat more detail in Chapter 6 of this book. The complete study is reported in James A. Inciardi, Ruth Horowitz, and Anne E. Pottieger, *Street Kids, Street Drugs, Street Crime: An Examination of Drug Use and Serious Delinquency in Miami* (Belmont, CA: Wadsworth, 1993).

Table 3.1
Dates of First Knowledge and Use of Crack Among 254 Drug-Using Street Delinquents, Miami, 1987.

	Number 254	Percent 100.0
When did you first hear about crack?		
November 1982 – December 1983	62	24.4
January – December 1984	82	32.2
January – December 1985	46	18.1
January 1986 – May 1987	64	25.2
When did you first try crack?		
By December 1984	116	45.7
January – November 1985	55	21.7
December 1985 – May 1987	73	29.5
Not Applicable/Never Tried It	8	3.1

Source: "Drug Use and Serious Delinquency," HHS Grant No. 1-RO1-DAO1827, from the National Institute on Drug Abuse, James A. Inciardi, Principal Investigator, Anne E. Pottieger, Co-Principal Investigator and Project Director.

They'll fight with each other over nothing — over a piece of dirt on the floor that they think is crack.

By 1989, the Drug Enforcement Administration estimated that there were no fewer than 700 operating crack houses in the greater Miami area.[2] As in other urban locales, the exchange of sex for drugs became a prominent feature of the Miami crack scene,[3] raising concerns about the increased potential for the further spread of the human immunodeficiency virus (HIV) in a metropolitan center already experiencing high rates of HIV and AIDS.[4] Much of the high AIDS-risk sex/drug bartering, furthermore, was occurring inside the walls of Miami's many crack houses.

Drug Houses Down Through the Ages

As a general thing, the men who are regular opium smokers have very little money, relying almost entirely upon the women, who spend their money freely upon the fiends. Beer and tobacco are generally sold [in opium dens], which considerably swells the revenue of the keepers.
                                          — *Thomas Byrnes, 1886*[5]

* * *

Roadhouses are nests of vice. The majority are nothing more than speakeasies which serve in some instances as gathering places, and even regular "hangouts" for a lawless and criminal element.
                                          — *Walter C. Reckless, 1933*[6]

* * *

Shooting galleries are as clean and attractive as yellow pissholes in the snow.

—A Chicago heroin addict, 1992

Edward Gibbon, the eighteenth century British historian well known for his five-volume *History of the Decline and Fall of the Roman Empire,* once referred to history as "little more than a register of the crimes, follies, and misfortunes of mankind." A century later, the American journalist Ambrose Bierce defined history as "an account, mostly false, of events, mostly unimportant, which are brought about by rulers, mostly knaves, and soldiers, mostly fools." Others have had equally unflattering comments about history. Voltaire saw history as "agreed-upon fables." For Napoleon it was "a bucket of ashes"; to Henry Ford it was simply "bunk"; and for Max Lerner history was made up of the rationalizations of yesterday's victors, written by its survivors. Yet despite these many epithets, there is one characteristic of history that seems to be true: it has a way of repeating itself. Such is the case with the retreats, haunts, and hollows of various sorts that have been used for the surreptitious preparation and ingestion of illegal substances over the years. The crack house of contemporary urban and rural America is but a recent manifestation of a genre that first appeared well over a century ago. First were the opium dens and hashish houses, then came the speakeasies and roadhouses, followed by the shooting galleries and get-off houses. All were antecedents in one way or another of the modern crack house.

Opium Dens in Nineteenth-Century America

Chinese emigration to San Francisco and elsewhere in California began during the summer of 1848, about five months after the discovery of gold at Sutter's Fort. Political turmoil and economic instability at home had provoked the Chinese relocation to America's West Coast, and the need for cheap labor in the mines made California a logical destination. By 1852 more than 10,000 Chinese had arrived.[7] The vast majority came from the area around Canton, a region long associated with opium trafficking, where opium smoking was commonplace and the opium den an institution.[8] Within a decade opium dens and lodging houses had become fixtures in those parts of the trans–Mississippi West where the Chinese immigrants were concentrated.[9] By the late 1870s the opium den had not only moved eastward, but was also being frequented by Chinese and Westerners alike. At about the same time, enterprising journalists and reformers began writing about the many "sins" of America's growing cities, and the "vice" of opium smoking was often mentioned.[10] In one volume, published in 1892 as *Darkness and Daylight; or, Lights and Shadows of New York Life,* the descriptions of the opium dens offered clear reflections of the Victorian climate of the time. For example:

Near the farther end of the room was a bunk occupied by four white women, three of them apparently being adept in the vice, and the fourth a novice. Four persons crowd a bunk very closely; two recline their heads upon pillows or headrests, and the other two make use of their companions for the same purpose. A party may consist of either men or women, or it may be made up of both sexes; opium smokers do not stand on ceremony with each other, and strangers will recline on the same bunk and draw intoxication from the same pipe without the least hesitation. The old adage says "Misery loves company"; this is certainly the case with debauchery, and especially of debauchery with opium.[11]

Although the use of opium was not a crime during those years, it was illegal in most locales to operate an opium-smoking parlor. Police efforts to close the establishments were vividly presented in a popular publication vehicle of the time, a "guidebook" through the urban underworlds of vice and crime, flophouses, brothels, gaming parlors, rat pits,* and "joints" for thieves, hoodlums, thugs, and "sharpers" (swindlers).[12] Moreover, spirited descriptions of the opium habit and opium dens appeared in the police literature of the day. In 1884, for example, in a lengthy volume written and published by New York journalist A. E. Costello, the dynamics of opium smoking were related with numerous vivid illustrations. In part of his commentary, Costello stated:

A comparatively new criminal agency has been at work in certain sections of the city, spreading the fruitful seeds of contamination, and throwing additional responsibilities on the already overburdened shoulders of the police. The agency in question is what is known as "the opium habit." In a remarkably short space of time this terrible vice has taken deep root, and it is feared that it has come to stay. Unfortunately, this pernicious habit is not confined to the children of the flowery kingdom [the Chinese]; many of them are people of respectability and refinement, and are slaves of the habit. The most debased and wretched practice of the habit is smoking, which is now engaged in in scores of "joints" in New York.[13]

---

*Rat-baiting was a premier betting sport during the second half of the nineteenth century. In 1875, for example, whereas admission to an illegal boxing match cost only 50 cents, to dogfights and cockfights the fee was $2, and to view a dog against rats cost upwards of $5. Perhaps the best known of the rat pits was Kit Burns' Sportsman's Hall, a three-story frame house located at 273 Water Street on New York City's Lower East Side. The first floor was arranged as a small amphitheater, with rough wooden benches for seats. In the center was a ring some fifteen feet in diameter, enclosed by a wooden fence three feet high. This was the famous pit in which the overgrown gray rats from the New York waterfront were sent to fight against fox terriers. Matches typically drew no less than a hundred betting spectators, with purses starting at well over $100. A good rat dog faced five rats at a time, and could kill a hundred of the rodents in thirty to forty minutes. Late in the century at Kit Burns' one could also wager events that pit rats against men wearing heavy boots. See Edward Winslow Martin, *Sins of the Great City: A Work Descriptive of the Virtues and Vices, the Mysteries, Miseries and Crimes of New York City* (Philadelphia: National, 1868), pp. 388–392; Herbert Asbury, *The Gangs of New York* (Garden City, NY: Garden City Publishing Co., 1928), pp. 49–51; Luc Sante, *Low Life: Lures and Snares of Old New York* (New York: Farrar, Straus and Giroux, 1991), p. 107.

By the 1880s, opium dens had become populated not only with "hop heads" (addicts), but gamblers, prostitutes, and thieves as well. As New York City Chief of Detectives Thomas Byrnes noted in 1886:

> The people who frequent these places are, with very few exceptions, thieves, sharpers, and sporting men, and a few bad actors; the women, without exception, are immoral. No respectable woman ever entered one of these places, notwithstanding the reports to the contrary. The language used is of the coarsest kind, full of profanity and obscenity.[14]

Importantly, the opium den, "dive," or "joint" was not only a place for smoking, but a meeting place, a sanctuary. For members of the underworld it was a place to gather in relative safety, to enjoy a smoke (of opium, hashish, or tobacco) with friends and associates. For the addict it was a place to find opium, opium-smoking paraphernalia, and the company of other opium smokers. In a sense, it had become a social institution.*

From the Urban Speakeasy to the Country Roadhouse

Prohibition, spirited by the passage of the Volstead Act in 1919, was made absolute and final at midnight on January 16, 1920, causing the closing of the many corner saloons, neighborhood pubs and bars, country inns, and downtown nightclubs that had been characteristic of American life for generations. Although many of these establishments remained unofficially open, most affected by the new law were the big city cabarets, unable to operate profitably with their spacious dance floors and highly paid entertainers. Perhaps New York City, the nation's center for cabaret night life, was hurt the most. Many of midtown Manhattan's most luxurious establishments were closed and invaded by wreckers. Most ironical was the fate that overtook Murray's Roman Gardens, celebrated for its revolving dance floor and wildly exotic decor. Murray's was replaced by an oddity known as Hubert's Museum and Flea Circus, where for thirty cents one could see an assortment of freaks and watch a corps of Professor Heckler's talented insects go through their complex routines.[15]

The pubs and clubs, bars and bistros, cafes and cabarets, as well as the saloons, taverns, public houses, taprooms, and dramshops of every type were replaced with the "speakeasy"—an illicit liquor shop. The word *speakeasy* wasn't really new in the American lexicon. The term had been suggested by the English "speak-softly-shop," an underworld expression for a smuggler's house where cheap liquor could be obtained (and the

---

*A more "respectable" but short-lived counterpart of the opium den were the "hashish clubs" of the 1880s. Catering to a clientele of writers, artists, and other members of the avant-garde, they could be found on the back streets of almost every major city from New York to San Francisco. For a lurid description of a hashish club, see H. H. Kane, "A Hashish-House in New York," *Harper's Monthly,* 67 (November 1883), pp. 944–949.

patron spoke softly when ordering it).[16] By the 1880s, *speakeasy* was fully a part of American slang.[17] Nor was the speakeasy as an illicit place for drinking new to the Prohibition Era. Temperance movements had been part of American life since the colonial era, and many locales were "dry" well before the passage of the Volstead Act.[18]

The "speaks,"† as many referred to them, were of numerous types. At the bottom of the scale in the big cities were the "clip joints," "cab joints," or "steer joints," which preyed on unwary locals or visitors unfamiliar with the ways of city life. Many of these establishments would pay cab and carriage drivers to "steer" in their victims. Picking a likely customer, the driver would suggest a speakeasy where "good booze and hot girls assured a happy evening."[19] The alcohol was always on hand, and so were the women, but the prices for both were always outrageously high. And if there was a protest when the bill finally came, the establishment's strong-arm crew would generally appear to end the argument.

The excitement and violence of New York City during the roaring twenties is sharply etched in a book-length account written by Paul Morand, French author and diplomat, who made a number of visits to the city during the Prohibition Era. Morand described the most typical of the city speaks, the more "uptown" establishments that were often found in brownstone residences and operated under the guise of "clubs":

> They are usually situated downstairs and are identifiable by the large number of empty cars standing at their doors. The door is closed, and is only opened after you have been scrutinized through a door-catch or barred opening. At night an electric torch suddenly gleams through a pink silk curtain. The interior is that of a criminal house; shutters are closed in full daylight, and one is caught in the smell of a cremation furnace, for the ventilation is defective and grills are prepared under the mantle piece of the fireplace . . . Facetious inscriptions grimace from the walls . . . The food is almost always poor, the service deplorable; the staff regard you with the eyes of confederates and care not two pins about you . . .[20]

There was a general consensus that during Prohibition speakeasies could be found just about everywhere. In fact, when a journalist was asked in 1929 where one could buy liquor, he responded:

---

†One of more curious slang terms from the Prohibition Era is *wiseguy*, meaning racketeer or mobster, and still in use today. It was first associated with Chicago bootlegger Earl Wajciechowski, also known as Hymie Weiss, Hymie the Polack, or just Hymie. During a regrouping of Chicago gangland allegiances in the twenties, those who followed Al Capone became known as "Capone guys" and those allied with Hymie Weiss were called "Weiss guys," and eventually "wiseguys." In time, the expression referred to mobsters regardless of their alliances. See Kenneth Allsop, *The Bootleggers: The Story of Prohibition* (New Rochelle, NY: Arlington House, 1968), pp. 87–90. For more contemporary information, see Nicholas Pileggi, *Wiseguy: Life in a Mafia Family* (New York: Simon and Schuster, 1985).

In open saloons, restaurants, night clubs, bars behind a peephole,
dancing academies, drug stores, delicatessens, cigar stores, confection-
eries, soda fountains, behind partitions of shoeshine parlors, back
rooms of barbershops, from hotel bellhops, from hotel headwaiters,
from hotel day-clerks, night clerks, in express offices, in motorcycle
delivery agencies, paint stores, malt shops, cider stubes [from the
German *stube*, meaning room or chamber], fruit stands, vegetable markets, taxi drivers, groceries, smoke shops, athletic clubs, grillrooms,
taverns, chophouses, importing firms, tearooms, moving-van companies, spaghetti houses, boarding houses, Republican clubs, Democratic
clubs, laundries, social clubs . . .[21]

While speakeasies were products of primarily city and suburban locales, rural areas had their "roadhouses." Before the advent of national
prohibition, some districts in American cities had closed their saloons,
which quickly relocated on the other side of the city line. In states and
counties that had elected to be "dry," a similar situation evolved. In
addition, given the many small-town attitudes toward drinking and
brawling and loud music and women in tight dresses, such "indecencies"
couldn't be tolerated right in the center of things. For those who wished to
drink and engage in all manner of making merry, being "sinful" somewhere other than in the town square was considered more desirable. As
such, roadhouses were country traditions, hidden (and not so hidden)
along the rural two-lanes. The liquor flowed freely and the jukeboxes were
loud, but the lights were typically low enough so no one would be
recognized.[22]

Even after the repeal of the Prohibition Amendment, roadhouses,
because of the nature of their roots, continued to flourish. In 1941, for
example, sociologists Mabel A. Elliott and Francis E. Merrill observed that
in addition to drunkenness, sexual impropriety, and gambling:

Laws against serving liquor to minors are openly flouted. Gambling is
carried on in direct conjunction with other entertainment facilities,
often with crooked roulette wheels and similar paraphernalia. Prostitution is openly practiced in some roadhouses and is encouraged through
available private rooms in many others. The entertainment and dancing
is often indecent and vulgar, with young girls employed as singers and
dancers. Unrestrained by integrated moral control and relatively
unhindered by the formal control of law, disorganization in its several
aspects is often fostered and abetted by the roadhouse.[23]

Inner-City Shooting Galleries

For the better part of the twentieth century in most urban locales where
rates of intravenous (IV) and other injection-drug use (IDU) are high,
common sites for injecting drugs (and sometimes purchasing drugs) are
the neighborhood "shooting galleries," typically referred to in some locales as "safe houses," and in Miami as "get-off houses." After purchasing
heroin, cocaine, amphetamines, or some other injectable substance in a

local "copping" (drug selling) area, users are faced with three logistical problems: how to get off the street quickly to avoid arrest for possession of drugs, where to obtain a set of "works" with which to administer the drugs, and where to find a safe place to "get off" (inject the drugs). As such, shooting galleries occupy a functional niche in the world of IV drug abuse, where for a fee of two or three dollars users can rent a set of works and relax while "getting off." After using a syringe and needle, the user generally returns them to a central storage place in the gallery where they are held until someone else rents them. On many occasions, however, these works are just passed to another user in the gallery.

In Miami and elsewhere, shooting galleries have not been systematically studied. However, based on the senior author's observations combined with reports from a variety of ethnographic and other research studies in drug communities in several parts of the United States, their more obvious roles and characteristics can be described.[24] Shooting galleries are situated in basements and back rooms in the rundown sections of cities where drug-use rates are high. Typically, they are only sparsely furnished and dirty. Sometimes they are run by drug users, drug dealers, and drug user/dealers. Neighborhood heroin and/or cocaine dealers may operate shooting galleries as a service to customers — providing them for just a few dollars with a nearby location to safely "shoot-up" (inject). More often, however, gallery operators are drug users who provide a service for a small fee or a "taste" (sample) of someone else's drugs.*

For the majority of drug "shooters" (injectors), galleries are considered to be the least desirable places to "get off." Most prefer to use their own homes or apartments or those of drug-using friends. These are considered safer than galleries, and there are few users who appreciate having to pay a fee to use someone else's drug paraphernalia. And for a minority of hardcore injectors, there is also the matter of personal hygiene. As one heroin user summed it up:

> Galleries ain't where it's at. We wasn't brought up like that. They be definitely hardcore junkies and they don't give a damn no more about how their appearance is or nothing like that. Ain't nobody want to give another two dollars. Their works . . . all dirty, man. An' people be shootin' blood all over you.[25]

For many IV drug users, however, the use of shooting galleries is routine and commonplace. Moreover, there are repeated occasions in the lives of all IV users — including the most hygienically fastidious types — when galleries become necessary. If users have no works of their own, or

---

*It should be noted here that there are many less formally structured shooting galleries, located in darkened hallways and empty rooms in abandoned buildings. Characterized by the stench of urine and littered with trash, human feces, garbage, and discarded injection paraphernalia, the conditions are extremely unsanitary and rarely is there heat, running water, or functional plumbing.

if friends or *running partners** have no works, then using a neighborhood gallery is the only recourse. Similarly, users who purchase drugs far from home also gravitate toward the galleries. This tendency is based on the heightened risk of arrest when carrying drugs and drug paraphernalia over long distances. Moreover, the gallery operator often serves as a middle-man between drug user and drug dealer, thus making the get off-house the locus of exchange. For example, as one Miami heroin user explained the situation in 1988:

> OK, let's say I'm white, but the only place I can cop some *smack* [heroin] is in the black neighborhoods, but I'm afraid that I'll be "ripped off" [robbed] there. But then there's this gallery an' I know the man there, he's right [trusted] by the buyers and sellers. So I go there an' he cops for me for a few dollars and maybe a taste. For another $3 I can use his works and house to lay up in for a little while.[26]

And finally, there are a few injection-drug users who actually prefer local galleries because of the opportunities they provide to socialize with other users. In short, despite their unsavory character, shooting galleries do indeed occupy a functional role in the street worlds of drug-taking and drug-seeking.

Rock Houses, Base Houses, and Crack Houses

> The crack house is a carnival of vice. It is one hell of a nasty place where the "kingrats" and "pay masters" rule, where the "gut buckets" give "slow necks" for a "penny", and where the "freaks," "rock monsters," and "bloodsuckers" will do anything for a hit on the "stem." It is the "hut" where anything goes — any drug, any kick, any perversion, any trip, even to heaven or to hell — if you have the "hard

---

*All forms of needle sharing tend to occur among "running partners" (or "running buddies") — IV drug users who are lovers, good friends, crime partners, or cohabitants. They serve as lookouts for one another — one watching for police and other intruders while the other "cops," prepares the drugs, or injects. Running partners also provide other elements of safety, such as monitoring each other's responses to the drugs they use in order to prevent overdoses or other acute reactions. As a 32-year-old former heroin-using prosti-tute in Miami related in late 1990, for some IV drug users having a running partner can mean the difference between life and death:

> Without my partner I'd be dead. He was big, and more than once he saved my ass from being beat on. . . . We weren't lovers or anything like that, although we did sleep together a few times when I was really down. He was no pimp either. We were just really good friends. We could depend on each other.
> One time I was cut up pretty bad and he got me patched up. One of my "dates" [customers] had really worked me over — one of them sado-blood freaks, tied me to a bed and worked over my "change purse" [vagina] with a coat hanger. Another time when I was bein' ripped off by a bunch of street kids who wanted all of my "shit" [money and drugs] he came to the rescue, like the fucking Lone Ranger.

white" or hard dollars to buy. It is that mystic place beyond the edge
of the world where dreams are really nightmares and where nightmares
are always real. And more, it is home—home to the wretched, the
depraved, and the perverted.*

—*A Miami "kingrat," December 1989*

The term "crack house" can mean any number of different things—a
place to use crack, or a place to sell or do both, a place to manufacture and
package crack. The location may be a house, an apartment, a small shack
at the back of an empty lot, an abandoned building, or even the rusting
hulk of a discarded automobile.†

Some crack houses, although relatively few in number, are fortified
structures where large quantities of crack are manufactured from
powder-cocaine, packaged in plastic bags or glass veils, and sold both
wholesale and retail. Typical fortifications include barred windows, reinforced door and window frames, steel doors with heavy slide bolts, and
walls reinforced from the inside with steel mesh and/or a layer of concrete
blocks. Such heavy fortifications are designed for the purpose of making
police raids difficult.

In addition to fortifications, most of these heavily secured establishments are well armed, with workers typically carrying automatic or semi-
automatic weapons at all times. Crack sales are accomplished with little
or no interaction. In some, exchanges are made through a slot or hole in
the fortified door, with the money passed in and the crack passed out. In

---

*In the Miami crack scene, *kingrats* are crack-house owners. Owners are also known as *rock masters* and *house men*. *Paymasters* are male crack house customers who purchase the sex. A *scrug* is a man who tries to get sex for free.

Gut buckets are women who trade sex for crack in crack houses. "Gut" refers to a vagina.

A *slow neck* is oral sex during which the penis is sucked very slowly, as compared to a *fast head* where the intent is to bring the customer to a climax as quickly as possible. *Slow necks* typically cost more than *fast heads*.

A *penny* is a single hit on a crack pipe, typically in exchange for sex.

A *freak* was originally a *crack whore* who would engage in oral sex with another woman. However, *freak* now refers to anyone who trades any type of sex for crack, and the *freak room* in a crack house is the locus of most of the sex.

Rock monsters, also known as *base heads*, *base whores*, *crackies*, *crack whores*, *head hunters*, *rock stars*, *skeeter heads*, and *skeezers*, are women who trade sex for crack.

A *bloodsucker* is a type of female *freak*, who will remove a tampon from a menstruating woman and then perform oral sex with her.

Stems, *skillets*, and *tools* refer to crack-smoking paraphernalia.

A *hut* is a crack house, or any house or apartment where people regularly congregate to use drugs.

Hard white is crack.

†The following descriptions are based on the senior author's observations in numerous Miami crack houses, combined with data from more than 85 informants, collected during the period January 1988 through February 1992. For a discussion of the methods of entry into crack houses, see Appendix A.

others, the transaction is accomplished by means of a basket or pail lowered from a second floor or attic window. Or as a Miami inner-city resident remarked in 1990:

> I remember one night a few years ago, 1983 or '84 maybe, I'm not sure. Anyway, I went out about 10 o'clock to walk the dog and get some smokes, an' I seen these people, kids mostly, by this house on the corner, lookin' up to an attic window. I thought it was real weird, because every so often a car would drive up, or somebody would walk up to the kids and say something. Then one of them would put somethin' in a cup that was tied to a rope and a pulley. And then the cup would be pulled up to that attic window and then come down again. I stood there watchin' a few minutes, 'til one of them from the house came over an' asked why I was hanging around. I told them that I was from just down the street, was walkin' the dog and "I mind my business." I really didn't know that they were dealin'. I'd seen dealing and copping and all kinds of drug deals go down in the neighborhood for twenty-five years, but I'd never seen anything like that before.

Whereas crack houses such as these admit no one except the owners and workers, there are "all-purpose drug joints" as one informant put it, that are used by many kinds of drug users, especially intravenous users. A variety of drugs are available, including crack. However, smoking crack is not the primary activity. Intravenous drug use (typically cocaine) is more commonly seen and accepted, and as such, such establishments are actually shooting galleries that have expanded into other areas.

Far more common is what many crack users refer to as the "resort" areas — one of the more customary types of crack houses in Miami. The physical layout is that of a small apartment adapted for crack use. The kitchen is used for cooking "rock," at least one bedroom is set aside for sex, and the living space is used for selling and smoking. As one user described the crack house resort:

> One of them was his main room and the other two he would rent out, one for sexuals and one for just smoking. And sometimes there wouldn't be nobody smoking and they just come to have sex in both of them. Inside, candles burning, pillows on the floor, it wouldn't be very good for a person in his right mind.

The owners of these crack houses seem to be concerned about two things — money and crack. Many of them are addicted to crack, and operating the houses supports their drug habits. Almost anything, furthermore, can happen in these crack houses. They were observed and described as filthy, chaotic, and crowded. The crack smokers got into fights, attempted to steal each other's drugs, and exhibited extreme paranoia. One informant noted:

> I only went there to do my drugs. But I actually see some people stay there, you know, in that shit. You know, crawling around roaches, you know, like they have a dog, the fucking dog poop is all over the floor.

Another observed:

> You see people looking at the floors, looking at their chairs, picking up
> little things and putting them in a pipe and smoking them and turning
> green and coughing because its not crack, and people falling on the
> floor and untying their shoes, and people hiding in closets and getting
> paranoid, peeking out windows and looking out the doors.

The complicated relationships that develop in crack houses and the
loyalties associated with them are reflected in the comments of yet another informant:

> He [a customer] was in the room with one of the tricks, right, one of
> the house ladies. She worked for the guy that was selling drugs in the
> house. She smoked, too, and she tried to rob him, and he caught her.
> And he hit her. He didn't know she was working for the people in the
> place where they was. And he hit her and she went screaming and ran
> back down to the pimp, right. And she told the story that the mother-
> fucker tried to take his money back. And the man [the customer] said,
> "No, this bitch went in my pocket, man, the bitch went in my
> pocket." So he started out hitting his head, the pimp did. I guess he
> didn't want to shoot him so he took the torch and stuck it right in that
> man's dick. You know they told him they were going to kill him. You
> don't go around there and beat their girl. When they say they will kill
> you I believe they will.

Yet in the end, the strongest loyalty is to the crack pipe. For example:

> One time I saw a girl raped beside me but I couldn't do nothing
> because I was all high and tripping you know, they tied her down to a
> bed and one got in front of her and the other got in back of her, and
> she was hollering and screaming you know, and while he was doing it
> to her he was beating her you know, because she was trying to steal
> one of the guy's drugs.

It should be added here that the crack houses known locally as "re-
sorts" are termed as such because of the variety of activities that occur
there. As one cocaine dealer reported:

> That they call it a "rock resort" has nothin' to do with music. Ha, ha.
> It's because you can really get into it there — drugs, sex, rock 'n roll,
> all three at once, whatever. You can smoke your brains out, fuck your
> brains out, get sexed any way you want, watch sex, get paranoid, fight,
> watch fights, cut somebody, get cut, get high, get killed, whatever the
> fuck you want.

The most common kinds of crack houses in both Miami and elsewhere are personal residences — houses or apartments where small groups
of people gather regularly to smoke crack. The operators are reluctant to
call these places "crack houses" because they are used as such only by
their friends. However, the activities are the same as those in other crack
houses, including sex-for-crack exchanges. The major differences revolve

around the payment system. Crack is not typically sold in these locations, only smoked. In the more traditional crack house, payment for using the house can be made either with money or crack, money being the preferred method. In these personal residences, however, payment is made only with crack. Visitors give crack, or, more often, share crack, with the owner of the house or apartment, in return for having a place to smoke or "turn tricks" (provide sexual services). There are usually fewer people in these crack houses than in others — five or six, compared to fifteen or twenty. They are also the same five or six individuals, whereas in other types of houses there is a greater turnover of people. Moreover, the visitors to other types of crack houses are "customers," whereas only "friends" are invited to these residences.

Finally, Miami's abandoned inner-city apartments and buildings that have been overrun by drug dealers and users are also used as crack houses. They are known locally as "graveyards." As a methadone client and active crack user reported in 1988:

> Now there are lots of graveyards in almost every part of the city — Liberty City, Overtown, Miami Beach, South Miami — every neighborhood where there's empty buildings and lots of crack. Crack, and lots of crack . . . that's what makes it a graveyard.

According to most informants, no one actually owns a particular graveyard, although there do seem to be turf issues associated with their use, based on squatters' rights. Crack users bring their own crack. Sex for money and/or drugs is performed in these buildings. For example:

> I know'd this one place off Miami Avenue where this lady set up in a burned-out house. She was sort of a whore/crack head/skeezer/bag lady who'd do anythin' for crack and for food for her "trick baby" [child of a prostitute fathered by a *john*], her "base baby" [a child conceived and gestated by a crack-using mother]. For a hit on your pipe or for some food or money or drugs or cigarettes she'd let you smoke in her digs . . .

And finally, somewhat related to graveyards are "base cars" — abandoned automobiles that serve as places to smoke crack, to have sex, or to exchange sex for crack.*

---

*For more detailed descriptions of crack houses (from which segments of this material were drawn), see James A. Inciardi, *The War on Drugs II: The Continuing Epic of Heroin, Cocaine, Crack, Crime, AIDS, and Public Policy* (Mountain View, CA: Mayfield Publishing Co., 1992), pp. 117–127; James A. Inciardi, "Kingrats, Chicken Heads, Slow Necks, Freaks, and Blood Suckers: A Glimpse at the Miami Sex for Crack Market," in Mitchell S. Ratner, ed., *Crack Pipe as Pimp* (Lexington, MA: Lexington Press, 1993).

Postscript

> I believe that one day, crack dealers will be kings and presidents and crack will rule the world.
>
> *—A Miami crack dealer, 1992*

Opium dens, speakeasies, and roadhouses had a number of characteristics in common. They were places just beyond the fringes of law-abiding society where illicit substances could be had—purchased, used, and even shared. Typically available in many were the prostitutes who congregated for the purposes of solicitation and theft. And too, the dens, speaks, and houses represented discrete locations where individuals with common interests or pursuits (usually drugs, alcohol, and/or sex) could congregate.

By contrast, shooting galleries—also the loci for illegal drug use and association, and sometimes prostitution—exist totally beyond the limits and borders of organized society. Although physically situated within cities and residential neighborhoods, they are a separate world nevertheless, since their use is restricted to a narrow subculture. Even further removed are the crack houses—places "beyond the edge of the world where dreams are really nightmares and where nightmares are always real," as the Miami "kingrat" quoted earlier in this chapter so eloquently put it. Or as a New York City crack user stated in 1991:

> I seen things in crack houses that I never seen anywhere else. They're the worst of places. No one cares about anybody, about what they do. I seen everything. I seen a girl get fucked fifty times in a row, 'till she was bloody and couldn't even stand, for a little rock. I saw a guy throw acid in a lady's face, all because she didn't want to go down on him any more. I seen a junkie get his balls blown off with a shotgun because he tried to steal some "white" [crack]. They're bad places, man, beyond the extremes, well beyond the extremes.

Among the most extreme and offbeat aspects of crack house life are the sexual activities and ventures that transpire in many. Prostitution, or the exchange of sex for some commodity—whether money or drugs—is central. Although prostitution has been central to drug-oriented environments for quite some time, "crack-house sex" would appear to reflect a new dimension. Without question, crack-house sex *is* prostitution. It involves the same risks typically associated with conventional street-prostitution—physical abuse, violence, sexually transmitted diseases, and arrest, as well as leading to concerns about health care, child care, and access to legitimate employment. But further, the seductive nature of *crack*-cocaine and the sexual barter system of the crack house combine to foster a "double dependency"—on crack *and* the crack house. For many crack-dependent women, trading sex for crack in crack houses becomes the only means of survival in a highly dangerous environment.

Endnotes

1. See *Miami Herald* ("Neighbors" Supplement), April 24, 1988, pp. 21–25.

2. *Crack/Cocaine: Overview 1989* (Washington, DC: Drug Enforcement Administration, 1989).

3. See "Sex for Crack: How the New Prostitution Affects Drug Abuse Treatment," *Substance Abuse Report* 19 November 15, 1988), pp. 1–4; "Syphilis and Gonorrhea on the Rise Among Inner-City Drug Addicts," *Substance Abuse Report* 20 (June 1, 1989), pp. 1–2; "Syphilis and Crack Linked in Connecticut," *Substance Abuse Report* 20 (August 1, 1989), pp. 1–2; *New York Times*, August 20, 1989, pp. 1, 36; *New York Times*, October 9, 1989, pp. A1, A30; *U.S. News & World Report*, October 23, 1989, pp. 29–30; *Newsweek*, September 25, 1989, p. 59; *Miami Herald*, October 22, 1989, pp. 1G, 6G; James A. Inciardi, "Trading Sex for Crack Among Juvenile Drug Users: A Research Note," *Contemporary Drug Problems* 16 (Winter 1989), pp. 689–700; Mary Ann Forney and T. Holloway, "Crack, Syphilis and AIDS: The Triple Threat to Rural Georgia," *Georgia Academy of Family Physicians Journal* 12 (1989), pp. 5–6; Robert T. Rolfs, Martin Goldberg, and Robert G. Sharrar, "Risk Factors for Syphilis: Cocaine Use and Prostitution," *American Journal of Public Health* 80 (July 1990), pp. 853–857.

4. Dale D. Chitwood, James A. Inciardi, Duane C. McBride, Clyde B. McCoy, H. Virginia McCoy, and Edward J. Trapido, *A Community Approach to AIDS Intervention: Exploring the Miami Outreach Project for Injecting Drug Users and Other High Risk Groups* (Westport, CT: Greenwood Press, 1991).

5. Thomas Byrnes, *Professional Criminals of America* (New York: G. W. Dillingham, 1886).

6. Walter Reckless, *Vice in Chicago* (Chicago: University of Chicago Press, 1933).

7. See Frank Soulé, John H. Gilran, and James Nisbet, *The Annals of San Francisco* (San Francisco: A. L. Bancroft, 1878).

8. David T. Courtwright, *Dark Paradise: Opiate Addiction in America Before 1940* (Cambridge: Harvard University Press, 1982), pp. 69–71.

9. H. Wayne Morgan, *Drugs in America: A Social History, 1800–1980* (Syracuse: Syracuse University Press, 1981), p. 35.

10. For example, see J.W. Buel, *Sunlight and Shadow of America's Great Cities* (Philadelphia: West Philadelphia Publishing Co., 1891); Edward Crapsey, *The Nether Side of New York* (New York: Sheldon, 1872); Gustav Lening, *The Dark Side of New York Life and Its Criminal Classes* (New York: Fred'k Gerhard, 1873); Thomas W. Knox, *Underground, or Life Below the Surface* (Hartford: J.B. Burr and Hyde, 1873); T. DeWitt Talmage, *The Masque Torn Off* (Chicago: Fairbanks, Palmer & Co., 1883); John H. Warren, *Thirty Years' Battle With Crime, or the Crying Shame of New York, as Seen Under the Broad Glare of an Old Detective's Lantern* (Poughkeepsie: A.J. White, 1874).

11. Helen Campbell, Thomas W. Knox, and Thomas Byrnes, *Darkness and Daylight; or, Lights and Shadows of New York Life* (Hartford: A. D. Worthington, 1892), p. 570.

12. For example, see A.P., *The Mysteries and Miseries of the Great Metropolis, With Some Adventures in the Country: Being the Disguises and Surprises of a New York Journalist* (New York: D. Appleton, 1874); Charles Sutton, *The New York Tombs: Its Secrets and Its Mysteries* (New York: United States Publishing Co., 1874).

13. A. E. Costello, *Our Police Protectors* (New York: Author's Edition, 1884), pp. 516–524.

14. Byrnes, *Professional Criminals*, p. 385.

15. Lloyd Morris, *Incredible New York: High Life and Low Life of the Last Hundred Years* (New York: Bonanza Books, 1951), p. 322.

16. H.L. Mencken, *The American Language: Supplement One* (New York: Alfred A. Knopf, 1975), p. 265; Eric Partridge, *A Dictionary of Slang and Unconventional English* (New York: Macmillan, 1970), p. 806.

17. See Josiah Flynt, *The World of Graft* (New York: McClure, Phillips & Co., 1901); Godfrey Irwin, *American Tramp and Underworld Slang* (New York: Sears Publishing Co., 1931).

18. See Frances E. Willard, *Women and Temperance: or, The Work and Workers of the Woman's Christian Temperance Union* (Hartford: Park Publishing Co., 1883); J.C. Furnas, *The Late Demon Rum* (New York: Capricorn Books, 1965); W.J. Rorabaugh, *The Alcoholic Republic: An American Tradition* (New York: Oxford University Press, 1979).

19. Morris, *Incredible New York*, p. 324.

20. Paul Morand, *New York* (New York: William Heinemann, Ltd, 1930), p. 174.

21. Quoted in Herbert Ashbury, *The Great Illusion: An Informal History of Prohibition* (Garden City, NY: Doubleday, 1950), p. 211. For a description of the more exotic speakeasy locations, see Izzy Einstein, *Prohibition Agent No. 1* (New York: Frederick A. Stokes, 1932).

22. See, for example, Reckless, *Vice in Chicago*, pp. 120–136.

23. Mabel A. Elliott and Francis E. Merrill, *Social Disorganization* (New York: Harper & Brothers, 1941), p. 882.

24. Michael H. Agar, *Ripping and Running: A Formal Ethnography of Urban Heroin Addicts* (New York: Seminar Press, 1973); Seymour Fiddle, *Portraits From a Shooting Gallery* (New York: Harper & Row, 1967); Leroy C. Gould, Andrew L. Walker, Lansing E. Crane, and Charles W. Lidz, *Connections: Notes from the Heroin World* (New Haven: Yale University Press, 1974); Bill Hanson, George Beschner, James M. Walters, and Elliott Bovelle, *Life With Heroin: Voices from the Inner City* (Lexington, MA: D.C. Heath, 1985); Bruce D. Johnson, Paul J. Goldstein, Edward Preble, James Schmeidler, Douglas S. Lipton, Barry Spunt, and Thomas Miller, *Taking Care of Business: The Economics of Crime by Heroin Users* (Lexington, MA: Lexington Books, 1985); Richard P. Rettig, Manual J. Torres, and Gerald R. Garrett, *Manny: A Criminal Addict's Story* (Boston: Houghton Mifflin, 1977).

25. Hanson, Beschner, Walters, and Bovelle, *Life With Heroin*, p. 43.

26. Chitwood, Inciardi, McBride, McCoy, McCoy, and Trapido, *Community Approach to AIDS*, pp. 36–37.

CHAPTER 4

Prostitution and Crack-House Sex

"It is generally recognized that immoral women and their 'cadets' (pimps) are addicted to the use of cocaine."
— *Vice Commission of Chicago, 1911*[1]

"Hurry up and come, or else I'm done."
— *A Miami crack-prostitute, 1991*

Drug use has been associated with prostitution for centuries.[2] In the United States, the use of cocaine by prostitutes dates to the earliest years of the drug's popularity,[3] and by the beginning of the twentieth century discussions of cocaine and prostitution began to appear in the literature.[4] Yet as researcher Paul J. Goldstein has pointed out in his well-known *Prostitution and Drugs*,[5] it would be difficult to describe the specific linkages between cocaine and prostitution, given the many different and varied patterns of both drug use *and* prostitution. Goldstein's conclusion was based on his own work as well as that of numerous others in the field. In 1976, for example, Karen File proposed a typology of female addicts, noting that "the correlation between addiction and prostitution is known to be high," but is not at all clear.[6] And similarly, to examine relationships between addiction and prostitution, Jennifer James interviewed one hundred women who were either prostitutes, addicts, or addict-prostitutes. She described the process of becoming an addict-prostitute, concluding that prostitution can lead to drug addiction, and that addiction frequently leads to prostitution.[7] Other studies, such as Marsha Rosenbaum's *Women on Heroin* and Eleanor Miller's *Street Woman*, also suggest that prostitution and addiction are frequently inextricable.[8]

The point is this; women who trade sex for drugs, or money to buy drugs, drift in and out of both drug use and prostitution. Due to the instability of their lifestyles, it is impossible to group them by either their drug use or their sexual practices. However, *drug use and prostitution do often vary according to where they occur*. In crack houses, prostitution takes on a very different character than soliciting on the streets. In the crack house a barter system exists in which sex and crack are the currency. Moreover, in the descriptions that follow, it becomes readily clear that there are a number of very real differences between *prostitutes who use crack* and *crack users who exchange sex for drugs.*

Throughout this book qualitative and quantitative data from the studies described in Appendix A are presented. The information comes from women who at the time of interview were either actively using crack or who were recent admissions to treatment for crack addiction. Overall, the women discussed in this book are young, between 19 and 30 years of age; uneducated, with only a third having completed high school; and almost all are dependent on prostitution as their only source of income. In addition, 70% of these women began using crack daily within two months of first trying it. For those still using crack at the time of the interview, most were daily users. The women in treatment reported daily crack use during the 30 days prior to entering treatment. For these women, crack was the primary drug used. For almost all of the women encountered, particularly those trading sex for crack in crack houses, the drug controlled their lives in that everthing they did revolved around seeking and smoking crack.

Conducting Business

Date?
— *Miami streetwalker, 1992*

* * *

How 'bout $3? Or a $3 rock? Just a $3 rock for some brains, you know, a blow job, 'till ya come, as long as it takes. Just a $3 rock. Please?
— *Miami crack addict, 1992*

Although there are many similarities between trading sex on the streets and in a crack house, the differences resulting from the unique nature of crack addiction and the crack-house environment are central to understanding crack addiction among women. The crack-house environment affects every aspect of the business of providing sexual services — the setting, the solicitation, the negotiation, the payment, the actual exchange of either money or drugs for sex, as well as the violence and cheating endemic to both the street and crack-house environments.

These similarities and differences emerged in interviews with 85 informants in Miami, the majority of whom traded sex either for crack or for money to buy crack. Although most of the respondents had traded sex in a variety of places for a variety of reasons, some had never traded sex in a crack house, whereas others had never solicited on the street. Their experiences illustrate both street prostitution and the barter system of the crack house.

The Setting

On the streets, sex usually occurs in cars, and less frequently in motels or rooming houses. This is confirmed by a study of 20 full-time career prostitutes in Camden, New Jersey, who were interviewed five times a day over a seven-month period.[9] For them, contact with customers was made on the streets and most sex was performed in the customer's vehicle. The Miami street prostitutes described similar arrangements. For example, one reported:

> I stroll* mostly for car dates, because I prefer that. He calls me over an' we talk, I get in an' off we go to find some dark spot, either by the water or on a side street. Most all they want is a quick blow job. An' that's what I want too. I'll do him quick too. He comes quick, I spit, I get out the car door, an' I'm gone. If it's late an' there's not many people around, I'll do it right when he's driving. Most dates act all nervous when they're drivin' an' you start gettin' 'em off right in the middle of everything. But they never argue, and with the excitement of doin' it in public makes 'em come quick.

And another stated:

> I always ask for $40 if they go to a hotel. But I mostly "car date" and it's just really, really quick. If we do it in the car, we go either to a park or to somewhere dark, you know, where not too many people come by. Sometimes they have guest houses. They have a guest house right behind my house so we go over to the guest house. It's a rooming house.

Most women providing sexual services on the street have a specific area in which they work. Case studies of street prostitution in the United States, Europe, and Australia indicate that it is common for prostitutes to consider a particular territory as their own and one that other street workers should respect.[10] These arrangements are certainly the case in Miami, with several prostitutes working the same area under an informal agreement. For example, a 32-year-old woman who had "worked" Miami's Biscayne Boulevard since she was 17 remarked in 1990:

> We have several of us all in the same place more or less, and there's a lot of reasons for it. You'll always see me and this bitch [another prostitute] along this street from here up to 40th [Street]. Mostly we'll be on the street, but sometimes in the bars and clubs, and sometimes in the motels. This way, nobody gets in our way an' we don't get in theirs. An' if our regulars [regular customers] want to find us they always know where.

Stroll can be a noun, referring to the streets and avenues where prostitutes solicit dates, whereas "to stroll" means "to solicit."

Crack-house sex occurs in different locations. In some houses, sex is restricted to a specific room, often called the freak room. The owner of the crack house—the "kingrat", "rock master", or "house man"— charges for use of this room, usually $5 to $10 paid by the customer, with a limit of thirty minutes to an hour. The freak room may be used by street prostitutes who visit crack houses solely as places to trick. They bring their own dates and stay only long enough to have sex. One street prostitute described a crack house as follows:

> One of the rooms is for base [crack], the other three rooms are for tricking and one of the first rooms inside the door, that's where the dude sit, that's where the G-man [security man or bouncer] sit. When you come in the house he pat you down. They pat you down, and when you come in you say "date." See, anyone was allowed to bring a date, anyone was allowed to bring a trick. When you go in you can bring a date in from the outside and use the room and get money from him and you got to do what you gotta do—$5 to use the room, $5 one hour, they say an hour but they only give you forty-five minutes with that motherfucker, I tell you.

In other crack houses sex occurs not only in freak rooms but also in the common areas where everyone else is smoking. During one visit to a crack house in 1989,* the main smoking area was observed to be a large living room/dining room combination covering about 1,000 square feet. There were 16 people in the room. Three men and four women were sitting or lying down by themselves, in various parts of the room—some were sitting on the floor in corners or by doorways, a few were just stretched out on the floor. Only two were smoking crack; the others appeared to be resting, or waiting, or watching what was going on elsewhere in the room. In a corner farthest away from the entrance, two men were sitting at opposite ends of a couch. Both were smoking and receiving oral sex from two women. Periodically, one of the women would interrupt her "chicken-heading"† to have a hit from the man's crack pipe. In another corner, two women were totally naked, with one straddling the other's face, receiving oral sex. They were "freaking" for crack. That is, they were being paid in crack to perform. Close by, a solitary man was watching them intently, smoking a cigarette with one hand, masturbating with the other.

Elsewhere, in a large bean-bag chair by a flickering television set a women was removing her clothes. She was alone, smoking crack. She kept complaining about the heat, that clothing and "base" just didn't mix and made her skin "crawl," and that she preferred to smoke in the nude. After she was fully undressed, she continued to complain about the heat and her

---

*These observations are from the senior author's field notes compiled after his observations in crack houses.

†Among numerous other names, fellatio is referred to as "chicken-heading" in some crack houses because the movement of the woman's head during the sex act is similiar to that of a chicken. As such, women who trade sex for crack are also referred to as *chickenheads*.

skin. In the midst of these activities, one of the operators of the house looked around from his post at the doorway to make sure that things were in order.

This scene continued for almost an hour. New customers would come and go — purchase crack, smoke crack, watch sex, engage in sex. Some would just look around and disappear into other rooms. The two men on the couch never spoke to each other, to the women, or to anyone else. Since they couldn't seem to climax or even maintain a complete erection, they just kept nudging the women on. The man who was masturbating and watching the two freaking women eventually got up and had vaginal sex with one of them — the one who had been on top, the straddler, the recipient. The other wiped her mouth, lit a cigarette, and watched — disinterested in all of the goings-on. The woman in the bean-bag chair eventually settled into a quiet smoking session. At one point a new visitor tried to solicit her for sex, but she waved him off. Later he was observed in another room engaging in vaginal intercourse with a young woman who apparently lived in the house and represented a "free service" of the house — freely available to anyone who regularly purchased sufficient amounts of crack, or who brought new customers to the house.

As is discussed in detail elsewhere in this book, crack seems to have a disinhibiting and degrading effect on women and men alike. Or as one crack user put it:

> Some of them don't care. Some women don't care, they'll suck off a
> guy or a woman.

In addition to the freak rooms and the smoking rooms, there are other locations where crack-house sex might occur — in bathrooms and closets, on porches and rooftops, in cars parked nearby, and, as one male customer noted, even in empty swimming pools:

> I don't do too much coke, so when I do I always want to get laid an'
> there's a rock crib [crack house] just down the way on 3rd that's pretty
> civilized. I mean no fuckin' in the middle of the room an' no freak an'
> blood shit right there for everyone to watch. Degenerate, sick, perverts
> in those. . . . Anyway, I go over to the place on 3rd so I can get a
> good nut [climax from oral sex] an' there's no space to get down when
> I get there this one time. I mean it was Friday night an' everybody was
> smokin' dope an' gettin' it on.
>   So the lady I want don't care where she do it, but I do, and she
> don't want to leave the fucking crib.‡ She don't want to get too far

---

‡ *Crib* is one of those designations that has had many meanings in the underworld and upperworld, including a brothel, a prostitute's room, a gambling dive, a cheap saloon, a back-street nightclub, a hangout for thieves and hoodlums, and a place patronized by prostitutes. See Josiah Flynt, *Tramping With Tramps: Studies and Sketches of Vagabond Life* (New York: The Century Co., 1899); John O'Connor, *Broadway Racketeers* (New York: Horace Liveright, 1928); Dean Stiff, *The Milk and Honey Route: A Handbook for Hobos* (New York: Vanguard Press, 1930); Godfrey Irwin, *American Tramp and Underworld Slang* (New York: Sears Publishing Co., 1933); Eric Partridge, *A Dictionary of the Underworld* (New York: Bonanza Books, 1961).

away from the crib. Maybe she was so loaded she was afraid she wouldn't find her way back. She says, "How about outside?" We go to the back of the house outside into one of those plastic pool things. There's no water in it, except for a little from rain . . .

To make a long story short, the whole thing was no good. She keeps sayin' it's like a private room under the stars. Fuck. I couldn't relax so I decide to just fuck her and get off quick an' easy. But when I'm climbing into the pig [having sex] all I can think of is snakes. I hate snakes, man, I just hate snakes. All niggers do! An' I'm thinking' about them and mosquitoes are pickin' at my balls and it was all just a waste.

Another aspect of crack-house sex is that there are some territorial issues that decide who tricks in one crack house as opposed to another. When the house is a residence in which only a small circle of friends or acquaintances are permitted to smoke, there are a few rules. Strangers aren't allowed, but they can be brought in as tricks by any member of the group. For these, there may be a freak room that can be used. For example:

Oh boy, I had a house, a nice big house. Everybody liked to come over to my house for some reason, to party or something. So they would come over there. Every room in my house I could lock with one key. I had freak rooms. It was crucial. I would lock people up in the freak room so they were alone. I would lock them up so no one would get in. I would give them thirty minutes for $10 in the freak room. It was nice. Thursday and Friday nights I would take my kids next door to the neighbor. As long as they [crack smokers] gonna use the house they give me drugs. It was like we all hit together, you make one hit you pass around, all around. You share the shit, we were friends. It's my house and I keep my house secure. If you were strung out and get in an argument, you gotta go.

In the more commercialized houses, territorial constraints are generally absent. Street prostitutes are permitted to solicit johns, as long as someone pays for the use of a room. Crack users soliciting or providing sex in the smoking rooms are permitted to do so as long as they have paid their entry fee to the house. In general, it is the crack-house owners who ultimately decide who tricks and who doesn't. And, too, although some women work in several crack houses, most focus on one or two.

The Solicitation

On the streets and in the crack houses, soliciting customers is primarily a matter of waiting. Prostitution is often portrayed as a "lively commerce,"[11] a colorful and exciting part of urban night life. However, for most prostitutes it can be extremely monotonous. Street prostitutes "hang out" on certain corners or "stroll" particular streets until approached by a potential customer. For example, a Miami Beach prostitute who works Ocean Drive in the newly rejuvenated "art deco" district commented in 1992:

You know, I work as a secretary at Barnett Bank during the day and to listen to the men there you'd think it would be easy to get dates. But it really isn't so, that every man out there wants to get laid all the time. And most of those that do either don't want it off the street, or don't want to have to pay for it, or they don't have the balls to be a john. That cuts your potential way down, so you do a lot of waiting and walking and watching.

Another reported:

You watch. Somebody looks at you and you'll wave. They'll beep the horn at you or they'll stop and ask you if you want a ride because what you actually try to do is act like you need a ride. And they'll stop and offer you a ride and when you get in the vehicle they'll either ask if you're dating or if you just want a ride. And you start conversating. You say, "Do you want a date?" and they say yes and then they say, "How much?"

It is at this point of solicitation that women on the street decide whether to pursue a situation and begin to negotiate the actual exchange of sexual services. The prostitutes encountered during the course of this study have been street-wise for quite some time and have developed a sense of whether situations are unsafe. One of them explained:

I been in the streets so long that when a guy talks to me I can get a feeling from the way that he talks to me whether he is gonna cause me a problem or not and with this feeling I won't go.

One concern of these women is the plainclothes police, the vice squad:

If I feel like you're a cop I would ask you what's the most you got, what you're spendin', and if you don't want to give me the price I know you're a cop. If you gives me a price, I know you're cool. I will get in the car and go.

In *Working Women*, Arlene Carmen and Howard Moody of the Judson Memorial Church in New York City have explored the relationship and interchange between police and prostitutes.[12] They discuss the unpredictable and illogical patterns of arrest as well as the frequent excessive force and violence used by police. They also indicate that most prostitutes are arrested when they begin working new areas. Similar to the comments made by the streetwalkers in Miami, the prostitutes in this New York City study quickly learned who were police officers and how to avoid them.

In contrast with the streetwalkers, women who exchange sex for crack in crack houses usually initiate the exchange when they are in need of a hit or rock. This solicitation is often informal and nonverbal. The women offer sexual services implicitly by sharing drugs bought by a man. For example:

Usually when a guy sees you running out of drugs he wouldn't have to ask you most of the time, you would just say "let me get a hit." And as soon as you ask him for that hit, he will give it to you, he will give you that first hit. And then after that he will let you see that he have plenty, and you don't even have to ask for another hit. He will just keep giving it to you. But then the time comes when you have to make the trade and that's usually how it works.

Similarly, as another explained:

She get to tripping and then don't have no more money but she want to keep on using this man's drugs, you know, and the man say, "Hey, you gotta give me pussy or something now, you know."

However, it is also not unusual for a man to approach a woman for the purpose of having a sex partner throughout a smoking encounter. Some men will enter a crack house, purchase enough rocks for two people for several hours, and then make it clear to every woman in the house what he has in mind. Usually someone will take him up on it. If not, someone else eventually comes by. In any case, the potential for soliciting an under-cover police officer is not the problem in the crack house that it is on the street. Streetwalkers, crack-house prostitutes, and police officers alike all agree that vice cops don't work crack houses. Or as a member of the *real* "Miami Vice" commented:

First of all, it's not safe. Officers are not particularly welcome in crack houses. There are guns, there are drugs, there are fugitives of all kinds, and there are who knows what else. If you go into a crack house for any reason, the reason is *not* going to be busting pathetic crack-whores. Everybody on the street knows that. When cops go into crack houses they go through the door in force, well armed, and the reason is to close the operation down.

The Negotiation

Although much of the soliciting in the sex industry is simply a matter of being in a particular place — on certain streets or in the crack houses — sex negotiations differ dramatically between the two settings. On the streets, prostitutes are active participants, if not the lead players, in the negotiating process. During the deliberations, the price and type of sex are determined. As noted above, to avoid vice arrests, street prostitutes insist that the customers quote the price.* Prostitutes also have prices to which

---

*If the john is an undercover police officer, and, depending on exactly *who* quotes the price, the outcome of the encounter might be either a legitimate arrest, or police entrapment, which is illegal. Entrapment is the *inducement* of an individual to commit a crime, under-taken for the sole purpose of instituting a criminal prosecution against the offender. Former Minneapolis Police Chief Anthony V. Bouza explained it this way:

If a cop comes up to a prostitute and engages in vague generalities or responses to her leads, this is not entrapment. The scenario might go something like this:

HE: Hi.

SHE: Hi, wanna party?

they generally adhere. For the most part, if the customer is unwilling to pay her set price, then no business is conducted. For example:

> They ask me how much I charge. It depends on the person. I charge $20 to $25 for oral sex, and I charge $25 and $30 for vaginal. I will not date for less than $20 and I don't like $20 dates, but there's girls, the chickenheads, who will date for $10 and $5. So a lot of men want to pay only $10 — maybe two out of five cars that stop will say, "I have $10" and I'll say, "You still got it," and I keep walking.

Other street workers, however, for a variety of reasons, are more flexible in their negotiations:

> If you are really lookin' good, haven't lost your good looks, an' you're out there just prancin' like some foxy bitch, sure you can hold your price. But when I need the money I'm bad up, I'm gonna go for $5.

In the crack house, on the other hand, there seems to be an expectation that if a man wants to have sex with a woman, she will not oppose the offer. The expectations are implicit. Everyone involved — the house owner, the male user/customer, and the female user/prostitute are all aware of what is expected. Because the rules and the roles are known to all parties, there is little negotiating. As mentioned above, it is also implied that if a woman uses the drugs bought by a man, she has agreed to provide sexual services — typically oral or vaginal sex but sometimes anal sex or participation in freaking or a sex show. One crack-house worker stated:

> And whatever he wants for her to do to get this crack that's what she gonna have to do. She gonna have to participate if she wants to get high and that's what happens.

And another indicated:

> They say to the house man: "I want that bitch over there, man." They say to the girl: "I want you for head [oral sex], get some head." So they go in the back room and then come back out after about ten minutes, fifteen minutes.

HE: Sure. What's the tariff, and what do you do?
SHE: Fifty dollars for a blow job.

This is a perfectly legitimate vignette for a legal arrest. The twist on this exchange would be:

HE: Hi.
SHE: Hi.
HE: I'm willing to give you $50 for a blow job. How about it?
SHE: Sure.

Because the officer initiated the action, the guilt of the target is not established. This arrest, if made, would be illegal.

Source: Anthony V. Bouza, *The Police Mystique: An Insider's Look at Cops, Crime, and the Criminal Justice System* (New York: Plenum Press, 1990), p. 165.

As such, women in crack houses resign all control of their bodies and their sexual self-determination to the crack-house owner and customer. Unless they can purchase crack on their own, they are permitted no input into either the fee or the act. What constitutes sex is decided by the customer.

Payment and Exchange

On the street, payment is received before services are rendered. Moreover, money is preferred and frequently demanded by street prostitutes. Although some will accept drugs in exchange for sex, most will not hear of it, feeling that they receive less for their services, particularly when the drug is crack. Other studies of prostitution confirm the existence of this preference.[13]

In the crack house, payment occurs before, during, and after the sexual service, and is usually a piece or hit of crack. Infrequently, a woman is paid with an entire rock. This barter system also defines the monetary exchange rate, which is much lower in the crack house than it is on the streets. The going rate for oral sex on the streets of Miami in the early 1990s was $20 or $25. In the crack house, it was $5 or $10, approximately the cost of a rock. As crack-house women become more desperate for rocks, however, they begin to perform oral sex for a single hit, sometimes for as little as 25 cents worth of crack.

The sexual exchange differs in two basic aspects—length of interaction and use of drugs. On the streets, the exchange doesn't take very long, and the use of drugs during the trade is uncommon. Such street-based interactions as car and motel tricks last between 10 and 20 minutes. For "working women" (prostitutes), time is money and they are anxious to move back onto the stroll and the next date.

> Get a quick head job, blow job, real quick. They'd give me money and crack and I'd go my way. They would go back to work and so would I. If they don't come in 15 minutes, I would say: "Hurry up and come or else I'm done."

In the crack house, both the customer and the woman providing sex use drugs during the sexual exchange. These exchanges last from 30 minutes to an hour or longer, depending on how long the crack-house owner rents the room. And if the encounter occurs in a common area, the sex might go on even longer. For example:

> He would let me get one good hit. I would enjoy my hit for a few seconds or a few minutes, whatever, and then while he was taking his hit that's when I would perform the oral sex.

For reasons that are not at all clear, crack users in general and male crack users in particular seem to enjoy oral sex while smoking. This is one of the reasons why crack is purported to engender some sort of "hypersexuality"—a matter examined later in this book. As a male crack user noted:

The cracks make a man want a woman all the time. An' it feel so
good—layin' back, smokin' and feelin' in control, and havin' a
woman's lips movin' up an' down on you.

Since the chronic use of crack tends to impair the ability to maintain an
erection and achieve a climax, the sexual contact often lasts for as long as
the crack-smoking session. And although it is the men in the crack house
who receive and control the sexual attention (because it is the men who
generally have the funds to purchase the drugs), a number of women have
expressed the same feelings about crack smoking and oral sex. For example, a 33-year-old street prostitute indicated:

Oh, I understand why the johns want a long slow blow job when
they're on the stem [smoking crack]. I like it myself. To me the best
sex is to be smokin' crack and layin' back in a big chair, my legs
spread over the arms, and a pretty young man or woman lickin' me up
and down. The crack makes the pussy feel better and the pussy makes
the crack feel better.

Three women crack users also commented on what is known as
"blowing bubbles." As one woman described it:

You take a hit, right, and you inhale the smoke and you hold the
smoke and you blow it into the vagina. And it makes a sound like
"pfffff." When it comes out the pussy flies. But if it's done wrong it
hurts. It has to be slow. It has to be slow, let it in there easy.

When asked about "blowing bubbles," a second woman reported:

Before I got addicted, me and my man would always smoke together,
and sex each other the whole time. We'd take turns giving each other a
blow job. When he was doin' me, every so often he'd take a hit and do
it [blow bubbles] an' I'd start to come right then.

Whether the sensual response to "blowing bubbles" is physical, psychological, or a combination of the two, is inconclusive. It is well-known
that a sprinkle of *powder*-cocaine on the clitoris will anesthetize the
tissues and retard a sexual climax, but with persistent stimulation, the
drug will ultimately promote an explosive orgasm.[14] Perhaps a similar
action is occurring with the complex interactions of smoking crack, oral
sex, and "blowing bubbles."

Cheating and Violence

Cheating and violence are as much a part of the crack scene as drugs and
sex are. Cheating and violence often go hand in hand, they occur with
considerable frequency, and they are often related to sex for drugs/money
exchanges. Moreover, the schemes used by prostitutes to cheat customers
are similar whether they occur on the streets or in the crack house. For
example, a downtown Miami prostitute recalled:

> OK, you sit in the car seat, right. He want some head, right. While he be pulling his pants down to get head you go in the pocket. While you giving him head you lean over to the left to suck his dick, right, you go in his pocket and take what he's got. The ones that want to be smart, they keep their pants up and just take out their dick.

Similar incidents occur in the crack house:

> Anyway, he had his pants on the bed while we were having sex. He was on top. . . . So I eased the pants up with my foot and I put my hand in the pocket and he couldn't feel nothing he was so busy. So when I put my hand in the pocket, I felt the paper, and I looked at it, it was a twenty dollar bill. I said well that's enough so I, like, pushed the pants back. Anyway, when we finished he said now we'll go to a few spots and we'll drink and everything. I'm holding the money in my hand trying to keep it hidden and everything. I got dressed real fast, you know, before he got into his pockets. So while he was inside getting dressed, I said, "I'm gonna take this beer," and I closed the door and I just went right out the front door and ran across the street.

Interestingly, it was found that Miami prostitutes on the streets and in the crack houses practiced the identical "badger," "panel," and "shakedown" extortion rackets that were characteristic in the Elizabethan underworld half a millennium ago. As described in *Martin Markall, Beadle of Bridewell*, published in 1610, extortion was undertaken in the following manner:

> Some base rogue . . . that keepeth a whore as a friend, or marries one to be his maintainer, consents or constrains those creatures to yield the use of their bodies to other men, that so, taking them together, they may strip the lecher of all the money in his purse or that he can presently make.[15]

Although this form of solicitation has likely been associated with prostitution for thousands of years, its invention was attributed to Laurence Crossbiter in 1491.

The Elizabethan pretense of the outraged husband of a prostitute represents the basis of the badger, panel, and shakedown rackets of the nineteenth and twentieth century in the United States.* The term *badger* seems to derive from the Anglo *badge*, first referred to in 1725. A *badge* was a "malefactor burned in the hand," or a tormented person. With the meanings of "torment," "annoy," or "malign," *badger* then appeared in

---

*This discussion of the etymology of *badger*, *panel*, and *shakedown* is drawn from George W. Matsell, *Vocabulum, or, The Rogue's Lexicon* (New York: George W. Matsell, 1859); Z.C. Judson, *The Mysteries and Miseries of New York* (New York: Berford, 1848); J.S. Farmer and W.E. Henley, *Slang and Its Analogues* (New York: Arno Press, 1970; reprint of the 1890–1904 editions, 7 volumes); Francis Grose, *A Classical Dictionary of the Vulgar Tongue* (New York: Barnes and Noble, 1963; reprint of the 1811 edition).

John O'Keeffe's *Wild Oats* (published in 1798), and Charles Dickens' *Pickwick Papers* and *Great Expectations* (published in 1836 and 1860, respectively). During the mid-1800s, *badger* had also become part of American underworld slang, referring to a "panel thief" — a person who robs a man's pocket after he has been enticed into bed with a woman.

The panel game was the basis of much of professional thieves' extortion rackets. There were several variations, usually involving the collective efforts of sneak thieves, prostitutes, and other types of criminals.[16] In the more typical situation, an attractively dressed woman approached a country gentleman, explaining that she was a victim of circumstances and was thus forced for the first time in her life to accost a man. After she named a modest sum for her charms, he would accompany her to her room, bolting the door. While he engaged in sexual relations with the young lady, a wall panel would slide open from which a thief would enter, replace the money in the victim's pocket with paper, and silently exit. After the theft had taken place a sound was heard which the woman claimed to be her husband. The gentleman would quickly dress and hastily leave through a rear door, unaware that his money had been taken. Variations of this practice were known in most of the larger cities in the United States in the last century.[17]

As early as 1848, a prostitute's room was known as a "panel-crib," perhaps from the fourteenth-century *parnel*, meaning prostitute, as found in William Langland's *The Vision of William Concerning Piers Plowman*. A panel-crib was also known as a "shakedown," hence, the shakedown racket. And the meaning of this term seems to be rooted in the descriptive context of an impoverished resting place. The late eighteenth- and early nineteenth-century sportswriter Pierce Egan described a shakedown as a temporary substitute for a bed, "a two-penny layer of straw."[18] Henry Mayhew, the founder of the English comic weekly magazine *Punch* used the term in 1841 with reference to the poor mattresses in lodging houses,[19] as did Dickens in his *Great Expectations*. More contemporary badger games rarely use the sliding panel, but rather, the "wronged husband" confronts the embracing couple, threatening to make the matter public, suggesting that money be paid in return for his silence. Although the use of the sliding panel seems to have disappeared, the "panel man" or "sneak thief" is still used. Known to some as "creeps," they sneak from under a bed, from an adjoining room, closet, or even a large trunk.

The late 1980s and early 1990s Miami crack scene variations of the panel, creep, badger, and shakedown schemes involve crack users' children or other accomplices coming from under beds or closets to steal money and/or drugs from the john's pants pockets while he is having sex, or an outraged "husband" or "pimp" (typically a *very* large and wild-eyed male accomplice) breaking down a door in a motel or freak room and threatening the john with mayhem or murder.

Although crack houses are violent environments, with numerous arguments and fights, and sometimes even stabbings and shootings—over money, drugs, and crack deals gone bad—violent situations involving women and sex/crack exchanges are typically the result of one party attempting to steal from the other. For example:

> . . . that night I was so stoned, so loaded, that I got real sloppy when I was givin' this guy head and tryin' to get a rock from his pocket. . . . He starts to come in my mouth so I start yellin' that I didn't like that an' he was supposed to tell me that he's comin' an' all. I was tryin' to distract the motherfucker. An' all the while I'm trying to get this rock he had in his shirt pocket, but I was loaded, an' he saw me. . . . He slapped me so hard that he knocked me down and broke my nose.

Or alternatively, violence is the result of misunderstandings of what is to be delivered:

> This guy I met tricking one night had some rocks and I bring him back to my house. I had my own base house then. Nobody was coming so I went out and found a customer. Somebody to smoke with. And these two guys came and they was smoking and shit. And when the shit was gone, it's time to go. The fucker was hitting on me for a fuck and that motherfucker grabbed me around my neck and told me he wanted some head. And I told him, he was in my house, fucker. "If you sweet, you better get your ass out of here," I said. And he punched me. And that tooth [respondent's gold tooth] fell straight out of my mouth. And he and his friend, they fucked me and I was screaming and all, and some lady knocked on the front door and they ran out the back door. And the gold part I sold that motherfucker for some rock.

Because so many crack users claim that the drug engenders sexual stimulation and consequently consider sex so much a part of using crack, house owners have a vested interest in keeping prostitutes in the house and will protect them to some degree. Sometimes they will try to mediate an argument before it gets out of control; sometimes they will intervene in the altercation to break it up; other times the house bouncer will eject the offending parties from the house.

By contrast, there seems to be more violence on the streets, especially rapes. Although some of the violence toward women trading sex on the streets is the result of attempted rip-offs, much of it appears to be uninstigated. Arlene Carmen and Howard Moody observed the most serious injuries being inflicted by customers for no apparent reason.[20] Suzanne Hatty, in her article "Violence Against the Prostitute," discusses how prostitutes are physically and sexually abused by customers and pimps as well as by police.[21] She also notes the difficulty in addressing such violence due to the stigma attached to prostitution. The criminal justice system frequently bases the legitimacy of a case on such factors as marital status, employment, living arrangements, and acquaintances. Such factors usually work against prostitutes. A study of newspaper articles about prostitutes who had been "viciously" raped revealed that the press, police, and other professionals often consider prostitutes to be "bad" women and "deserving" victims.[22] Such attitudes make it difficult if not impossible for women to respond to or seek protection from assault and rape. Regardless of the situation, street prostitutes appear desensitized toward the physical abuse they experience. As a prostitute in New York remarked, "But while you're working, you really can't worry about the danger or you'll just freak out."[23] It is part of the world in which they live and work, and usually the world in which they grew up.* They learn quickly to sense whether a potential customer is going to be violent. Nevertheless, violent situations occur with seeming regularity. For example:

> I got raped and beat up, put in a hospital for two months while I was out there. Four, five times, six, seven eight times. . . . I've had them take them money back but I fight them back. I've been stabbed nine times.

Another remarked:

> One guy wanted head, paid me $40, gave me the money. He couldn't get hard. There was something about him. Apparently, he must have been ripped off by a lot of girls, because he goes, "Why do you bitches steal, why do you bitches steal?" And I said, "Wait a minute buddy. You know, what's up? I didn't steal anything from you." As I started to get out of the car he grabbed me by the back of my hair and took a billy club and whacked me in the head and honey, he, um, that was the worst, the worst of my life. He whacked me with that billy club and made me take off my clothes, tied my hands with a T-shirt of his and made me lay on the passenger seat, pulled the seat down and made me lay there. There was no doubt in my mind this man was going to kill me because he said, "I'm going to teach you bitches what a rip-off gets you." He took me to 89th Street and Collins Avenue to the ocean and he said to me: "I'm gonna open the car door and you're gonna go to the ocean." As soon as he opened the door, I ran.

Sex With Friends

There are many crack-using women who have sex with people they know, people they call "friends" as opposed to "customers," in order to support their drug habit. They are not considered "sex partners" in the same sense as a spouse, lover, or "significant other," but *friends* with whom they have sex. As "customers," to use consistent terminology, they are individuals befriended in pre-crack drug networks or social settings. And although they are referred to as "friends," the friendship seems to be contingent on bartering sexual services for drugs. The women must be willing

---

*In addition to the sexual abuse and rape of prostitutes, not to be ignored is the high incidence of child sexual abuse among women who later become prostitutes. For further discussion, see Mimi H. Silbert and Ayala M. Pines, "Early Sexual Exploitation as an Influence in Prostitution," *Social Work*, (July–August, 1983), pp. 285–289.

to perform sexual favors; the men must provide the drugs. There are no particular rules or procedures associated with these exchanges. They are very casual, informal, and spontaneous. The women rarely set out to solicit sex; they take advantage of an opportunity to get drugs or to obtain a few dollars to buy drugs from people they know. For example:

> I left the house that night and I ended up running into a guy that went to school with me. Okay, he probably spent maybe $80 on me that night. He wanted to sex me all night and we were on the street. He bought drugs with the $80. And then I started doing a lot of weird things. I sexed him up under a tree.

Also:

> There was this guy that I went to high school with. He gave me some crack, you know. I knew him and he said: "You know, I'd like to fuck your brains out." And I wanted the drug so bad I went and fucked his brains out and he gave me $50. One time I was out, I met this guy at the Jamaican Club and I knew him a long time ago, and he wanted just a mate for the night and I told him: "I'll live with you how long you want me to, you know, but I want two ounces of cocaine, for about two days in a motel room."

For the women exchanging sex for drugs or money with "friends," this arrangement is not considered "prostitution." Since these women usually have other sources of income, they are simply taking advantage of the opportunity to obtain crack at no cost. However, they face the same risks of violence and/or rape as women in other crack/sex barter arrangements. Violence seems to be a common occurrence when crack is involved, regardless of the environment or relationships between those smoking. For example, a 19-year-old woman in treatment for crack addiction recalled:

> There was this motherfucker I worked with at the Burger King. We did a lot of crack together. Sometimes I would sex him for the rocks, or give him hand jobs or blow jobs right in the kitchen of the place, at Burger King, and he would give me a rock. One time after work we started to get high and he wanted me to give him head, and I didn't want to just that time. So he hits me between the shoulders and knocks me down and fucks me, he raped me . . . . He hurt me, and I really felt dirty.

Prostitutes Who Smoke Crack and Crack Addicts Who Prostitute

> Sex is my business, my profession, and I pride myself on the fact that I give one of the best blow jobs in all of Florida.
> —*A Miami prostitute, 1991*

* * *

Crack is a pimp drug. Crack is a fucking pimp, and he's my pimp.
                                        —*A Miami crack house girl, 1991*

COYOTE (Call Off Your Old Tired Ethics), a group organized to promote the interests of prostitutes, argues that for some women, prostitution is a legitimate business and profession, that prostitutes *choose* to do what they do, and that many continue to be prostitutes for as long as they can because the money is good.* Although the street women encountered in this study are far from the elite of their profession, many indeed reflect attitudes espoused by members of COYOTE. Moreover, a comparison of a few of the day-to-day activities of *prostitutes who smoke crack* suggests that they are indeed different from *crack addicts who prostitute* in crack houses.

In the first place, the fact that prostitution has its monetary rewards appears throughout the literature.[24] Moreover, the same view is readily evident in the remarks of many of the street women encountered in Miami. For example:

> I went out on the streets and started walking the sidewalks dressed like a hooker and flaunted it around until a guy asked me if I wanted a ride. And that was the start. I get $20 to $30, sometimes more if I go home with the guy. It's easy and good money.
>
> I had a pimp for one year. After that I was prostituting on my own. I was paying a hotel room $40 a day, I was eating good and I was buying new clothes.

The daily routines of street workers are not all that different than those of women working night shifts in legitimate jobs. Their crack smoking, furthermore, is often considered as no more than a means of relaxing. For example:

> I wake up in the morning, I cook breakfast, I go out and walk, ride my bike, watch my soap operas, sleep, eat. About 6 or 7 in the night, sometimes I go out in the afternoon. It depends how I feel. Well, I don't spend a lot of hours out there, you know. I'll catch one or two dates and I'll go home for an hour or two and then I'll come back out. It's not like I'm standing out there constantly, because you don't want the police to look at you too much. I end about 6 or 7 in the morning,

---

*COYOTE consists of women and men from diverse backgrounds and interests including prostitutes, lawyers, housewives, and feminists. It was established in 1973 by ex-prostitute Margo St. James, and is the oldest and probably best-known national group advocating for rights, protection, and decent health care for prostitutes in the United States. Currently, it has thirteen branches nationwide and several affiliate groups. COYOTE members have been active with the National Task Force on Prostitution and the International Committee for Prostitute's Rights. See Valerie Jenness, "From Sex as Sin to Sex as Work: COYOTE and the Reorganization of Prostitution as a Social Problem," *Social Problems* 37 (August 1990), pp. 403–419.

and then I smoke a couple of hours. Whatever I buy, it lasts me, because you know I don't just smoke. I smoke slow and I go to sleep while I'm smoking.

Another explained:

Darn, I'm out there trying to make a living. So I take care of business first. And then after I take care of my business, that's when the enjoyment comes. I smoke crack.

The schedules and daily routines of women who trade sex for crack in crack houses are driven by their addiction to the drug. Their lives are chaotic, revolving exclusively around crack-smoking and crack-seeking. There are feeble attempts to fulfill responsibilities to children and family, but these are secondary to crack use. Days and nights are spent in and out of crack houses, alternating between tricking and using, sexing and smoking. If there are customers in the crack house, then crack-addicted women will remain there. If there are none, they will leave, but only to find customers. And if they cannot find customers, then they will sell personal belongings or steal in order to keep themselves high. For example:

I would get up early in the morning and get my hit. I would get up early because my son has to go to school. I would get crack from the crack dude. And come back home and smoke. And that's what I would do all day long. I would take something out of the house and sell it to the crack dealer. A TV, my living room set, my glass table, my bedroom set. I sold everything in my house.

Another stated:

Okay, I'll go through a day. When I'd leave the house my mother would always give me money, I don't know, maybe $10. I would catch the jitney. I would go to the city. I would buy one rock, one $5 rock, smoke that, that first rock. They call it the first hit. Then after that I'd trick. I'd stop somewhere, take a hit, go in one of the empty houses, you know, and I would get somebody. And they got something, too, and they got something and we'd share it.

Not surprisingly, street prostitutes have little respect for their crack-addicted counterparts in crack houses. For example, a 35-year-old woman who had been prostituting on the streets of Miami for 17 years and earned on the average of $4,500 a month doing so, offered this description:

She's a girl put in a predicament. . . . Her brain is all fucked up. She's young and naive. Right out of high school, 18 years old and they'll get her started, see. They'll give her hits free. She's staying in there getting high for free and she doesn't know why. Now she wants another hit. She doesn't understand what you have to do for that guy to get a hit. He wants you to give him head for an hour and then the motherfucker can't get hard. He's so into the rock, you see. They make people vulnerable like that.

Another seasoned prostitute added:

> They call them "rock heads," "strawberrys," "skeezers," and the like.
> They ought to call them dog piss and dog shit, 'cause that's what they are
> —just dirty street turds. They'll do *anything* for a hit of crack. For a
> hit I seen one suck off a dog and lick diarrhea.

As a final point here, some comment seems warranted on the role of
the pimp—the "street man," "street hustler," "player," or "meat
salesman"—the man who is regularly in the company of prostitutes, who
seems to exercise control over their activities, and who derives all or part
of his livelihood from their earnings. There was a time when prostitution
and pimping went hand in hand, so much so that one student of prostitution estimated in 1935 that Chicago's population of 3 million included
some 8,800 prostitutes and 6,300 pimps.[25] The roles of the pimp, then and
now, include staying alert for police, attempting to divert or bribe police,
posting bail and obtaining an attorney when necessary, helping to steal
from johns, and protecting the prostitute from beatings by tricks.

During the 1980s, the pimp/prostitute relationship was frequently
used to demonstrate the patriarchal and repressive nature of prostitution.[26] Pimps have been portrayed as not only recruiting women unwill-
ingly into prostitution, but also as keeping them in the business through
violence, threats, and dependency. There is evidence, however, that the
role of the pimp in the sex industry may be diminishing. Karen File noted
this trend in 1976 with female addicts seeming to "depart from the
male-dominated role structure."[27] Similarly, of the six prostitutes interviewed in Zausner's *The Streets*, only one had a pimp.[28]

In the Miami sex-for-crack scene, none of the women encountered
used a pimp. All were "outlaws," whether they walked the streets or
worked the crack houses. Repeatedly, they made the statement, "Crack is
my pimp." Almost all, furthermore, were quite turned off by the idea of
giving part of their earnings or drugs to someone who did nothing for
them in return. For example:

> I ain't going to sell my body and give blow jobs and then go back and
> say here's the money. No way! I don't work for no mens. I survive. If I
> want to smoke I go get it. I ain't gonna go get it for his habit.

Similarly, another emphasized:

> He [the john] paid me $25. I bought two rocks and kept five, put the
> money away. I don't even give my boyfriend money because to me
> that's a pimp and I refuse, you know.

However, women tricking or trading sex in a crack house do give a
share of their earnings (or drugs) to the crack-house owner. They do not
consider the owner to be a pimp, and, at least officially, he does not play
the pimp's role. Nonetheless, the women are paying to use the house and,
indirectly, for protection. As one of the informants reported:

Each time I brought in a date, I had to pay $5 to use the house and another $5 for a room. The john would pay for the room, but I paid the house. And it was every time I went in the door. If I went in five different times in a night, it was five times $5.

The advantage, however, was the protection offered:

I would feel safest at those places because he [the crack house owner] would make sure nobody bothered me.

In *Street Woman*, sociologist Eleanor Miller notes that Milwaukee women active in both street crime and drug networks rarely use the term *pimp*.[29] Rather, one hears the expression "my man" when they speak of male confederates or companions. Their "man" is usually a drug dealer, and frequently is the one who introduced these women to the fast life. Similar to the women in Milwaukee, those in Miami are typically introduced to crack by male drug-using friends, many of whom are dealers and/or crack-house owners. These same "friends" are often the gateway to crack-house prostitution. Although the women do not refer to the men as "pimps" or even as "my man," male dealers are often the conduit to drug use and prostitution. For example:

I smoked and smoked till my money was gone. No one was left in the house except the dealer. So I told him I wanted a hit. He said you are going to have to do something for a hit. So I had oral sex with him. That's how I got started.

Postscript

In many ways, crack is just another drug on the street. For the women in this study, it was neither the first, the second, nor even the third drug ever used. Most had been users of marijuana, heroin and other narcotics, barbiturates and other sedatives, and *powder*-cocaine before they first encountered *crack*-cocaine. Many had also been in the sex industry for years before crack came along. Neither drug use nor prostitution was new to them.

But in other ways, crack and the crack house are fundamentally different from anything previously known in the street-drug scene. Crack is likely the most seductive street drug ever, and the crack-house environment creates an interdependence among users, and between users and dealers, in which the bartering of sexual services is central. Moreover, although many of the women providing sex in crack houses may have occasionally bartered sex for money or drugs in the past, most are young, have little or no legitimate employment experience, and are addicted to crack. As a result, they have no control over what happens to them. This is poignantly illustrated in the following quotation, drawn from the tran-

script of a 28-year-old female crack user. This woman had been a marijuana user since age 15, a cocaine user since age 18, and a crack user since
age 26. In her comments below, she details her first exchange of sex for
crack and how it came about, and how it drew her into the crack-house
environment.

I had my last paycheck, that was $107. That day I went straight from
there [work] with a friend-guy and copped some drugs. I bought
$25 — five nickel rocks. I walked up to the apartment, me and the
same guy. We drunk a beer, we needed the can to smoke on. So we sat
there and we smoked those five rocks and you know, like they say,
one is too much and a thousand is never enough. And that's the truth.
Those five rocks went like this [snaps fingers] and I immediately, I had
maybe about $80 left. I had intentions of takin' my grandmother some
money home for the kids. But I had it in my mind — you know, I was,
I was just sick. I wanted to continue to get high, so push come to
shove and I smoked up that — that whole day me and him we smoke
up. It didn't last till maybe about 8:00 PM 'cause we started maybe
about 12:00 that afternoon.

Okay, all the money was gone, all the drugs was gone. About 9:00
we went and sat in the park. Usually when we set in the park people
will come over and they'll have drugs. Some friends came over and
they had drugs. He walked home. I stayed out because I couldn't give
an account for what I had did with the money. My grandmother done
thought that I was goin' to pick up my check and comin' back. So I
walked around and I walked down this street, you know you got
people that will pick you up. So this guy stopped and I got in the car,
and I never did any prostituting but I wanted more drugs. So this guy
he stopped and he picked me up and he asked me, "How much would
you charge me for a head?" That's oral sex. And I told him $40. And
so he say, "How much would you charge me for two hours to have to
just sex, not oral sex?" And so I told him $40 so he say, "Okay get in,"
and he took me to this hotel.

He had about six rocks. I didn't wanna sex. I wanted to get high,
so we smoked the rocks and durin' the time I sexed with him. So after
I sexed him he gave me the money and after the rocks was gone I still
wanted to get high. So this man, he gave me his car and his keys and
gave me more money to go get more drugs. We went into another
hotel. By that time it was maybe 6:00 in the morning. He ended up
leaving me in the hotel. By that time I done spent all my $40. It wasn't
nothing I had, I'd wasted the money. So later on that afternoon, my
grandmother done let me get sleep and everything. I think later on that
day and the next day I went to my godfather's house and I earned $15,
I helped him do some work around the house so he gave me $15.

So I went and stayed home with the kids and waited till they got
ready to go to bed that night. I went and got three rocks with that $15.
I started off smokin' by myself, but when you sittin' in the park
people come to know you and they be tryin' to horn in on what you
doin'. So I ended up smokin' I think about a rock-and-a-half with

somebody that was sittin' in the park. Later on I ended up walkin' down the main strip again and this guy came by and he say, "Well, how much money do you want for a head?" So I told him $10. I was really desperate this time around so I told him $10. He say well, I don't have but $5. I say okay, I'll take that, you know I settle for little or nothin'. So we went down the street and parked in this parkin' lot and I gave him a head. And I immediately went to the drug house, and bought a nickel rock.

The woman eventually became a regular crack-house "chickenhead," exchanging oral, vaginal, and anal sex for small amounts of crack.

Endnotes

1. Vice Commission of Chicago, *The Social Evil in Chicago* (Chicago: Gunthorp-Warren, 1911).
2. For a discussion of drug use among prostitutes during medieval times see Fernando Henriques, *Prostitution and Society: Primitive, Classical and Oriental* (New York: Grove Press, 1962); Fernando Henriques, *Prostitution in Europe and the Americas* (New York: Citadel Press, 1965).
3. For a history of cocaine, see Lester Grinspoon and James B. Bakalar, *Cocaine: A Drug and Its Social Evolution* (New York: Basic Books, 1976); John C. Flynn, *Cocaine* (New York: Birch Lane Press, 1991).
4. George J. Kneeland, *Commercialized Prostitution in New York City* (New York: The Century Co., 1913); Vice Commission of Chicago.
5. Paul J. Goldstein, *Prostitution and Drugs* (Lexington, MA: Lexington Books, 1979).
6. Karen N. File, "Sex Roles and Street Roles," *International Journal of the Addictions* 11 (1976), pp. 263–268.
7. Jennifer James, "Prostitution and Addiction: An Interdisciplinary Approach," *Addictive Diseases: An International Journal* 2 (1976), pp. 601–618.
8. Marsha Rosenbaum, *Women on Heroin*, (New Brunswick, NJ: Rutgers University Press, 1981); Eleanor Miller, *Street Woman* (Philadelphia: Temple University Press, 1986).
9. Matthew Freund, Terri L. Leonard, and Nancy Lee, "Sexual Behavior of Resident Street Prostitutes with Their Clients in Camden, New Jersey," *Journal of Sex Research* 26 (November 1989), pp. 460–478.
10. See Michael Zausner, *The Streets* (New York: St. Martin's Press, 1986); Roberta Perkins and Garry Bennett, *Being a Prostitute* (Boston: Allen & Unwin Publishers, 1985); Eileen McLeod, *Women Working: Prostitution Now* (London: Croom Helm, 1982); Anonymous, *Streetwalker* (New York: Viking Press, 1960).
11. Charles Winick and Paul M. Kinsie, *The Lively Commerce: Prostitution in the United States* (Chicago: Quadrangle Books, 1971).
12. Arlene Carmen and Howard Moody, *Working Women: The Subterranean World of Street Prostitution* (New York: Harper & Row, 1985), pp. 133–161.
13. See Zausner, *The Streets*; Lewis Diana, *The Prostitute and Her Clients* (Springfield, IL Charles C. Thomas, 1985).
14. See James A. Inciardi, *The War on Drugs II: The Continuing Epic of Heroin, Cocaine, Crack, Crime, AIDS, and Public Policy* (Mountain View, CA: Mayfield, 1992), pp. 93–94.
15. See Arthur V. Judges, *The Elizabethan Underworld* (London: George Routledge, 1930), p. 418.
16. See James A. Inciardi, *Careers in Crime* (Chicago: Rand McNally, 1975).

17. Edward Crapsey, *The Nether Side of New York* (New York: Sheldon, 1872); William W. Sanger, *The History of Prostitution: Its Extent, Causes and Effects Throughout the World* (New York: Medical Publishing Co., 1897); Clifton R. Wooldridge, *Hands Up! In the World of Crime, or 12 Years a Detective* (Chicago: Thompson, 1901).

18. Pierce Egan, *Real Life in London, or, The Further Rambles and Adventures of Bob Tallyho, Esq., and his Cousin the Hon. Tom Dashall, etc., Through the Metropolis; Exhibiting a Living Picture of Fashionable Characters, Manners, and Amusements in High and Low Life* (London: Jones & Co., 1821), p. 164.

19. Henry Mayhew, *London Labour and the London Poor* (New York: Dover Publications, 1986; reprint of the 1861 edition).

20. Carmen and Moody, *Working Women*, pp. 43–44.

21. Suzanne Hatty, "Violence Against the Prostitute: Social and Legal Dilemmas," *Australian Journal of Social Issues* 24 (November 1989), pp. 235–248.

22. Helen M. Roberts, "Trap the Ripper," *New Society* 44 (April 6, 1978), pp. 11–12.

23. In Zausner, *The Streets*, p. 37.

24. Lionel James, "On the Game," *New Society* 24 (May 24, 1973), pp. 426–429; Zausner, *The Streets*.

25. Ben L. Reitman, *The Second Oldest Profession* (New York: Vanguard, 1936).

26. See Kim Romenesko and Eleanor M. Miller, "The Second Step in Double Jeopardy: Appropriating the Labor of Female Street Hustlers," *Crime and Delinquency* 35 (January 1989), pp. 109–135.

27. File, "Sex Roles and Street Roles."

28. Zausner, *The Streets*.

29. Miller, *Street Woman*.

CHAPTER 5

Drugs, Sex, and AIDS: The Crack-House Connection

"Around 1980, suddenly and much to their own great
astonishment, physicians detected the existence of an illness
that seemed "new." New because they thought they had never
seen it before. New because to understand it they were forced
to resort to explanatory models unknown in classical pathology
and epidemiology."[1]

Toward the end of 1979, Dr. Joel Weisman of Los Angeles was finding that an increasing number of his patients were suffering from a mononucleosis-like disease—marked by hectic fever, weight loss, and swollen lymph nodes. Many also had diarrhea, respiratory distress, and oral and anal thrush (a fungus infection characterized by whiteish spots). The patients were young, and all were from California's growing gay community. "I was stumped," Weisman later recalled. "Before the great advances in medicine, doctors were essentially documenters of what happened. With these patients, that's essentially all I could do."[2] At about the same time, a New York homosexual began to experience an illness that left his physicians perplexed—lassitude, weight loss, spiking fevers, and a seemingly slow consumption of his whole body—but all without any specific signs. A number of his gay friends were ill with similar symptoms. And when he lapsed into unconsciousness one afternoon, a brain scan showed cerebral lesions.[3]

Not surprisingly, observers considered the possibility that the new disease was limited to homosexual men. Within a brief period of time, however, the notion that it was some form of "gay plague" was quickly extinguished. The disease was suddenly being reported in other populations—intravenous drug users, blood-transfusion patients, hemophiliacs, and the sex partners of all three groups.[4] And given the populations in which the affliction was concentrated, some observers began claiming it was "nature's revenge" for the "crime" of homosexuality, or "God's retribution for the perversions committed by junkies and perverts and queers and whores." And to many more it became like syphilis, leprosy, and plague—a contemporary metaphor for corruption, decay, and consummate evil.[5]

Sex, Drugs, and AIDS

By October 2, 1985, the morning Rock Hudson died, the word was familiar to almost every household in the Western world. AIDS.
—*Journalist Randy Shilts, 1987*

The first actual description of *Acquired Immune Deficiency Syndrome* (AIDS) as a new and distinct clinical entity came during the late spring and early summer of 1981. First, clinical investigators in Los Angeles reported five cases to the Centers for Disease Control of *Pneumocystis carinii* pneumonia among homosexual men.[6] None of these patients had an underlying disease that might have been associated with *Pneumocystis*, or a history of treatment for a compromised immune system. All, however, had other clinical manifestations and laboratory evidence of immunosuppression. Second, and within a month, 26 cases of Kaposi's sarcoma were reported among homosexual men in New York and California.[7]

What was so unusual was that prior to these reports, the appearance of both *Pneumocystis* pneumonia and Kaposi's sarcoma in populations of previously healthy young men was unprecedented. *Pneumocystis* is an infection caused by the parasite *P. carinii*, previously seen almost exclusively in cancer and transplant patients receiving immunosuppressive drugs.[8] Kaposi's sarcoma, a tumor of the blood vessel walls that often appears as blue-violet to brownish skin blotches, had been quite rare in the United States—occurring primarily in elderly men, usually of Mediterranean origin. Like *Pneumocystis* pneumonia, furthermore, Kaposi's sarcoma had also been reported among organ transplant recipients and others receiving immunosuppressive therapy.[9] This quickly led to the hypothesis that the increased occurrences of the two disorders in homosexual men were due to some underlying immune system dysfunction. This hypothesis was further supported by the incidence among homosexuals of numerous and varied "opportunistic infections"—infections caused by microorganisms that rarely generate disease in persons with normal immune-defense mechanisms.[10] It is for this reason that the occurrence of *Pneumocystis* pneumonia, Kaposi's sarcoma, and/or other opportunistic infections in a person with unexplained immune dysfunction became known as the *Acquired Immune Deficiency Syndrome*, or more simply, *AIDS*.

In 1983, scientists at the Institute Pasteur in Paris identified and isolated the cause of AIDS—Lymphadenophy-Associated Virus. Later, it was renamed *Human Immunodeficiency Virus*, more commonly known as "HIV."[11] Subsequent studies demonstrated that HIV is transmitted when virus particles or infected cells gain direct access to the blood-stream. This can occur through all forms of sexual intercourse, the sharing of contaminated needles, blood, and blood products, and the passing of the virus from infected mothers to their unborn or newborn children.* Within this context, HIV is a continuum of conditions associated with immune dysfunction, and AIDS is best described as a severe manifestation of infection with HIV.

The primary spread of HIV and AIDS in the drug-using community occurs among intravenous and other injection-drug users as the result of drug-sharing and needle-sharing practices. The sharing of hypodermic needles and syringes is a major route of HIV transmission. The mechanism is the exchange of the blood of the previous user that is lodged in the needle, the syringe, or some other part of the "works" (drug paraphernalia). Levels of risk vary, however, depending on the particular injection practice. Of lesser risk, for example, is "skin-popping" — the intramuscular (into the muscle) or subcutaneous (under the skin) injection of cocaine, narcotics, and other drugs. At the opposite end of the risk spectrum is "booting," a process involving the use of a syringe to draw blood from the user's arm, then mixing the drawn blood with the drug already taken into the syringe, and then "mainlining" — intravenous injection (and in the case of "booting," the injection of the blood/drug mixture directly into the vein). Many injecting users believe that this practice potentiates a drug's effects. Importantly, however, booting leaves traces of blood in the needle and syringe, thus placing subsequent users of the injection equipment at risk.[12] And although most injection drug users are generally aware of the risks associated with booting and needle-sharing, they often ignore them.

Further, drug users typically give little thought to the risks associated with other aspects of the injection process. Studies have indicated that HIV can survive in ordinary tap water for extended periods of time.[13] Injection-drug users require water to both rinse their syringes and mix with their drugs to liquify them for injection. Rinsing, for example, is not for hygienic purposes, but to make sure a syringe does not become clogged with blood and drug residue, so that it can be used again. And the rinse water is often shared. Similarly, "spoons," "cookers," and "cottons" are parts of the injecting kit that also represent potential reservoirs of disease. "Spoons" and "cookers" are the bottle caps, spoons, baby food jars, and other small containers used for mixing the drug, while "cottons" refer to any materials placed in the spoon to filter out undissolved drug particles. Filtering is considered necessary since undissolved particles tend to clog

---

*HIV has been isolated from the blood, semen, vaginal secretions, urine, cerebrospinal fluid, saliva, tears, and breast milk of infected individuals. Transmission could theoretically occur from contact with any of these fluids, but the concentration of HIV found in saliva and tears is extremely low. Moreover, no cases of HIV infection have been traced to saliva or tears.

injection equipment. The risks of HIV infection from spoons and cottons are due to their frequent sharing, even by drug users who carry their own syringes.[14] In addition, users often mix their drugs together in the same containers before drawing them into their syringes, or they exchange drugs from one set of works to another.[15] In both situations, the potential for contamination with HIV is present.

Pertinent to this discussion is the potential for HIV transmission through prostitution. Since the early 1970s, a significant number of prostitutes in the United States have been using condoms, initially in response to the spread of herpes and later to HIV and AIDS.[16] This has been especially common among prostitutes who use neither narcotics nor cocaine. A recent study in this regard examined the prevalence of HIV infection among a group of call girls and women working in massage parlors in New York City.[17] In the 78 subjects studied, the mean age was 31.6 years and the mean duration of prostitution was 5.1 years. Study participants reported a median of some 200 different sex partners during the preceding year. Six had a history of intravenous drug use, and none had a history of any other recognized risk factor for AIDS. Ninety percent of the women studied used condoms during intercourse with at least some of their partners. One of the women with a history of intravenous drug use and none of the 72 non-users were HIV positive, that is, infected with the virus that causes AIDS. The study clearly suggests that despite their promiscuity, among non-drug-using prostitutes the rates of HIV infection may nevertheless be low.

Prostitutes at the greatest risk for HIV and AIDS are those who use drugs, particularly intravenous drugs — not only because of their own drug use, but also because of the HIV risk behaviors of the populations with whom they work. Most intravenous drug-using prostitutes tend to work the streets — an estimated 20% of the sex industry, with the other 80% comprised of workers in massage parlors, escort services, and brothels. Moreover, some 20% to 60% of street walkers use injection drugs or have had a long-term relationship with an injection-drug user.[18] A Centers for Disease Control review of 19 studies conducted in more than 15 cities and communities found that almost all of the prostitutes who tested positive for HIV had a history of injection-drug use.[19] These studies also demonstrated that HIV infection was more than twice as high for black and Hispanic prostitutes as for white and other prostitutes, and that the highest rates were found in inner-city areas where injection-drug use was common.

Within this context, crack use is becoming more and more associated with HIV/AIDS acquisition and transmission. Health clinics in several parts of the United States have linked increased rates of sexually transmitted diseases to crack use.[20] These reports note that it is not the smoking of crack, but the sexual activities associated with crack use that are placing users at risk.

Crack and Hypersexuality

> I probably had sex maybe 10,000 times in the last two years. A lot of it was blow jobs, and I did a lot of it with the same mens over an' over. But I bet I sexed with a couple of thousand different guys, an' a few dozen ladies . . . . Lots of times it was vaginals, and sometimes it was anals, an' the guys who would do that they'd come inside me . . . . I never once had no condoms.
>
> —*A Miami crack-house addict, 1991*

Drugs have been found to influence sexual behavior and functioning in a variety of ways. First, there are the direct pharmacological effects of drugs which can alter psychological inclinations and physical propensity for sexual activity.[21] Second, since drug use often occurs within a social-recreational context, it is frequently intermingled with sexual opportunities — occasions and locales where sexual encounters may not only be permitted, but expected and sought after as well.[22]

Among many drug users there is the view that certain drugs enhance sexual effects. Marijuana's reputation as an aphrodisiac dates back to ancient times.[23] Many novice and recreational users report that marijuana stimulates desire, enhances enjoyment, and may even improve sexual performance.[24] Similarly, cocaine has the reputation of being a spectacular aphrodisiac: it is believed by many to create sexual desire, to heighten it, to increase sexual endurance, and to cure frigidity and impotence.[25] Alcohol, amphetamines, barbiturates and other sedatives, and even opiate drugs have all been reported to enhance sexual functioning in some users,[26] but as has been documented at length in the literature, disturbed sexuality is a typical outcome of most chronic drug use.[27]

Recent research has suggested that as an aphrodisiac, cocaine in either its hydrochloride (powder) or base (crack and freebase) forms is problematic. For example, it has been found that there are considerable differences in sexual responsiveness to the same dosage level of cocaine, depending primarily on the setting of the use and the background experiences of the user. Among recreational users, the male sexual response to cocaine is not unlike that of women. For men, cocaine not only helps to prevent premature ejaculation, but at the same time permits prolonged intercourse before orgasm. Among women, achieving a climax under the influence of cocaine is often quite difficult, but when it occurs it is quite intense. But finally, as is the case with other drugs, research also demonstrates that chronic, heavy users of cocaine typically experience sexual dysfunction.[28]

A strong association between crack use and apparent "hypersexual behaviors" is evident in the observations and interviews in Miami, as well as in other ethnographic analyses of the crack scene.[29] As has been documented at length in Chapter 4, many crack-addicted women engage in any manner of sexual activity, under *any* circumstances, in private or in public, and with multiple partners of either sex (or both sexes simultaneously). Indeed, the tendency of crack users to engage in high-frequency sex with numerous anonymous partners is a feature of crack dependence and crack-house life in a myriad of locales. Sex-for-drugs exchanges are far more common among female crack addicts now than they ever were among female narcotics addicts — even at the height of the 1967–1974 heroin epidemics.[30] Moreover, neither the "strawberries," "skeezers," "head hunters," and "toss-ups" (the crack "house girls" who provide oral sex for just a few cents worth of drugs), nor the crack-house "freaks" (the "house girls" who have public sex with other women for similarly small amounts of drugs), have any parallel in either the heroin subculture or that of the old-style brothels.

The question is whether the crack-sex association is primarily pharmacological or sociocultural in nature. That is, do crack users exhibit hypersexual behavior because their drug provides hypersexual stimulation and enjoyment? Or is the aphrodisiac effect of crack a mythical explanation for behavior that actually results from economic and street-subculture factors? The best answer appears to be that both pharmacological and sociocultural factors are involved.

The pharmacological explanation of the crack/sex association begins with psychopharmacology: one effect of all forms of cocaine, including crack, is the release of normal inhibitions on behavior, including sexual behavior. The disinhibiting effect of cocaine is markedly stronger than that of depressants such as alcohol, Valium, or heroin. While the latter drugs typically cause a release from worry and an accompanying increase in self-confidence, cocaine typically causes a feeling of elation and an accompanying gross over-estimation of one's own capabilities. Further, since effects have a rapid onset, so, too, does the related release of inhibitions. Moreover, as one male crack user in Miami reported:

> There is definitely something about crack, something very sexual about it when you are smoking. When you're smoking you want to have sex, and when you're smoking sex seems to be better, stronger, with the crack high.

Similarly, a woman crack user indicated:

> One of the first times I had crack, I was with a girlfriend from high school. Before, a lot a times we'd been high together, on other drugs, on pot mostly. We'd get hot, and we'd talk about sex. But this time it was really something. We really got hot, both of us, and we started talkin' about sex things we'd done. I asked her if she ever did it with a girl, and she said no. Me neither. We talked more, and we ended up havin' sex with each other. It was so good, felt so good. It was the crack that did it.

Medical authorities generally concede that because of the disinhibiting effects of cocaine, its use among new users does indeed enhance sexual enjoyment and improve sexual functioning, including more intense orgasms.[31] These same reports maintain, however, that among long-term addicts, cocaine decreases both sexual desire and performance.

Going further, the crack/sex association involves the need of female crack addicts to pay for their drug. Even this connection has a pharmacological component — crack's rapid onset, extremely short duration of effects, and high addiction liability combine to result in compulsive use and a willingness to obtain the drug through any means. In addition, although overdose is a constant threat, crack use does not pose the kind of physiological limit on the maximum (or possible) daily dosage. Whereas the heroin addict typically needs four doses a day, for example, and an alcoholic not uncommonly passes out after reaching a certain stage of intoxication, the heavy crack user typically uses until the supply is gone — be that minutes, hours, or days. The consequent financial burden can be staggering.

Other parts of the economic crack/sex relationship, however, are strictly sociocultural. As in the legitimate job market, the access of women in the street subcultures to income is typically more limited than that of men. Prostitution has long been the easiest, most lucrative, and most reliable means for women to finance drug use.[32]

The combined pharmacological and sociocultural effects of crack use can put female users in severe jeopardy. Because crack makes its users ecstatic and yet is so short-acting, it has an extremely high addiction potential. *Use* rapidly becomes *compulsive use*. Crack acquisition thus becomes enormously more important than family, work, social responsibility, health, values, modesty, morality, or self-respect. This makes sex-for-crack exchanges psychologically tolerable as an economic necessity. Further, the disinhibiting effects of crack enable users to engage in sexual acts they might not otherwise even consider. For the female crack addict, the consequences may be extreme sexual behavior, but the term "hypersexuality" is very deceptive. For example, one Miami woman reported in 1990:

> When I first started smoking it, I'd go to a crack house, I would want to get laid. Then I got down to the last year-and-a-half of smoking it, I just didn't want to fuck anymore.

Moreover, a 22-year-old Miami woman reported in early 1991:

> There been days when I sexed 20, 30, 40 different men, an' weeks when I gave head a thousand times. . . . But I ain't no superwoman, no superwhore, no supernympho. It's the cracks. I done so, so many things. But its the cracks. I done things, sex things, an' other things too, that I wouldn't have done but for the cracks. An' it's so degrading. . . . It's got so that I hate the cracks now, an' I hate sex, an' men, an' myself, too. But I need the cracks, I'm caught by the drug, and I got to do it.

Regardless of whether the hypersexuality of crack is real or imagined, the overwhelming majority of the women encountered in this study were not bartering sex for crack for the sake of sensual pleasure. Many depended on bartering sex as their only way of getting crack. Most reported performing sexual acts that they would only do while *on* crack or *for* crack. For example:

> I had a date that wanted me to find a girlfriend that enjoys females. I said sure, I knew a girl that enjoyed females, so I got her. We made a date and time where I was supposed to meet this guy and we did and it was $30 apiece. Just for him to watch us. She went down on me for about five minutes and I went down on her for, like, five minutes. I was trying not to do it but then it was like he wanted to watch. He was, like, right there on top. So I had no choice but to do it if I wanted my money, because I was high at the time.

Similarly:

> Three years ago I would not have believed the things I seen and the things I done in rock houses. I seen all kind of sex — men with women, men with little girls an' boys, women with girls an' little boys, an' even women with women an' men with men. Even with animals. I do a lot of that, too, but not with kids. I'll never do that, you know, not with kids. Not me. But I done most everything else for rocks.

Crack Houses and HIV Risk

The biological variables that determine HIV "infectivity" (the tendency to spread from host to host) and "susceptibility" (the tendency for a host to become infected) are incompletely understood. HIV has been isolated from the semen of infected men, and it appears that it may be harbored in the cells of pre-ejaculated fluids or sequestered in inflammatory lesions.[33] Furthermore, it appears that women can harbor HIV in vaginal and cervical secretions at varying times during the menstrual cycle.[34] The probability of sexual transmission of HIV among homosexual and bisexual men through anal intercourse, and to women through vaginal intercourse, has been well documented.[35] However, although there is the potential for viral transmission from female secretions, the absolute amounts of virus in these secretions appear to be relatively low. The efficiency of transmission of male-to-female versus female-to-male is likely affected by the relative infectivity of these different secretions, as well as sex during menses, specific sexual practices, the relative integrity of skin and mucosal surfaces involved, and possibly the presence of other sexually transmitted diseases. Within this context, the character of crack-house sex, both vaginal and oral, likely facilitates the heterosexual transmission of HIV.

The potential for transmission of HIV from women to men during vaginal intercourse in crack houses is related to aspects of the cocaine/sexuality connection. Male customers as well as female providers in sex/crack exchange networks report the difficulties associated with ejaculating under the influence of crack. Some men can climax only through extremely vigorous masturbation. A woman who resided in a Miami crack house and regularly provided sex for crack commented:

> Some of these mens have trouble gettin' it up and keepin' it up, and it's hard to get them to come, although sometimes even that happens.

Other women similarly reported:

> The cracks causes problems for men. They can get a hard-on, but they don't come quick like when they're straight. So first they want heads, and when that don't work, they want vaginal sex. Then it still takes 'em forever, pumpin' away until he gets sore, I get sore, and then I get pissed. But I can't say anything, because he already gave me the cracks. . . .

> * * *

> One time this Hispanic dude was taking so long that he sees blood and starts yelling, "What the fuck's goin' on with you, lady, you on the rag or something?" But it was him that was bleedin' in me. He was goin' in and out of me so long that he rubbed himself raw. . . .

> * * *

> I had this guy once who they should've named him "horse cock." He was so big that it really hurt . . . . I figured it'd be over quick. But he don't come. Fuck, Fuck, fuck, and he still don't come. Then he starts jerkin' himself off fast, doin' it 'till ya can see his cock is bleedin' on his hand. His dick has blood on it an' so does his hand. And then he rams himself back in me and fuck, fuck, fuck. . . . He never did come.

It is within such a situation that a high potential for female-to-male transmission of HIV likely exists. During vaginal intercourse, the friction of the penis against the clitoris, labia minora, and vaginal vestibule, opening, and canal causes stimulation that can generate copious amounts of vaginal secretions. And, as noted above, HIV has been isolated from vaginal/cervical secretions. Furthermore, since women who exchange sex for crack in crack houses do so with many different men during the course of a day or night, potentially HIV-infected semen from a previous customer can still be present in the vagina. Still another female-to-male route is suggested in the report of one crack-house customer who ruptured the skin on his penis while having intercourse with a crack-house prostitute while she was menstruating:

> I really didn't think much about it. I was high, and I had been high most of the night, and porking [having vaginal intercourse with] a

> crack-house prostitute while she was on the rag [menstruating] was
> something I had done more than once in my time. . . . She was
> bleeding, and I was bleeding, first from a bad blow job and then from
> too much sex. . . . After a while, the blood, hers, got too much, so I
> turned her over and put it in her chute [anus].

As such, genital secretions as well as semen and blood come into direct
contact with the traumatized skin of a client's penis during crack-house
sex.

Although vaginal and anal intercourse often occur, much of the sex
that occurs in crack houses involves women performing oral sex on men.
To date, however, evidence for an oral route of HIV has been unconvinc-
ing.[36] In most of the investigations of homosexual practices where a full
range of sexual activities was carefully considered, for example, the risk
from either insertive or receptive orogenital contact was uncertain, although it was regarded to be quite low.[37] The data concerning heterosexual spread of the virus by oral sex are also limited. For example, in one
study of the spouses of AIDS patients, HIV seropositivity among spouses
was higher for couples who practiced oral sex in addition to penile/vaginal
sex, as compared with couples who practiced *only* penile/vaginal sex.[38]

There is an accumulating body of evidence that impaired host immu-
nity, as well as concomitant sexually transmitted diseases, and particularly genital ulceration, may potentiate the transmission of HIV by increasing both infectivity and susceptibility.[39] All three of these cofactors
are apparent in crack-house oral sex. A fourth cofactor is that open sores
on the lips and tongues of chronic users of crack are not uncommon, a
result of burns and skin ulcerations caused by the heated stems of crack-
smoking paraphernalia. Given the high concentrations of virus in the
semen of men infected with HIV,[40] the potential for transmission of
infection under these circumstances is considerable. Because most women
who perform repeated acts of oral sex in crack houses refuse to swallow a
customer's semen as it is ejaculated, the potential for HIV transmission
from infected semen via the open sores on the lips and tongue becomes
apparent. For example, one 22-year-old crack-using woman who claimed
to have more than 30,000 episodes of oral sex over a three-year-period
commented:

> I may have swallowed a lot of cock in my time, but I don't swallow
> nobody's come. You can tell when a man is gonna come, so you try to
> get his cock out of your mouth so it ends up somewhere else. Most of
> the time it ends up on your face, hair, chest. . . . Either that or he
> surprises me and I end up with a mouth full of jizz [semen]. So I wait
> 'till he's done and then I let it out all at once.*

---

* It should be noted here that this particular women also reported having an open sore on the
inside of her lower lip, which she assumed was from a crack pipe.

Another reported:

> Yeah, I really don't want to swallow any of it. I don't like that, not at
> all. I hold it, see, in my mouth. Sometimes it dribbles out while he's
> still workin' at it. But when he's all done I don't fuck the dog [waste
> time]. I get rid of it quick. Spit it out.

As such, it would appear that the potential for the transmission of HIV
infection via crack-house oral sex is quite substantial.

Crack, AIDS, and Condoms

Even in the crack house there is a high rate of awareness and concern
about AIDS. Almost all of the women encountered who traded sex for
crack or money to buy crack had concern about contracting HIV and
AIDS. Most claimed to have had an AIDS test, several knew that they
were already HIV-positive, but a significant number of those who *had*
been tested never bothered to get their test results. Moreover, few of these
women even discussed AIDS with their peers. One reported:

> Everybody that goes by, they holler AIDS out their windows, that's
> about the only discussion about AIDS.

Another said:

> It never came up as the topic of a conversation, but right away when a
> person says "rubber" they know what you mean. But you really don't
> want to say it because you really don't want to turn the guy off, you
> know. You know what I'm saying here is a guy who's really turned on
> and you know he really wants to sex you right, you really don't want
> to say stuff like AIDS.

Moreover:

> I try not to think about it. I just try to be safe. It's scary, I'm out there
> scared all the time.

Although they did not discuss AIDS, women trading sex for crack did
have a fairly high level of knowledge about HIV infection and its routes of
transmission.† Most of those interviewed were aware that there is a
latency period between becoming infected, testing positive for HIV, and
showing symptoms. They also knew that AIDS is not spread through
kissing or sneezing. Most were aware that condoms could help prevent
the spread of AIDS and the majority knew that cleaning needles with
bleach is also an effective prevention effort. By contrast, however, they

---

†Although these crack users appeared knowledgeable about HIV transmission, they are not
as informed about the origins of the disease. According to many, AIDS was the result of
everything from people eating infected green monkeys, to gays having sex with the monkeys, to pilots carrying the virus from Africa back to the United States.

harbored a variety of myths about how to protect themselves from infection, as was apparent in such comments as: "I won't fuck somebody who looks sick"; "I'll only give blow jobs to people I gave blow jobs to before"; "I don't fool around with queers"; "No anal sex anymore, just mouth and pussy"; "If he won't put on a rubber, he can't put it in my cunt, only in my ass or a blow job."

The use of condoms, furthermore, did not appear to be widespread. While a few street prostitutes insisted on them, most did not press the issue if it appeared that they would lose a trick. In crack houses, the use of condoms was quite rare.

Postscript

Recent data from a population of 235 women who came to the attention of a University of Miami School of Medicine AIDS prevention/intervention project dramatically illustrates the HIV infection potential associated with crack use.[41] Although the majority of these women were the sex partners of injection-drug users, none of them were drug injectors themselves. Most importantly, 40.9% were crack users while the rest were not. The exchange of sex for *money* was reported by 64.5% of crack users and only 18.4% of non-users. The difference is even more pronounced when exchanges of sex for *drugs* are considered—reported by 24.2% of the crack users but only 2.7% of non-users.

Both groups in this study had a high degree of HIV risk associated with having sex partners who were injection-drug users. Almost 90% of the non-crack users and 96% of the crack users reported having one or more drug injectors as sex partners—an expected finding since the Miami prevention/intervention effort targeted injection-drug users and their sex partners from the outset. As such, almost all in both groups faced that particular risk factor. However, their histories of sexually transmitted diseases (STDs) were quite different. The proportions of crack users reporting genital herpes, gonorrhea, syphilis, and genital sores were significantly higher than those of the non-users. For example:

STD	Crack Users	Non-Users
Genital Herpes	1.0%	0.7%
Gonorrhea	42.7%	23.7%
Syphilis	30.2%	13.8%
Genital Sores	17.7%	3.6%

And most importantly, while 10.8% of the non-crack-using women were HIV positive, 19.8% of the crack users—almost double—were HIV-positive.

Endnotes

1. Mirko D. Grmek, *History of AIDS: Emergence and Origin of a Modern Pandemic* (Princeton, NJ: Princeton University Press, 1990), p. 3.
2. David Black, *The Plague Years: A Chronicle of AIDS, the Epidemic of Our Times* (New York: Simon and Schuster, 1986), pp. 36–38.
3. Black, pp. 35–56.
4. M. S. Gottlieb, R. Schroff, H. Schanker, J. D. Weismal, P. T. Fan, R. A. Wolf, and A. Saxon, "Pneumocystis Carinii Pneumonia and Mucosal Candidiasis in Previously Healthy Homosexual Men: Evidence of a New Acquired Cellular Immunodeficiency," *New England Journal of Medicine* 305 (10 December 1981), pp. 1425–1431; H. Masur, M. A. Michelis, J. B. Greene, I. Onorato, R. A. Vande Stouwe, R. T. Holzman, G. Wormser, L. Brettmen, M. Lange, H. W. Murray, and S. Cunningham-Rundles, "An Outbreak of Community-Acquired Pneumocystis Carinii Pneumonia: Initial Manifestation of Cellular Immune Dysfunction," *New England Journal of Medicine* 305 (10 December 1981), pp. 1431–1438; Centers for Disease Control, "Epidemiologic Aspects of the Current Outbreak of Kaposi's Sarcoma and Opportunistic Infections." *New England Journal of Medicine* 306 (28 January 1982), pp. 248–252; Randy Shilts, *And the Band Played On: Politics, People, and the AIDS Epidemic* (New York: St. Martin's Press, 1987), pp. 18–19; Ann Giudici Fettner, "The Discovery of AIDS: Perspectives from a Medical Journalist," in Gary P. Wormser, Rosalyn E. Stahl, and Edward J. Bottone, eds., *AIDS and Other Manifestations of HIV Infection* (Park Ridge, NJ: Noyes Publications, 1987), pp. 2–17.
5. See Susan Sontag, *AIDS and Its Metaphors* (New York: Farrar, Straus and Giroux, 1988).
6. Centers for Disease Control, "Pneumocystis Pneumonia — Los Angeles," *Morbidity and Mortality Weekly Report* 30 (June 5, 1981), pp. 250–252.
7. Centers for Disease Control, "Kaposi's Sarcoma and Pneumocystis Pneumonia Among Homosexual Men — New York City and California," *Morbidity and Mortality Weekly Report* 30 (July 3, 1981), pp. 305–308.
8. See W.T. Hughes, "Pneumosystis Carinii," in G.L. Mandell, R.G. Douglous, and J.E. Bennett, eds., *Principles and Practice of Infectious Diseases* (New York: Wiley, 1979), pp. 2137–2142; J.A. Golden, "Pulmonary Complications of AIDS," in Jay A. Levy, ed., *AIDS: Pathogenesis and Treatment*, New York: Marcel Dekker, 1989), pp. 403–447.
9. See Paul A. Volberding, "Kaposi's Sarcoma in AIDS" in Jay A. Levy, ed., *AIDS: Pathogenesis and Treatment*, pp. 345–358.
10. Institute of Medicine, National Academy of Sciences, *Mobilizing Against AIDS: The Unfinished Story of a Virus* (Cambridge: Harvard University Press, 1986), p. 195.
11. S. Connor and S. Kingman, *The Search for the Virus: The Scientific Discovery of AIDS and the Quest for a Cure* (London: Penguin, 1989).
12. Don C. Des Jarlais and Samuel R. Friedman, "Intravenous Cocaine, Crack, and HIV Infection," *Journal of the American Medical Association* 259 (1988), pp. 1945–1946; Don C. Des Jarlais and Samuel R. Friedman, "HIV Infection Among Persons Who Inject Illicit Drugs: Problems and Prospects," *Journal of the Acquired Immune Deficiency Syndromes* 1 (1988), pp. 267–273; Don C. Des Jarlais, Samuel R. Friedman and William Hopkins, "Risk Reduction for Acquired Immunodeficiency Syndrome Among Intravenous Drug Users," *Annals of Internal Medicine* 103 (1985), pp. 755–59.
13. L. Resnick, L. K. Veren, S. Z. Salahuddin, S. Tondreau, and P. D. Karkham, "Stability and Inactivation of HTLV-III/LAV Under Clinical and Laboratory Environments," *Journal of the American Medical Association* 255 (11 April 1986), pp. 1887–1891.
14. Dale D. Chitwood, James A. Inciardi, Duane C. McBride, Clyde B. McCoy, H. Virginia McCoy, and Edward Trapido, *A Community Approach to AIDS Intervention: Exploring the Miami Outreach Project for Injecting Drug Users and Other High-Risk Populations* (Westport, CT: Greenwood Press), pp. 29–50.

15. Jean-Paul Grund, Charles Kaplan, and Nico F. P. Adriaans, "Needle Exchange and Drug Sharing: A View from Rotterdam," *Newsletter of the International Working Group on AIDS and IV Drug Use* 4 (1989), pp. 4–5; Jean-Paul C. Grund, Charles D. Kaplan, Nico F. P. Adriaans, Peter Blanken, and Jan Huismanm, "The Limitations of the Concept of Needle Sharing: The Practice of Frontloading," *AIDS* 4 (August 1990), pp. 819–821; James A. Inciardi and J. Bryan Page, "Drug Sharing Among Intravenous Drug Users," *AIDS* 9 (June 1991), pp. 772–773.

16. Arlene Carmen and Howard Moody, *Working Women: The Subterranean World of Street Prostitution* (New York: Harper & Row, 1985).

17. M. Seidlin, K. Krasinski, D. Bebenroth, V. Itri, A.M. Paolind and F. Valentine, "Prevalence of HIV Infection in New York Call Girls." *Journal of Acquired Immune Deficiency Syndromes* 1 (1988), pp. 150–154.

18. J. Cohen, P. Alexander, and C. Wofsy, "Prostitutes and AIDS: Public Policy Issues," *AIDS and Public Policy Journal* 3 (1988), pp. 16–21; J.P. Cohen, C. Wofsy, P. Gill, S. Aguilar, J. Witte, W. Bigler, R.K. Sikes, T. Leonard, J. French, C. Sterk., O. Ravenholt, R. Reich, C. Campbell, J. Potterat and L. Phillips, "Antibody to Human Immunodeficiency Virus in Female Prostitutes," *Morbidity and Mortality Weekly Report* 36 (March 27, 1987), pp. 157–161.

19. Centers for Disease Control, "Human Immunodeficiency Virus Infection in the United States: A Review of Current Knowledge," *Morbidity and Mortality Weekly Report* 36 (December 18, 1987, Supplement S-6).

20. Marsha F. Goldsmith, "Sex Tied to Drugs = STD Spread," *Medical News & Perspective* 260 (Oct. 14, 1988), p. 2009; "Relationship of Syphilis to Drug Use and Prostitution — Connecticut and Philadelphia, Pennsylvania," *Journal of the American Medical Association* 261 (January 20, 1989), p. 353; "Syphilis and Crack Linked in Connecticut," *Substance Abuse Report*, August 1, 1989, pp. 1–3; "Congenital Syphilis — New York City, 1986–1988," *American Journal of Diseases of Children* 144 (March, 1990), p. 279; Robert T. Rolfs, Martin Goldberg, and Robert G. Sharrar, "Risk Factors for Syphilis: Cocaine Use and Prostitution," *American Journal of Public Health* 80 (July 1990), pp. 853–857; "Cocaine Use Linked to Congenital Syphilis in New York City," *Substance Abuse Report*, December 1, 1991, pp. 3–5; Mary E. Guinan, "Women and Crack Addiction," *Journal of American Medical Women's Association* 44 (1989), p. 129; S. Schultz, M. Zweig, T. Sing, and M. Htoo, "Congenital Syphilis: New York City, 1986–1988," *American Journal of Diseases of Children* 144 (1990), p. 279; R.E. Fullilove, M.T. Fullilove, B.P. Bowser, S.A. Gross, "Risk of Sexually Transmitted Disease Among Black Adolescent Crack Users in Oakland and San Francisco, California," *Journal of the American Medical Association* 263 (1990) pp. 851–855.

21. Moira L. Plant, Martin A. Plant, David F. Peck, and Jo Setters, "The Sex Industry, Alcohol and Illicit Drugs: Implications for the Spread of HIV Infection," *British Journal of Addiction* 84 (1989), pp. 53–59; John Buffum, "Pharmacosexology: The Effects of Drugs on Sexual Function," *Journal of Psychoactive Drugs* 14 (1982), pp. 5–44; G.T. Wilson and Lawson, "The Effects of Alcohol on Sexual Arousal in Women," *Journal of Abnormal Psychology* 89 (1976), pp. 489–497; G.T. Wilson, G.T. and D.G. Lawson, "Expectancies, Alcohol and Sexual Arousal in Male Social Drinkers," *Journal of Abnormal Psychology* 89 (1976), pp. 587–594.

22. E.M. Adlaf and R.G. Smart, "Risk-Taking and Drug Use Behavior," *Drug and Alcohol Dependence* 11 (1983), pp. 287–296; A. Lang, "The Social Psychology of Drinking and Human Sexuality," *Journal of Drug Issues* 15 (1985), pp. 273–289.

23. Helen C. Jones and Paul W. Lovinger, *The Marijuana Question* (New York: Dodd, Mead, 1985).

24. David E. Smith, "Marijuana and Sex," *Medical Aspects of Human Sexuality* 8 (1974), p. 39.

25. Arnold M. Washton and Mark S. Gold, *Cocaine: A Clinician's Handbook* (New York: Guilford Press, 1987).

26. Thomas E. Piemme, "Sex and Illicit Drugs," *Medical Aspects of Human Sexuality* 10 (1976), pp. 85–86.

27. Robert Seecof and Forest S. Tennant, "Subjective Perceptions to the Intravenous 'Rush' of Heroin and Cocaine in Opioid Addicts," *American Journal of Drug and Alcohol Abuse* 12 (1986), pp. 79–87; Burton Angrist and Samuel Gershon, "Clinical Effects of Amphetamine and L-DOPA on Sexuality and Aggression," *Comprehensive Psychiatry* 17 (1976), pp. 715–722; D.S. Bell and W.H. Trethosan, "Amphetamine Addiction and Disturbed Sexuality," *Archives of General Psychiatry* 4 (1961), pp. 74–78; Ronald K. Siegel, "Cocaine and Sexual Dysfunction: The Curse of Mama Coca," *Journal of Psychoactive Drugs* 14 (1982), pp. 71–74.

28. Patrick T. Macdonald, Dan Waldorf, Craig Reinarman, and Sheigla Murphy (1988) "Heavy Cocaine Use and Sexual Behavior," *Journal of Drug Issues* 18 (1988), pp. 437–455.

29. For example, see Phillipe Bourgois and Eloise Dunlap, "Sex-for-Crack in Harlem, New York" (Paper presented at the Annual Meeting of the Society for Applied Anthropology, Charleston, South Carolina, March 13–17, 1991); Stephen Koester and Judith Schwartz, "Crack Cocaine and Sex" (Paper presented at the Annual Meeting of the Society for Applied Anthropology, Charleston, South Carolina, March 13–17, 1991).

30. John C. Ball and Carl D. Chambers, *The Epidemiology of Opiate Addiction in the United States* (Springfield, IL: Charles C. Thomas, 1970); Marsha Rosenbaum, *Women on Heroin* (New Brunswick, NJ: Rutgers University Press, 1981).

31. Roger D. Weiss and Steven M. Mirin, *Cocaine* (Washington, DC: American Psychiatric Press, 1987); Lester Grinspoon and James B. Bakalar, *Cocaine: A Drug and Its Social Evolution* (New York: Basic Books, 1985).

32. See Paul J. Goldstein, *Prostitution and Drugs* (Lexington, MA: Heath, 1979). Also, see Chapter 6.

33. Margaret A. Fischl, "Prevention of Transmission of AIDS During Sexual Intercourse," in Vincent T. DeVita, Samuel Hellman, and Steven A. Rosenberg, eds., *AIDS: Etiology, Diagnosis, Treatment, and Prevention* (Philadelphia: Lippincott, 1988), pp. 369–374.

34. M.W. Vogt, D.E. Craven, D.S. Crawford, D.J. Witt, R. Byington, R.T. Schooley, and M.S. Hirsch, "Isolation of HTLV-III/LAV from Cervical Secretions of Women at Risk for AIDS," *Lancet* i (1986), pp. 525–527; M.W. Vogt, D.J. Witt, D.E. Craven, R. Byington, D.S. Crawford, M.S. Hutchinson, R.T. Schooley, and M.S. Hirsch, "Isolation Patterns of the Human Immunodeficiency Virus from Cervical Secretions During the Menstrual Cycle of Women at Risk for the Acquired Immunodeficiency Syndrome," *Annals of Internal Medicine* 106 (1987), pp. 380–382; C.B. Wofsy, J.B. Cohen, L.B. Hauer, N. Padian, B. Michaelis, J. Evans, and J.A. Levy, "Isolation of AIDS-Associated Retrovirus from Genital Secretions of Women with Antibodies to the Virus," *Lancet* i (1986), pp. 527–529.

35. See, for example, Pearl Ma and Donald Armstrong, eds., *AIDS and Infections of Homosexual Men* (Boston: Butterworths, 1989); Judith B. Cohen and Constance B. Wofsy, "Heterosexual Transmission of HIV," in Jay A. Levy, ed., *AIDS: Pathogenesis and Treatment*, pp. 135–157.

36. Thomas A. Peterson, "Facilitators of HIV Transmission During Sexual Contact," in Nancy J. Alexander, Henry L. Gabelnick, and Jeffrey M. Speiler, eds., *Heterosexual Transmission of AIDS* (New York: Wiley-Liss, 1990), pp. 55–68.

37. Richard A. Kaslow and Donald P. Francis, *The Epidemiology of AIDS: Expression, Occurrence, and Control of Human Immunodeficiency Virus Type 1 Infection* (New York: Oxford University Press, 1989), p. 98.

38. M. Fischl, T. Fayne, S. Flanagan, M. Ledan, R. Stevens, M. Fletcher, L. La Voie, and E. Trapido, "Seroprevalence and Risks of HIV Infection in Spouses of Persons Infected With HIV," *IV International Conference on AIDS*, June 1988, Stockholm.

39. Anne M. Johnson and Marie Laga, "Heterosexual Transmission of HIV," *AIDS*, 2 (Supplement 1, 1988), pp. S49–S56.

40. Giora M. Mavligit, Moshe Talpaz, Flora T. Hsia, Wendy Wong, Benjamin Lichtiger, Peter W. A. Mansell, and David M. Mumford, "Chronic Immune Stimulation by Sperm Alloantigens: Support for the Hypothesis That Spermatozoa Induce Immune Dysregula-

tion in Homosexual Men," *Journal of the American Medical Association* 251 (1984), pp. 237–241; Robert R. Redfield, Phillip D. Markham, Syed Zaki Salahuddin, M. G. Sarngadharan, Anne J. Bodner, Thomas N. Folks, William R. Ballou, D. Craig Wright, and Robert C. Gallo, "Frequent Transmission of HTLV-III Among Spouses of Patients With AIDS-Related Complex and AIDS," *Journal of the American Medical Association* 253 (1985), pp. 1571–1573; Jay A. Levy, ed., *AIDS: Pathogenesis and Treatment*, pp. 159–229.

41. H. Virginia McCoy, Christine Miles, and James A. Inciardi, "Survival Sex: Inner-City Women and Crack-Cocaine," under review.

CHAPTER 6

Women, Crack, and Crime

"Hustling is how I get by. What that means is that I get up at noon, boost [shoplift] something at the OMNI* on my way to cop some drugs. I'll sell half the drugs at a profit, and sell the watch or perfume that I boosted to someone on the street. Then some car date will wave me down an' I'll give him a quick blow and if he's careless I'll empty his pockets. Later in the day I might help in a breakin'-in, deliver some coke for a Montana [a Cuban drug dealer, see Glossary]. . . . At night I'll be back on the stroll."

—A Miami prostitute/hustler, 1991

The most commonly perceived linkage between drug use and crime is that of crime as a means of financing drug use. As discussed in Chapter 2, this economic connection is confined to the use of expensive drugs — heroin and cocaine — and, although it is not as inevitable as popularly assumed, prior research has established that it is a very common phenomenon among heroin and cocaine users of both genders. However, the ways in which the economic drugs/crime connection actually works are less well understood for women than men, because most of the research on this issue has dealt with men.[1] The economic drugs/crime linkage is at least different — and possibly more complicated — for women because of differences in the economic options typically open to them as compared to men.

Before looking at the particulars of this connection for women, however, it should be noted that crime to finance drug use is by no means the only linkage operating between drug use and crime. Other connections explain how the economic linkage came to be established in the first place and help to clarify its nature by describing ways in which it is actually a convoluted two-way interaction.

---

*The OMNI is a hotel/shopping mall complex in downtown Miami located within walking distance of a high drug-use/high crime area.

Women, Drugs/Crime Linkages, and History

> The walking of the street prostitutes after nightfall has become an alarming evil. Nowhere else is the class so degraded. . . . accosting people on the streets, picking pockets in public bar-rooms, stupefied by drugs and alcohol . . .
>
> —*Edward Crapsey, 1872*[2]

As discussed in Chapter 3, highly deviant drug use in America — opium smoking, recreational morphine use, and then heroin injection — has long been associated with exotic underworld locations, criminal subcultures, and the availability of women for sexual services. Until about 1920, however, this drugs/crime linkage involved only an extremely small percentage of chemically dependent women. A number of analyses indicate that at least by 1850, large numbers of American women were addicted to opiates — strong pain-killers of the same general drug class as heroin.[3] The opiate most commonly involved was opium, as a major component in some prescription or over-the-counter medication; the women most commonly involved were middle-aged and of middle- or upper-class background (and hence white) who probably disapproved of alcohol use and would never have seen themselves as drug addicts; and the most prominent cause of the problem was the astounding ubiquity of these preparations and the degree to which they were advertised and accepted as cures for any ailment a woman might have. It is generally agreed that from 1850 to 1920, women addicted to opiates outnumbered male addicts two to one, and the great majority of addicts were respectable law-abiding citizens.

Then, in the decade after the Harrison Act of 1914, a growing anti-opiate hysteria resulted in federal enforcement policies which turned this legislation — a fairly liberal tax and licensing regulation with many loopholes — into a war on opiate use.[4] By the 1920s, the availability of legal opiates to conventional citizens had been dramatically reduced. Legal possession required a prescription, but relatively few physicians were willing to risk violating the new laws and many were unwilling to put up with addicted patients, who were commonly defined as troublesome; physicians willing to write prescriptions were strongly pressured to reduce the number of prescriptions they wrote; and the idea of maintenance dosages for patients who were already addicted was strongly discouraged.[5] The out-patient clinics set up in 1919 at federal urging were all closed by 1923, again at federal urging, due to assorted scandals — huge profits, allegedly inadequate efforts at forcing withdrawal, and extremely high relapse rates among discharged patients. Increasingly, it was argued that only in-patient treatment could possibly cure addicts — but no hospitals were set up to replace the clinics until 12 years later.

This time period illustrates a major historical drugs/crime connection

—the thoroughness with which opiate use was criminalized, both legally and socioculturally. In this process, more and more power was turned over to the criminal justice system. This in turn had the effect of making heroin the opiate of choice for black-market entrepreneurs because its potency meant both easier distribution and bigger profits. Heroin replacing other opiates only inflamed public fear and emotionalism, since heroin, like opium, was by then associated in the public mind with use by disreputable if not outright criminal groups. More furor was added when apparent increases in crime rates after World War I could conveniently be blamed on heroin use by youths.[6] And, as enforcement of narcotics laws was stepped up, some of these stereotypes began to come true. Heroin became increasingly expensive and more likely to be the only opiate available on the black market, making it likelier that an addict would need to commit crime to support a habit. Women went from the clear majority of opiate users to a small minority. Opiate addiction was driven out of middle-class homes and into inner-city neighborhoods, a fact which soon accounted for increasing numbers of poor and minority group addicts with much younger ages at the onset of use. And, as heroin prices continued to rise, a solid opiate-crime association became established where only a weak one had existed before. Unlike in the old pattern of female opiate addiction, the majority of the new opiate users had arrest records by the time they entered treatment.

Such a dramatic change took a long time. When the first genuine studies of the drugs/crime relationship among women were done, in the 1960s, both patterns still existed. A study of admissions to the federal narcotics hospitals found that fewer than 5% of addicts from Alabama, Georgia, and Kentucky were heroin users.[7] These people were whites from small towns, very few had incomes from crime, and they began and continued their dependence on opiates—most typically morphine—through prescriptions from physicians. Very few had ever even used marijuana. Even as late as 1969–73, records indicated that patients from the southeastern states were less likely than those from any other region to have the arrest records typical of other addicts.[8] The two-pattern findings held for women as well as men. For example, a study of female patients at the Lexington Hospital showed that 45% of the white women first obtained opiates through medical sources, while 89% of the black women had peers as their first source; while 91% of the black women bought their opiates from street dealers, many of the white women were still getting them from physicians (33%) or pharmacists (19%).[9]

Another historical connection is that even as fields of study, women's drug use and women's crime have a number of striking similarities and interconnections. First, both had extremely small literatures until the early 1970s, when both were given major boosts by the impact of the women's movement on social science research. Second, each has traditionally been conducted as if the other didn't exist. Criminology—

whether concerned with studying males or females, adults or adolescents —has been especially prone to ignoring drug use as a topic, and reference to crime in research on female drug users has only rarely been more than a mention. Consequently, several literature surveys in the early 1980s concluded that the combined topic of women, drug use, and crime was in need of considerably more research attention.[10]

Third, these research areas, even though separated, nonetheless were very similar in their early topics of study. As discussed in Chapter 2, the great majority of pre-1970 work on women drug users concentrated on two kinds of subject matter—the impact of a pregnant woman's alcohol or heroin addiction on the health of the fetus, and clinical descriptions of the personality problems of female addicts. That is, to a dismaying degree this literature reduced women and drug use to (a) complications for a fetus, (b) disturbed personalities, and (c) very little otherwise worth studying.

A strikingly similar viewpoint can be seen in the criminology literature up to about the same point. A number of extensive reviews conclude that while women were not totally ignored in studies of crime and deviance before 1970, they were most commonly included only by vague implication.[11] Empirical studies of specifically criminal (or delinquent) populations were highly unlikely to include females at all, since only general population self-report studies routinely included both sexes. Similarly, women and girls are strikingly absent from the modern classics of criminology, regardless of focus or perspective—anomie, organized crime, professional theft, the delinquency classics, labelling theory, the radical critiques. But the most problematic aspect of the pre-1970 literature on women and crime is that those few studies which did focus on women were guided by startlingly sexist assumptions and viewpoints. In particular, women's crime was repeatedly explained by reference to the physiology of female reproductive systems and its impact on women's emotions. Thus, crime was said to be rare among women due to their (physiologically based) passivity and/or maternal instincts; when women did commit crimes, problems in the physiology/emotions linkage were used to explain the particulars.

Early criminological studies of women were also peculiar in their almost exclusive focus on only three offense types: shoplifting, prostitution, and adolescent promiscuity/(sexual) "ungovernability." Two of these are explicitly sexual; all three are ostensibly trivial. The justification for this narrow focus was the prominence of these offense types in female arrest rates, which means that the highly problematic relationship of these three offense types to law enforcement was most commonly ignored. It now seems especially astonishing that prostitution and promiscuity could be seen as predominantly female activities, in apparent total disregard of male clients and partners.

Only in the particulars, then, is the literature on women and crime different from that on women and drug use prior to about 1970. Both reflect an assumption that women are, most essentially, mothers or at least potential mothers — hence the strong focus in both literatures on female reproductive functions: pregnancy and the fetus for studies of addicts, hormonally induced emotional problems or disapproved sexual behavior in the criminology literature. Even more clearly, both also rest on an assumption of necessarily psychopathological origins for female deviant behavior: women as the sickest addicts, delinquent girls as subject to (physiologically based) emotional turmoil. And, both reflect an assumption that serious social problems are essentially problems of male behavior, since each literature was of such small size relative to the total work on addiction or crime.

Current Drugs/Crime Linkages

> The evidence indicates that female drug users commit a significant amount of crime. . . .
> —*Susan K. Datesman, 1981*[12]

The initial drugs/crime linkage for current users of expensive street drugs is that both drug use and crime typically begin together in adolescence. These activities most often appear as parts of a larger behavioral complex involving a variety of misbehaviors, most undertaken as experimentation with testing limits, trying new behaviors, and attempting to deal with the difficulties inherent in making the transition from childhood to adulthood. Personality disorders or psychological adjustment problems may be present but they certainly are not a requirement. In fact, relatively trivial misbehaviors — an occasional petty theft, experimentation with alcohol and marijuana, skipping classes — are so common during adolescence as to be the norm. For children growing up in neighborhoods where both drug use and crime are common and highly visible, initial involvement is likely to include the influence of slightly older peers and established youth versions of drug/crime subcultures; it is particularly easy for these youths to just drift into both drug use and crime. For children growing up in rural and suburban areas, initial drug use and crime are still likely to be partially subcultural in origin, but with fellow students rather than adults as the local drug dealers, and fewer role models for intensive drug/crime involvement.

Generally, the criminal behavior of adolescents stays relatively minor and then is discarded by the time of young adulthood. Similarly, youth drug use does not usually go beyond alcohol use and perhaps marijuana experimentation. But for those relatively few young people who persist in these behaviors, escalation in one is usually accompanied by escalation in the other. Numerous small-scale and several very large-scale studies of teenagers are unanimous in showing a significant positive correlation between drug involvement and both minor and serious delinquency.[13]

For purposes of looking at women's crack use, this correlation means that by the time a woman is using crack, she is extremely likely not only to have used other drugs but also to have had some kind of criminal involvement. By the same token, for those relatively few women who continue crime beyond adolescence, initial criminality typically has occurred within a pattern of drug involvement. Thus, as adult criminal involvement escalates into a career, drug use is likely to continue, permitting causal relationships to develop even if there were none before.

Increased crime to help finance greater drug involvement is only one kind of drugs/crime causal effect. The direction can also go the other way, with crime increasing or decreasing drug use. An addict who initiates a criminal enterprise may be willing (or able) to go only so far in the effort, restricting drug intake to a level possible within that crime profit-level. On the other hand, a criminal activity may prove much more profitable than ever anticipated, resulting in a decreased concern for how to pay for drug expenses and hence increasing usage levels. Drug use can also affect crime directly by making risky or otherwise difficult offenses psychologically easier — for example, prostitution, theft, or assault.[14]

Still another kind of drug/crime interaction results from what Paul Goldstein has called "systemic violence," a phenomenon that has come to characterize street-drug sales in recent years.[15] Buyers as well as dealers are at risk of assault, robbery, and death just by participating in the drug market, because fear of getting cheated during the sale is such a major concern that arguments escalate to violence quite easily. In the case of cocaine, an additional factor is that large scale sales are such a recent phenomenon that local and even regional markets are still unstable, subject to bids for power from new entrants into "the cocaine wars."[16]

Over time, any single heroin or cocaine addict experiences many of these drug/crime interactions, leading to a sometimes chaotic existence. Anything that changes one factor — drug use or crime — will have an impact on the other. The social and psychological consequences of this chaos amount to further dedication to a street-addict lifestyle. Contacts with other people are increasingly limited to other addicts; values are altered as needed to fit behaviors; crime is accepted as not just a means of obtaining drugs but as part of the addict's self-concept; and conventional people and conventional values are defined as "square": pathetically out of touch with what is really important and enjoyable.[17]

Commitment to a street-addict way of life is, in fact, the most important way in which crime and expensive drug use are linked. Both behaviors are major requirements for participation in a subculture that provides its participants with activities they enjoy, social expectations they can meet, and social support for their values and behaviors. Resisting the addict lifestyle — to the point of developing rituals and values incompatible with this world, as well as keeping non-user friends — is thus one way in which occasional cocaine or heroin users resist addiction.[18] Conversely, commitment to the street-addict lifestyle is a primary reason heroin addicts generally resist methadone-maintenance programs: being a clinic patient would take care of a heroin habit, but it would restrict too many other elements of the addict's lifestyle. Studies of street addicts who do abandon heroin thus indicate that for them, the rewards of the lifestyle have been surpassed by its problems.[19]

A final kind of current drugs/crime linkage requiring discussion is that of convergence — the possibility that street addicts and "career criminals" are increasingly the same people, and that the heroin/cocaine addict's world and the street crime underworld have essentially converged into one. A primary source of evidence for this convergence is the increasing percentages of persons taken into police custody who test positive for drugs. Between 1984 and 1988, increases in cocaine use were especially apparent, both among males and females, and among adults and juveniles.[20]

Another indicator of convergence is provided by our own experience with street interviews of active female criminals at two different points in time, in the same cities, with the same kind of methodology. When we conducted street interviews in Miami in 1977–78, we wanted two kinds of comparison samples for the heroin users we were most concerned with: criminals involved with nonopiate street drugs, and criminals who were not using street drugs at all. What we found was that almost everyone, male or female, heroin user or not, smoked marijuana. Thus, of the 124 women interviewed who were not heroin users, only 20% used no drugs at all or used only alcohol and hence no street drugs. But when we went back to Miami in 1983–84, even a "no more than alcohol and/or marijuana" pattern was much rarer. While this described the drug use of 43% of the female nonheroin sample (total 124) in 1977–78, it fit only 21% of the (184) women not using opiates in 1983–84. The primary reason was increased use of cocaine. Current use of cocaine among women in the nonopiate sample was reported by 49% in 1977–78, but 73% in 1983–84. The increase in daily cocaine use was even larger: 22% in 1977–78 but 42% in 1983–84. This was not just a matter of Miami's prominence as a cocaine-import site, either, since the alcohol/marijuana pattern was even more rare among our 1983–84 New York respondents than it was in Miami: a mere 5% of the 98 nonopiate users, versus 21% (of 184) in Miami. In short, the comparison of our findings at two different times suggests that serious drug involvement by female criminals is more extensive now than in even the very recent past.

Further, when we went back to Miami in 1988–1990 to locate adolescents who were seriously crime involved, we found that 98.8% of the 511 males (age 12–17) were current users of cocaine, as were 96.0% of the 100 females (age 14–17). In fact, drug use was so pervasive among these 611 young criminal offenders that when they were asked about their use of seven different drug types, the mean number of types for which they reported current use was 4.6, and they were using a mean of 2.6 different types *regularly* (three or more times a week).[21]

Crime Patterns of Female Street Addicts

> I done everything — *hustling* (prostitution), boosting, robberies, some dealing . . . stealing from dates . . . an' I cut a few people.
> — *a Miami heroin user, 1989*

Given that female heroin and cocaine users not uncommonly engage in crime — for an apparent multiplicity of reasons — what kinds of crime are involved? How extensive is the involvement? How commonly does it result in arrest? Several stereotypic expectations are contradicted in the answers provided by our street interviews with female heroin users in Miami.[22] First, like their male counterparts, female heroin users engage in a wide variety of offense types — including robbery, burglary, shoplifting, a wide variety of other property crimes, and drug sales. Prostitution was the single most common offense type, but it accounted for only a little over half (54%) of all offenses committed by 133 female heroin users interviewed on the street in 1983–1984 and even fewer (38%) for a similar cohort of 153 women interviewed in 1977–1978.

Second, these women committed a large number of crimes, including property offenses and drug sales. This is evident in the totals shown below for crimes during a *12-month* time period for the 153 members of the 1977–1978 cohort, and in a *6-month* time period for the 133 women in the 1983–1984 sample.

Crime Type	1977–79	1983–84
Robbery, assault	890	260
Property crimes	15,797	6,188
Prostitution, procuring	22,835	33,770
Drug sales	15,126	21,067
Grand Total	**54,548**	**61,285**

Third, even though prostitution — the most frequent crime type for these women — tends to be a sufficiently visible crime to make arrest relatively easy, only an extremely small percentage of these crimes resulted in arrest. For the 1977–1978 cohort, 131 offenses (60 of them prostitution) resulted in arrest — a mere 0.2% of the total crimes committed. For the 1983–1984 cohort, arrest was even less likely—47 offenses (27 of them prostitution) resulted in arrest, which is 0.1% of the total crimes committed. The shorter time frame for the second study may be part of the explanation but it is by no means all of it, since 43.6% of this extremely crime-involved cohort had *never* been arrested.

Similar characteristics—multiple offense types, high-frequency crime, low probability of arrest for any given offense—are reported in other studies of female heroin users.[23] However, prior research on *cocaine* users, male or female, appears more equivocal. A number of studies have found that low-level dealing is common among persons using cocaine at moderate to heavy levels, but that even heavy cocaine users tend to avoid involvement in other offenses.[24] The samples on which these conclusions are based, however, are the easiest kind of noninstitutionalized respondents for researchers to access: persons of relatively stable income with little or no criminal involvement prior to their cocaine use. This serves as a back door verification of the assertion made earlier that the single most important drugs/crime linkage is their joint occurrence as part of the street-addict lifestyle. Cocaine users unwilling to commit themselves to this lifestyle are not driven by cocaine usage as such to a life of crime. As Dana Hunt has observed, the relevant cocaine/heroin difference here is probably that cocaine has become much more widely available to—and prevalent among—ordinary conventional working-class and middle-class people than heroin has ever been.[25]

Studies of cocaine users in publicly funded treatment programs, however, find a clear association between degree of cocaine involvement and amount of criminal activity. These cocaine users tend to have socioeconomic and criminal justice profiles which resemble those for heroin users in the same programs—high rates of unemployment, low levels of educational attainment, and a prior arrest record.[26] A cocaine/crime relationship has also been reported for women from similar economic backgrounds who were interviewed on the street.[27]

Finally, it should be noted that there is a paucity of research on the linkage of crime with specifically *crack*-cocaine. Most of the work cited above was done prior to the advent of plentiful crack; the respondents were people who used *powder*-cocaine, primarily by snorting. This kind of cocaine use has maintained a certain degree of association with Hollywood, the jet set, professional athletes, glamour, and power—but crack's image has remained associated with ghettos and gutters. As discussed in Chapter 2, prevalence rates for these two cocaine types in the general household population appear to reflect the street-life association of crack: only *powder*-cocaine is used by significant percentages of young adults, whereas crack use is confined to less than 0.5% of even the most likely age/gender subpopulations. Consequently, one would expect to see specifically *crack*/crime associations highly similar to those found for heroin and crime.

Crack/Crime Connections Among Women

> I once killed a man over crack. He was a dealer, he wanted too much
> for it, and he made me mad.
> —*A woman crack user, 1992*

In response to the dearth of information about crack/crime relationships, including differences between *crack*-cocaine and *powder*-cocaine, a new study of cocaine users was conducted in Miami between April 1988 and March 1990.[28] A total of 699 cocaine users were interviewed, half (N = 349) in residential treatment programs and half (N = 350) on the street. Of the 237 women included, a subsample of 197 were identified as "female crack users" because crack was at least 75% of their total cocaine usage during their last 90 days on the street—the 90 days prior to interview for active respondents or, for treatment respondents, the 90 days prior to program entry. Crack usage was analyzed in a three-category variable based on computed total dosage: days (number of days crack was used in the last 90 days on the street) multiplied by doses (number of usual crack doses per day). High levels of crack use were the norm for this sample, as indicated by the category definitions and the sample percentages:

"**Moderate**" — Less than 360 doses total (N = 49, 25%)

"**Typical**" — 360-719 doses total (N = 90, 46%)

"**Heavy**" — 720 or more doses total (N = 58, 29%)

Of the total 197 women, 92% were using crack at a level that averaged 2+ doses a day (180+ doses); this level described 69% of even women in the Moderate category. However, crack is often used on a binge basis— multiple doses per day for several days running, and then none at all for a day or two. Thus, even with their high total dosages, 19% of Heavy users and 8% of Typical users did not use crack on every one of their last 90 days on the street. They did all use "regularly," defined as 3+ days a week (or 35+ of the 90-day time period). Of the Moderate users, 57% used crack every day, 29% used regularly but less than daily, 12% used only occasionally (7–34 days), and 2% used infrequently (6 or fewer days).

The sociodemographic background of these female crack users was highly similar to that generally seen for female heroin users. Over half (56%) had not graduated from high school, over half (52%) had *never* held a legitimate job, and only 11% were employed even part of their last 90 days on the street. Most (60%) were receiving at least some financial support from people they were living with; most were living with either parents (45%), a husband/boyfriend (31%), or other people (13%) rather than alone (11%). Only 13% had their children living with them.

Many sociodemographic variables were significantly associated with crack-usage level, but—as indicated on Table 6.1—race was not. The

Table 6.1
Demographic Characteristics by Crack Usage Level for 197 Female
Crack Users

	Crack Usage Last 90 Days			Total Sample (N = 197)	Rho*
	Moderate (N = 49)	Typical (N = 90)	Heavy (N = 58)		
Ethnicity					
Black	57%	49%	57%	53%	
White	43%	51%	43%	47%	
Sample					
Street	61%	87%	28%	63%	.29
Treatment	39%	13%	72%	37%	
Age					
13–17	51%	17%	0%	20%	.40
18–24	10%	40%	22%	27%	
25–34	35%	36%	60%	43%	
35–49	4%	8%	17%	10%	
Mean Age	21.3	24.2	28.5	24.7	.42
High School Graduate	29%	44%	57%	44%	.21
Mean Years of Education	10.4	11.1	11.6	11.1	.27

*Rho is the Spearman Correlation Coefficient significant at p < .01 between crack usage and the other variables as reported, except that the full range of age and years of education data was used for the correlations reported on the lines that report mean age and mean years.

sample design called for equal numbers of black and white women, and the split for all 197 female crack users was roughly even, at 53% black, 47% white. Breakdowns within the three crack usage-levels were not significantly different from these overall percentages. However, heavier use was significantly correlated with older age. The Moderate users had a mean age of 21.3 years and over half of them (51%) were under age 18. The Typical users were a mean of 24.2 years old and 76% were in the 18–34 age range, as one would expect for a street sample of female heroin users. The Heavy users were clearly older, since they had a mean age of 28.5 years, none were under age 18, and only 22% were under age 25.

Crack usage-level was also related to sample type — treatment versus street. Heavy users were almost twice as likely as Moderate users — 72% versus 39% — to have been in treatment at the time of interview, but the great majority (87%) of the Typical users were not then — and had never been — in any kind of substance abuse treatment. However, while still significant, the relationship between treatment and crack usage-level was not as strong for *prior* treatment experience. About 48% of Heavy crack users who were interviewed in treatment — and 58% of Moderate crack users in treatment — had never been in treatment before. Thus, percentages of women with prior treatment experience in the Heavy, Moderate, and Typical categories were 38%, 16%, and 7% — indicating the same kind of difference seen in the street/treatment sample percentages, but not as extreme.

Further, it might be noted that low rates of treatment entry for the Typical users were not attributable to fewer problems with cocaine. Three out of four Typical users (77%) had been to a hospital emergency room because of an acute cocaine problem of some type — a much higher figure than the 40% of Heavy users or the 22% of Moderate users. The most common problem for all groups was an overdose — 68% of Typical users, 33% of Heavy users and 16% of Moderate users had at least one such cocaine-related emergency room visit. Comparison of these figures to figures related to total cocaine overdoses indicates that the great majority of these experiences resulted in an emergency room visit. Total reports also show that for both Heavy and Typical users, cocaine overdoses were at least as likely to be from snorting as from crack. About one in four Heavy and Typical users who ever overdosed on any cocaine actually reported that because of their last overdoses, they switched to crack as a "safer" drug.

If the greater percentage of Heavy users in treatment was related to more problems for them, it would appear to have been problems with social support.[29] They had the least stable living circumstances during their last 90 days on the street — 31% had two or more different living arrangements in this time compared to only 8% of both Moderate and Typical users. Possibly as a result, Heavy users were also most likely to get *no* financial support from other people — 34% compared to only 6% of both Moderate and Typical users.

Turning to the question of whether greater crack usage means more crime, Table 6.2 shows that most Typical and Heavy users (but only one in four Moderate users) lived with another cocaine user and many of those users were also dealers. Heavy users were twice as likely as Moderate users to live with someone selling cocaine — 33% compared to 16% — and Typical users were even more likely to do so, with almost half (46%) living with a dealer. However, this did not mean heavier users had all of their drug use needs supplied by dealer friends or husbands. Only 6–9% of the Typical and Heavy users reported *no* drug use expenses were met with criminal activities and two out of three reported that *almost all* of their drug use expenses were satisfied in this way. This was markedly more crime to support drug use than reported by women in the Moderate crack usage category. The primary drug expense, it might be noted, was cocaine — only 5% of these 197 women were using heroin or other street opiates, and only two women used them on more than 31 of their last 90 days on the street.

While crack usage-level was significantly correlated with crime for drug expenses, it was even more strongly related to crime for ordinary

Table 6.2
Selected Living Arrangements and Expenses Variables by Crack Usage
Level for 197 Female Crack Users

	Crack Usage Last 90 Days			Total Sample (N = 197)	Rho*
	Moderate (N = 49)	Typical (N = 90)	Heavy (N = 58)		
Last Week on the Street, Live with (% Yes):					
Cocaine User	24%	70%	59%	55%	.23
Cocaine Dealer	16%	46%	33%	35%	
Last 90 Days on the Street, How Much of Living Expenses from Crime					
None	96%	41%	40%	54%	.45
5–20%	2%	21%	5%	12%	
25–45%	0%	14%	7%	9%	
50–75%	2%	13%	12%	10%	
90%+	0%	10%	36%	15%	
Drug Expenses From Crime					
None	27%	6%	9%	12%	.33
5–20%	14%	3%	3%	6%	
25–45%	12%	11%	3%	9%	
50–75%	20%	16%	16%	17%	
90%+	27%	64%	69%	56%	

*Rho (reported if p < .01) is Spearman (Rank Order) Correlation Coefficient.

living expenses. Only two Moderate users (4%) earned *any* of their living expenses from crime — compared to 59–60% of Typical and Heavy users; further, 23% of Typical users and 48% of Heavy users earned half or more of their living expenses by engaging in crime.

Altogether, 20% of Moderate users reported committing no crime at all in their last 90 days on the street, although the 80% who committed crimes did a median of 544 offenses each (and a total 25,845 offenses) during those three months. Heavy crack users were considerably more crime-involved — the 93% who committed crimes had a median of 978 offenses each (and a total 114,441 offenses). The most crime-involved were women using at the Typical level, with the 98% who committed crimes doing a median of 2,723 offenses each (totalling 238,284 offenses). Thus, these female crack users demonstrate the same kind of high-volume criminal activity previously discussed as common among female heroin users.

The difference in totals by crack usage-level was apparently due to greater drug business involvement for the Typical users, since 60% of these women committed 1,950 or more such offenses in the last 90 days —twice as many women operating at this level as seen among the Heavy users (29%) and 15 times as many as for the Moderate users (4%). Responses about particular drugs sold indicated that most of the 197 female crack users (75%) specifically sold crack during their last 90 days on the street, although a few (13%) sold marijuana and most (76%) had sold marijuana at some previous time. These general reports of crack and marijuana sales were not related to crack usage-level, but history of selling *powder*-cocaine was. This activity was common in the past histories of Typical (70%) and Heavy (59%) crack users, but not for Moderate users (20%); in the last 90 days on the street, sales of *powder*-cocaine were unusual for all three groups, although more likely for Heavy crack users (12%) than Typical or Moderate users (3% and 4% respectively). The difference was probably because snorting *powder*-cocaine was more common among Heavy crack users (19%) than it was for Typical or Moderate users (9% and 10% respectively), as was injecting cocaine—7% of Heavy crack users versus none of the other women. Less than 2% of the sample sold any drug type other than cocaine or marijuana in their last 90 days on the street.

Looking at the range of particular crime types committed, the diversity seen among female heroin users also appears among these female crack users. Table 6.3 indicates that during their last 90 days on the street, 3 out of 4 women engaged in drug business offenses (76%) and the same proportion committed petty property crimes (77%)—in both instances, then, a greater participation rate than reported for prostitution (51%). Many fewer women committed any violence-related offenses or major property crimes, but this is also typical of female heroin users.[30] Even more importantly, participation in violence-related offenses and major property crimes—as well as in prostitutes' thefts from clients, con games, stealing drugs, and selling or trading stolen goods—is significantly correlated with crack usage-level: the heavier the crack use, the likelier it is that at least one such crime was committed. This did not hold, however, for participation in any of the drug business offense types or in petty property crime in general. By far the strongest association with crack usage-level appears for prostitution. Only 14% of Moderate crack users did any prostitution in their last 90 days on the street, compared to 58% of Typical users and 71% of Heavy users.

One way in which the criminal activity of these female crack users appears to be less diverse than that of the female heroin users previously discussed is that drug business offenses represent a considerably greater percentage of their total crimes—94% as opposed to 28% of the 1977–1978 heroin cohort's total offenses and 34% for those interviewed in

Table 6.3
Particular Crimes Done in the Last 90 Days on the Street (Subtotals and Specifics, % "Yes") by Crack Usage Level for 197 Female Crack Users

	Crack Usage Last 90 Days			Total Sample (N = 197)	Rho*
	Moderate (N = 49)	Typical (N = 90)	Heavy (N = 58)		
Violence-Related	4%	31%	31%	24%	.22
Robberies	0%	4%	9%	5%	
Assaults	0%	7%	7%	5%	
Weapon Show/Use	4%	23%	21%	18%	
Major Property Crimes	2%	3%	14%	6%	.19
Burglaries	2%	3%	10%	5%	
Motor Vehicle Thefts	0%	0%	5%	2%	
Petty Property Crimes	63%	86%	74%	77%	
Thefts from Vehicle	12%	32%	16%	22%	
Shoplifting	43%	72%	36%	54%	
Prostitute's Thefts	2%	30%	26%	22%	.20
Con Games	0%	10%	21%	11%	.25
Pickpocketing	0%	1%	27%	1%	
"Bad Paper" Crimes	16%	52%	38%	39%	
Other Sneak Thefts	12%	6%	12%	9%	
Drug Thefts	2%	4%	16%	7%	.20
Stolen Goods Offenses	12%	24%	33%	24%	.18
Drug Business	67%	88%	66%	76%	
Sales in Weight	2%	1%	9%	4%	
Manufacture/Smuggling	2%	0%	9%	3%	
Sales To Users	67%	88%	60%	75%	
Vice	16%	58%	71%	51%	.39
Prostitution	14%	54%	69%	49%	.39
Procuring	10%	50%	29%	34%	
Any Crime	80%	98%	93%	92%	.17

*Rho = Spearman Correlation Coefficient significant at p < .01 between crack usage and Yes = 1, No = 0.

1983–1984. Figures for prostitution and petty property crimes were correspondingly lower. The specifics are as follows:

	H/77–78	H/83–84	Crack
Drug business	28%	34%	94%
Prostitution	38%	54%	3%
Petty property crime	28%	9%	2%

At least part of the explanation for this heroin/crack difference may be provided by two factors discussed in the analysis of differences between the two heroin cohorts. One is that the climate of attitudes toward, and handling of, drug-involved property crime offenders in Miami has gotten increasingly chilly — and street addicts know it. Thus, addicts have turned away from such crimes toward offenses that are less likely to involve the conventional citizenry and hence less likely to result in arrest —namely, prostitution and drug sales. This apparent difference between 1977–78 and 1983–84 appears to have continued into the crack era, which is hardly surprising given the amount of media attention given to, and general public outrage about, the dangers of crack use and crack users.

Second, many female heroin users told us that they considered drug sales highly preferable to prostitution as a money-making activity, but in times of drug shortages they were unable to entertain this preference and instead turned to prostitution. Once engaged in regular prostitution, they discovered that it provided not only a more consistent income but a higher one as well. At least part of the dramatically larger drug-business involvement of the crack users, compared to the heroin users, is thus likely to be explained by the dramatically greater availability of crack compared to heroin. That is, more female crack users sell crack because, simply, they can obtain it to sell. Another part of the explanation may be that the advent of freely available crack has made prostitution a less attractive income source because more of a prostitute's customers are likely to be high on cocaine, making this way of life more dangerous. Some support for this hypothesis is provided by research done by Paul J. Goldstein and his associates. These studies indicate that women who use crack more frequently are more likely to be engaged in prostitution, that prostitutes are at a high risk of being the victims of violent sex crimes, and that men who use higher volumes of crack are likelier to be the perpetrators of violence.[31]

While drug-business offenses represented 94% of all crimes for the 197 female crack users, the percentage was somewhat lower for Heavy users — 88% compared to 97–98% for Moderate and Typical users. The difference was made up in vice offenses — prostitution and procuring — which comprised 8% of all crimes for Heavy users, 2% for Typical users, and 1% for Moderate users. These percentages imply small numbers of

Table 6.4
Crimes and Arrests in the Last 90 Days on the Street by
Crack Usage Level for 197 Female Crack Users

	Crack Usage Last 90 Days			Total Sample (N = 197)
	Moderate (N = 49)	Typical (N = 90)	Heavy (N = 58)	
Number Done				
Violence-Related	5	159	173	337
Major Property Crime	3	15	204	222
Petty Property Crime	295	2,588	4,574	7,457
Prostitution/Procure	325	4,864	9,066	14,255
Drug Business	25,217	230,658	100,424	356,299
Grand Total	25,845	238,284	114,441	378,570
Percent of Total Done				
Violence-Related	<0.1%	0.1%	0.2%	<0.1%
Major Property Crime	<0.1%	<0.1%	0.2%	<0.1%
Petty Property Crime	1.1%	1.1%	4.0%	2.0%
Prostitution/Procure	1.3%	2.0%	7.9%	3.8%
Drug Business	97.6%	96.8%	87.8%	94.1%
Percent Arrested For				
Violence-Related	0%	0%	2%	0.5%
Major Property Crime	0%	0%	3%	1.0%
Petty Property Crime	0%	2%	5%	2.5%
Prostitution/Procure	0%	0%	2%	0.5%
Drug Business	0%	0%	2%	0.5%
Any Offense	0%	2%	10%	4.1%
Number of Offenses				
Resulting in Arrest				
Violence-Related	0	0	10	10
Major Property Crime	0	0	5	5
Petty Property Crime	0	2	8	10
Prostitution/Procure	0	0	3	3
Drug Business	0	0	1	1
Total Crimes –> Arrest	0	2	27	29
Percent of Offenses				
Resulting in Arrest				
Any/All Crime	0.00%	<0.01%	0.02%	0.01%

even vice offenses, let alone crimes against persons and property, but this is misleading because the numbers of drug-business offenses were astronomical. As Table 6.4 shows, these 197 women committed 14,255 prostitution and procuring offenses and 7,679 property crimes in just 90 days. Per offender, this includes medians of 9, 32, and 90 prostitution offenses for women in the Moderate, Typical, and Heavy crack usage categories respectively, as well as 7, 17, and 36 petty property crimes and 3, 3, and 13 major property crimes. As the progressions in these medians imply, greater crack usage was associated not only with a greater likelihood of participation in these crime types (as shown on Table 6.3), but also with a greater number of crimes per offender.*

Finally, Table 6.4 also shows that the probability of a female crack user being arrested for criminal activity is extremely slight. Drug business activities were particularly likely to operate without police interference, since the 356,299 drug-business offenses resulted in 1 arrest. Heavier crack use appears to mean greater likelihood of arrest, but even the Heavy crack users had an extremely low probability of arrest, with only 1 out of every 4,239 of their offenses leading to arrest. The great majority of all 197 female crack users (86%) had been arrested at some time, but the charges leading to arrest were most likely to be drug-*possession* offenses (69% were arrested on such charges) rather than drug-*business* offenses (13%). The Typical users, for whom large-scale drug business was an especially likely offense, were the *most* likely to have been arrested for drug-business offenses (18%), but they were considerably *more* likely to have been arrested for larceny/theft (62%) or prostitution (57%). As these figures suggest, Typical users almost always had an arrest record — 96% did, compared to 78–79% of Moderate and Heavy users.

Altogether, the female crack users interviewed for this study had both the sociodemographic backgrounds and current crime involvement generally found among female heroin users. Further, like female heroin users, the criminal patterns of these women show a wide variety of offense types, a large number of total crimes committed, an extremely low probability of any given crime leading to arrest, and a clear relationship between the degree of their criminal involvement and the usage level for their drug of choice.

---

*Specifically, Spearman Correlation Coefficients between the three-category crack usage variable and the full range of crime data (0 through maximum) for each crime type are: .21 for violence-related offenses, .19 for major property crimes, .29 for petty property crimes, and .44 for prostitution and procuring. All are significant at the .01 level, which did not hold for the correlation with total number of drug business offenses.

Adolescent Females and the Crack Business

> When I started selling crack, I started using more of it, or maybe,
> maybe it was the other way around.
>
> —*A Miami adolescent, 1988*

Further details about the criminal involvement of female crack users are provided in a study of serious delinquents in Miami. Beginning in December 1985, some 611 seriously crime-involved teenagers were interviewed on the street about their drug use and criminal activities. Preliminary analysis of the first 200 interviews indicated an unexpectedly high degree of crack usage among these youths. Consequently, a set of supplementary questions about crack was put together and used during the final 254 interviews, from October 1986 through November 1987. Of this crack-supplement subsample, 38 respondents (15%) were females age 14–17, about the same percentage as had been targeted for the total 611 interviews for the larger study.[32]

The final crack supplement question was "Do you deal in crack or help a crack dealer or anything like that?" Answers fell into four general categories: (1) no crack-business involvement (17% of males, 34% of females); (2) only minor involvement — selling only to friends or working for dealers only as lookouts or people to steer customers to crack houses (9% of males, 3% of females); (3) dealers — direct involvement in the retail sale of crack (54% of males, 58% of females); and (4) "dealer+" — crack dealers who also manufactured, smuggled, or wholesaled the drug (20% of males, 5% of females).[33] As these percentages indicate, male participation in the crack trade was clearly greater than that for females, but still, two out of three females were involved in the crack business to some extent.

In order to look more closely at female crack business participation, the four crack business categories were reduced to a "Crack Dealer?" dichotomy: *No* versus *Yes*. The one girl with "only minor involvement" was omitted from the analysis, and all female crack dealers — including the two in the "dealer+" group — were assigned to the same category. Thus, of the 37 respondents included in the analysis, 65% were crack dealers and 35% were not. About half (54%) of the total 37 girls were age 14–15 and the remainder (46%) were age 16–17; age was not related to being a crack dealer. Nor was race significantly related — 65% of the total 37 girls were black and 35% were white.† Most of these respondents (70%) were living with families rather than with friends or alone; living arrangements were not related to crack dealing, either.

---

†Hispanic females were not interviewed in this study.

Initiation into drug and crime involvement, however, was very strongly related to crack dealing. It should be kept in mind that all respondents for this study were seriously involved in drug use and crime. All 37 girls were using marijuana regularly (three or more days a week); 97% had used alcohol to the point of intoxication; 92% were current users of some form of cocaine; and 100% were committing some type of crime regularly. Nonetheless, as shown in Table 6.5, crack dealing was associated with more and earlier use of a wide variety of drugs, and more and earlier involvement in a diversity of crimes — specifically including regular use of prescription depressants, heroin, *powder*-cocaine, and *crack*-cocaine as well as involvement in theft, prostitution, and robbery. The crack dealers, at a mean age of 15.6, were thus girls who had been using some kind of illicit drug *regularly*, since a mean age of 9.7 (compared to 13.4 for the other girls) and had been doing some kind of crime *regularly*, since a mean age of 10.2 (compared to 12.7 for the other girls). Not surprisingly, most (83%) of these young female crack dealers had been incarcerated (compared to 8% of the other girls); more of a surprise was the finding that absolutely none (0%) of these 37 girls had ever been in treatment for substance abuse.

Crack dealing was not significantly related to *current use* of alcohol (92% using, 43% using regularly), marijuana (92% using every single day, 100% using regularly), hallucinogens or inhalants (8% using occasionally), or speed (5% using occasionally). But crack dealing was related to greater prescription drug use (89% of dealers using and 33% using regularly, compared to 54% and 8% for nondealers), more heroin use (54% of dealers using at least occasionally, compared to 8% of nondealers), and much greater use of crack (96% of crack dealers using crack on every one of the last 90 days, compared to *no* crack use for 62% of the nondealers and only 8% using daily). Nondealers used slightly more *powder*-cocaine than crack dealers did, so that when all forms of cocaine were considered together, 69% of even nondealers were using some form of cocaine regularly. However, 100% of crack dealers were *daily* users of some form of cocaine, compared to 38% of nondealers.

The dealers' greater use of cocaine, particularly *crack*-cocaine, suggests that their dealing permitted them to use more. This is confirmed in the series of supplemental crack questions concerning how respondents acquired the crack they had used in the last 12 months, with answer categories of Never, 1–5 Times, and 6+ Times. Virtually all the dealers (96%) reported 6+ occasions of receiving crack as payment for drug sales, compared to none of the five nondealer crack users. However, crack sales did not supply all of their crack use needs. Most dealers also traded stolen goods for crack on 6+ occasions (79%, compared to none of the nondealer crack users); almost all got crack at least a few times by theft or robbery from a dealer (96%, compared to none of the nondealer users), and most

Table 6.5
Drug and Crime History by Crack Dealing Involvement
for 37 Seriously Delinquent Females

	Crack Dealer?		Total Sample (N = 37)	Rho*
	No (N = 13)	Yes (N = 24)		
Percentage Ever				
Regular Alcohol	69%	92%	84%	+.29
Any Rx Depressant	69%	100%	89%	+.47
Regular Rx Depressant	23%	92%	68%	+.70
Any Heroin	15%	75%	54%	+.57
Regular Heroin	8%	50%	35%	+.42
Any Powder Cocaine	85%	100%	95%	+.32
Regular Powder Cocaine	77%	100%	92%	+.40
Any Crack	62%	100%	86%	+.54
Regular Crack	38%	100%	78%	+.71
Any Marijuana Sale	77%	100%	92%	+.40
Any Other Drug Sale	38%	100%	78%	+.71
Regular Drug Sales	69%	100%	89%	+.47
Any Theft	77%	100%	92%	+.32
Regular Thefts	77%	100%	92%	+.40
Any Prostitution	69%	100%	89%	+.47
Regular Prostitution	46%	100%	81%	+.66
Any Robbery	15%	79%	57%	+.61
Tenth Robbery	0%	50%	32%	+.51
Age First Time (Means)				
Any Alcohol	11.8	5.5	7.7	−.77
Regular Alcohol	14.0	8.3	10.0	−.70
Any Marijuana	12.5	8.8	10.1	−.76
Regular Marijuana	13.4	9.7	11.0	−.79
Any Rx Depressant	14.0	12.3	12.8	−.53
Any Heroin	13.5	11.2	11.4	−.45
Any Powder Cocaine	13.7	10.9	11.8	−.75
Regular Powder Cocaine	13.9	12.0	12.5	−.62
Any Crack	14.0	12.9	13.2	−.32
Any Marijuana Sale	13.6	9.5	10.7	−.73
Any Other Drug Sale	14.2	10.8	11.4	−.59
Regular Drug Sales	14.1	10.9	11.8	−.72
Any Theft	10.8	9.9	10.1	−.30
Regular Thefts	12.8	10.9	11.4	−.56
Any Prostitution	13.2	10.3	11.1	−.57
Regular Prostitution	13.0	11.2	11.5	−.39
Any Robbery	15.0	11.6	11.9	−.49

*"Regular" means three or more times per week. Rho is the Spearman (Rank Order) Correlation Coefficient significant at p < .05 between Dealer (No = 0, Yes = 1) and Ever (No = 0, Yes = 1) or specific age first.

received crack as payment for sex on 6+ occasions (67%, compared to none of the other users).

Further, even though 46% of these adolescent female crack dealers had committed 500 or more drug business offenses in the prior 12 months (and 83% had done at least 250), this type of crime accounted for only 31% of their total criminal activities. This figure was actually slightly smaller than the 36% of crimes attributable to the drug business for the girls who were *not* crack dealers. In fact, the percentage distribution of offenses was quite similar on all counts. About half of all crimes were prostitution and procuring offenses for both the dealers (49%) and the nondealers (50%); petty property crimes were less numerous, at 19% for dealers and 13% for others, and major felonies — robbery, assault, burglary, and motor vehicle theft — made up 1% or less of all crimes for each group. The difference, rather, was in how many girls were committing each offense type and how many crimes per offender were typical.

Just as the crack dealers committed large numbers of drug-business offenses, they also committed large numbers of vice offenses and petty property crimes. As shown in Table 6.6, two out of three dealers committed 350+ prostitution and procuring offenses in the prior 12 months, compared to 8% of nondealers; further, every dealer committed at least 100 vice offenses, compared to 46% of nondealers. Similarly, 50% of the crack dealers committed 300 or more petty property crimes — a level achieved by none of the nondealers — and 96% of dealers reported committing at least 150 such offenses, compared to 8% of nondealers. Even the most serious crime category, major felonies, saw more involvement by crack dealers — 92% committed at least one such crime, compared to 38% of nondealers; and 42% of dealers committed more than 12 such offenses, compared to 8% of nondealers. The total crime summaries on Table 6.6 indicate that although the 13 girls who did not deal crack were sufficiently crime-involved to be eligible for a sample of serious delinquents, most (62%) qualified only at the lowest level of such involvement. None of the crack dealers qualified *only* at the minimum level of serious delinquency. Further, none of the nondealers were classified in the highest total-crime category, while 83% of the crack dealers were. This indicates an extremely high correlation between *any* crack dealing and *total* crime.

Altogether, then, these adolescent female crack dealers demonstrate a degree and diversity of criminal involvement that is highly similar to that of (adult) female heroin users. They also had a similarly low level of offenses resulting in arrest. Of their total 40,392 offenses in the prior 12 months, only 40 resulted in arrest — 0.1%, or one arrest per every 1,010 crimes. This is twice as high an arrest probability as that for the 13 nondealers — 3 of 6,188 crimes leading to arrest, which is 0.05%, or one arrest per every 2,063 crimes. However, the 24 dealers committed not merely twice as many total crimes but rather 3.5 times as many crimes per offender (means of 1,683 versus 476).

Table 6.6
Crime During the Last 12 Months by Crack Dealing Involvement for 37 Seriously Delinquent Females

	Crack Dealer		Total Sample ($N = 37$)	Rho*
	No ($N = 13$)	Yes ($N = 24$)		
Major Felony Score				
(0) None	62%	8%	27%	+.54
(1) 1–12	31%	50%	43%	
(2) 13–24	0%	17%	11%	
(4) 25–47	8%	8%	8%	
(8) 50+	0%	17%	11%	
Petty Property Crime				
(0) 0–12	15%	0%	5%	+.79
(1) 13–74	54%	4%	22%	
(2) 75–145	23%	0%	8%	
(4) 150–298	8%	46%	32%	
(8) 300+	0%	50%	32%	
Prostitution/Procuring Score				
(0) None	31%	0%	11%	+.69
(1) 1–72	23%	0%	8%	
(2) 100–160	8%	4%	5%	
(4) 175–320	31%	29%	30%	
(8) 350+	8%	67%	46%	
Drug Business Score				
(0) 0–20	38%	0%	14%	+.57
(1) 25–120	8%	4%	5%	
(2) 125–225	23%	13%	16%	
(4) 250–475	23%	38%	32%	
(8) 500+	8%	46%	32%	
Total Crime Level				
Lowest (1–5)	62%	0%	22%	+.86
Typical (6–15)	38%	17%	24%	
Highest (16+)	0%	83%	54%	
Mean Total Crime Score	6	20	15	+.80

*Rho is the Spearman (Rank-Order) Correlation Coefficient significant at $p < .001$ between Dealer (No = 0, Yes = 1) and each score as listed. Numbers in parentheses are the points assigned for each crime level. Total Crime Score is the sum of the points for the four specific crime types; its actual range (for both the total 611 respondents and the 100 female respondents in the larger study) is 1–32.

Taken together, Tables 6.5 and 6.6 suggest a complex of interconnections between crack and crime in a female adolescent subsample. *First, the girls with the earliest involvement in crime, as well as in use of drugs other than crack, were the most likely to become crack dealers.* It should be recalled in this context that, as shown on Table 6.5, crack was the *last* drug type used by these respondents. As an accident of when crack happened to become widely available, the girls now dealing crack didn't even try crack until they were at a mean age of about 13 — two years older than their mean age for starting regular drug sales, regular theft, and regular prostitution. This means, in other words, that crack use did not lure them into lives of crime — they were already there when crack became widely available. Instead, their prior crime and drug involvement apparently put them in a position to become crack dealers.

Second, crack dealing is not necessarily some kind of profitable specialization for juvenile offenders. Even though they averaged over 500 drug sales each in the prior 12 months, during the same time period they *also* committed significant numbers of prostitution and petty property offenses, most (92%) had committed a major felony, and they used a number of different approaches to getting crack for their personal use — including sex-for-crack exchanges, trading stolen goods, and stealing from other dealers.

Third, dealing crack, in particular, is associated with more significant drug and crime involvement than is just any kind of drug business offense. As Table 6.5 shows, most girls who did *not* deal crack nonetheless had some experience with drug-business offenses — 77% had sold marijuana, 38% had sold some other drug, and 69% had engaged in *regular* drug-business offenses. Further, as indicated on Table 6.6, 54% of them committed at least 125 drug-business offenses in the last 12 months. Yet although these 13 offenders were seriously delinquent — with, as noted, a mean of 476 criminal offenses in the prior 12 months — they were not nearly so enmeshed in dealing, thefts, prostitution, and even major felonies as were their crack-dealing peers. Similarly, although 85% of the girls not dealing crack had at least experimented with cocaine use and 69% were using cocaine regularly, the crack dealers were using not only much more cocaine but also significantly more prescription depressants and heroin.

Fourth, crack dealing itself may very well be the reason that crack dealing is associated with greater drug and crime involvement. The primary logic chain is that crack dealing increases opportunities for crack acquisition and thus more crack use, more crack use encourages solidification of an addictive crack use pattern which in turn leads to the need for more money to support crack use, and this need for money leads to more involvement in all kinds of crime — not only more drug sales but also petty property crimes, prostitution, and major felonies. In addition to this classic drugs/crime interactive cycle, crack dealing may also encourage greater criminality because it constitutes one more set of reasons for being attracted to a drugs/crime lifestyle. Street addict subcultures used to be essentially closed to adolescents except for the few teenage drug dealers whose supplier was an adult rather than a slightly older teenager. With the advent of plentiful crack, and substantial rates of crack use among inner-city youth populations, adult crack suppliers very commonly use teenagers as street-level dealers. Thus, crack dealing is the most rapid means available for an adolescent to be integrated into the world of adult street addicts.

Postscript

> Drugs drive crime!
>
> *—David N. Nurco, 1985*[34]

Researchers have suggested that *narcotics users* may be responsible for as many as 50 million crimes each year in the United States, and that an even greater level of criminality may be attributable to *cocaine and other drug users*.[35] Although the universe of drug-related crime has yet to be fully measured, recent research on narcotics users has drawn a number of reliable conclusions: 1) that narcotics users are involved in crime with a greater frequency, intensity, diversity, and severity than any other law-breaking group; 2) that heroin users represent a large cohort of habitual offenders who engage in repeated crimes against both property and persons when actively using drugs; and, 3) that narcotics and cocaine tend to freeze street-drug users into criminal careers that are more profound and extreme and that endure for longer periods of time than they might otherwise have.

The data from this study suggest a number of the same conclusions with respect to *crack*-cocaine. Among the adolescent crack users studied, for example, it would appear that the crack business tends to be highly criminogenic, leading many serious delinquents to be even more seriously involved in crime. That is, the more these youths were associated with the crack business, the more crack they used and the more crimes they committed. What was occurring was the classical cyclical pattern of crime financing use, use encouraging more use, and more use encouraging more crime.

It would also appear that among the women crack users studied, *crack drives crime!* Those most heavily using crack committed more crimes not only to support their drug use, but their general living costs as well. Moreover, and perhaps most importantly, participation in major property offenses, violent crimes, petty thefts, confidence games, and dealing in stolen goods was strongly correlated to intensity of crack use. And this, too, involved cyclical patterns of crime/drugs/more drugs/more crime, as is clearly reflected in the recollections of Suzanne M., a 32-year-old Miami crack user contacted in a residential drug treatment program in early 1992:

> I used to work at a downtown hotel travel agency, you know, because I could look good for the clients and speak well on the phone and all that. Little did the people at the agency know what I was really like on my own time. At night I'd do some tricking on the street not too far from the hotel. Of course I'd look very different. I'd do my hair up, and my clothes and make-up would be different, and I walked and talked different. And you know, one time I even went to the window of the agency on a dare, just to see if anything happened. A few people looked up, and you could read their expressions, "lady of the night" on their faces, but they didn't know who it was . . . .
>
> Yeah I *was* using dope, but I was tricking dates because I wanted other things, not because I was bad off with cocaine. I had a little but nice apartment in Coconut Grove, and I had a nice car, and I sold a little drugs, had a few dates, emptied a few pockets, just to keep it all going. But I guess it started to be different starting around when I was 27 or 28. What was that? 1988, I guess.
>
> I got into a lot of freebase and crack, and that really fucked me up. First I started to use coke kind of heavy. I managed to keep up with it by staying out on the streets later, doing more dates. I was working out and keeping in shape, so I was getting good money — $100 to $150 on a weekday night, sometimes $1,000 on a weekend. I looked really good. The freebase really cost, though. You go through it fast. It got to the point that I would be basing and tricking and stealing from johns all night. I was coming in to work late because I was out all night and still pretty fucked up from coke in the morning. And I'd get into fights with the people at work, and I'd get pissed because the job began to interfere with my cocaine use. Can you imagine that? I'd get pissed at the boss because I couldn't freebase on the job. So one day I just didn't show up for work.
>
> Then I got busted. I was a little high, and I guess I was careless, because this john turns out to be a fucking vice cop. This was the first time I ever got popped [arrested]. I was so scared. I knew I was bound to be picked up sooner or later, but did it have to be a time when I was carrying a half a gram of cocaine? I made so many deals with God about how I'd change and do better if I could just walk away this one time. He must have known that I was a fucking liar, because I ended up doing 60 days.
>
> I ended up losing my apartment, I sold my car to try to get myself set up again, and that's when I started doing crack instead of cocaine and base. I ended up selling most everything I had, I had no job, and just a shithole of a place to live in. I started to steal — I was stealing from the johns, I was stealing from the shopping malls, from the supermarket, I was breaking into cars, I was carrying crack for this guy I knew, I was doing cons [confidence games] on tourists, I was picking pockets and stealing luggage at the airport. Everything.

When I finally ended up as a skeezer, giving head for a nickel rock or freaking for a dime rock, you'd think I'd do something about it. No. What finally did it was when I tried to get this guy's wallet. We were in this room on 55th Street. He caught me, and we got into a fight. He started to beat me, and I pulled a knife, but he got it from me. He hit me so hard then that he broke my jaw and practically knocked me out. Then he takes this bottle off the floor and breaks the top off it. I still had no clothes on, and he breaks off the end and rams it into my vagina. He starts cursing me — "filthy whore" — and he's twisting it around, tearing me up. . . .

I was screaming. Nothing ever hurt so much, but I must have fainted. I woke up at Jackson [Jackson Memorial Hospital]. I had lost a lot of blood, and they had to sew me up, and they kept me there a while. I couldn't walk, or even piss for a long time. It was after that that I came into [drug] treatment.

Endnotes

1. Eric D. Wish and Bruce D. Johnson, "The Impact of Substance Abuse on Criminal Careers," in Alfred Blumstein, Jacqueline Cohen, Jeffrey A. Roth, and Christy A. Visher, eds., *Criminal Careers and "Career Criminals,"* Vol II (Washington, D.C.: National Academy Press, 1986), pp. 52–88.

2. Edward Crapsey, *The Nether Side of New York; or, The Vice, Crime and Poverty of the Great Metropolis* (New York: Sheldon & Co., 1872).

3. David T. Courtwright, *Dark Paradise: Opiate Addiction in America Before 1940* (Cambridge, MA: Harvard University Press, 1982); Walter R. Cuskey, T. Premkumar, and Lois Sigel, "Survey of Opiate Addiction Among Females in the United States Between 1850 and 1970," reprinted from *Public Health Reviews,* 1972 (pp. 8–13, 16–39) in Freda Adler and Rita J. Simon, eds., *The Criminology of Deviant Women,* (Boston: Houghton Mifflin, 1979), pp. 223–247; David F. Musto, *The American Disease: Origins of Narcotic Control* (New Haven: Yale University Press, 1973).

4. See Courtwright; Musto, *The American Disease;* Rufus King, *The Drug Hang-Up: America's Fifty-Year Folly* (New York: W. W. Norton, 1972).

5. See Musto, *The American Disease,* pp. 92–94, 121–150.

6. David F. Musto, "Early History of Heroin in the United States," in Peter G. Bourne, ed., *Addiction* (New York: Academic Press, 1974), pp. 175–185.

7. John C. Ball, "Two Patterns of Narcotic Drug Addiction in the United States," *Journal of Criminal Law, Criminology, and Police Science* 56 (1965), pp. 203–211.

8. John C. Ball, Betsy K. Levine, Robert G. Demaree, and Janice F. Neman, "Pretreatment Criminality of Male and Female Drug Abuse Patients in the United States," *Addictive Diseases* 1 (1975), pp. 481–489.

9. Carl D. Chambers, R. Kent Hinesley, and Mary Moldestad, "Narcotic Addiction in Females: A Race Comparison," *International Journal of the Addictions* 5 (1970), pp. 257–278.

10. Susan K. Datesman, "Women, Crime, and Drugs," in James A. Inciardi, ed., *The Drugs-Crime Connection* (Beverly Hills, CA: Sage, 1981), pp. 85–104; Thomas J. Glynn, Helen Wallenstein Pearson, and Mollie Sayers, eds., *Women and Drugs* (Rockville, MD: National Institute on Drug Abuse, 1983); Ira J. Silverman, "Women, Crime and Drugs," *Journal of Drug Issues* 12 (1982), pp. 167–183.

11. Frances M. Heidensohn, *Women and Crime* (New York: New York University Press, 1985), pp. 110–162; Dorie Klein, "The Etiology of Female Crime: A Review of the

Literature," *Issues in Criminology* 8 (1973), pp. 3–30; Coramae Richey Mann, *Female Crime and Delinquency* (University, AL: University of Alabama Press, 1984), pp. 55–112; Marcia Millman, "She Did It All for Love: A Feminist View of the Sociology of Deviance," in Marcia Millman and Rosabeth Moss Kanter, eds., *Another Voice: Feminist Perspectives on Social Life and Social Science* (Garden City, NY: Anchor Books, 1975), pp. 251–279; Christine E. Rasche, "The Female Offender as an Object of Criminological Research," *Criminal Justice and Behavior* 1 (1974), pp. 301–320; Carol Smart, *Women, Crime and Criminology: A Feminist Critique* (London: Routledge & Kegan Paul, 1976).

12. Susan K. Datesman, "Women, Crime, and Drugs," p. 99.

13. See Richard R. Clayton, "The Delinquency and Drug Use Relationship Among Adolescents: A Critical Review," in Dan J. Lettieri and Jaqueline P. Ludford, eds., *Drug Abuse and the American Adolescent* (Rockville, MD: National Institute on Drug Abuse, 1981), pp. 82–103; Delbert S. Elliott, David Huizinga, and Suzanne S. Ageton, *Explaining Delinquency and Drug Use* (Beverly Hills, CA: Sage, 1985); Delbert S. Elliott, Delbert S., David Huizinga, and Scott Menard, *Multiple Problem Youth: Delinquency, Substance Use, and Mental Health Problems* (New York: Springer-Verlag, 1989); Jeffry Fagan, Joseph G. Weis, and Yu-Teh Cheng, "Delinquency and Substance Use Among Inner-City Students," *Journal of Drug Issues* 20 (1990), pp. 351–402; James A. Inciardi, Ruth Horowitz, and Anne E. Pottieger, *Street Kids, Street Drugs, Street Crime* (Belmont, CA: Wadsworth, 1993); John K. Watters, Craig Reinarman, and Jeffrey Fagan, "Causality, Context, and Contingency: Relationships between Drug Abuse and Delinquency," *Contemporary Drug Problems* 12 (1985), pp. 351–373; Helene Raskin White, "The Drug Use–Delinquency Connection in Adolescence," in Ralph Weisheit, ed., *Drugs, Crime and the Criminal Justice System* (Cincinnati: Anderson, 1990), pp. 215–256.

14. See Paul J. Goldstein, "The Drugs/Violence Nexus: A Tripartite Conceptual Framework," *Journal of Drug Issues* 15 (1985), pp. 493–506; James A. Inciardi and Brian R. Russe, "Professional Thieves and Drugs," *International Journal of the Addictions* 12 (1977), pp. 1087–1095; Jennifer James, "Prostitution and Addiction: An Interdisciplinary Approach," *Addictive Diseases* 2 (1976), pp. 601–618.

15. Goldstein, "The Drugs/Violence Nexus"; also see Duane C. McBride, "Drugs and Violence," in James A. Inciardi, ed., *The Drugs-Crime Connection* (Beverly Hills, CA: Sage, 1981), pp. 105–123; Duane C. McBride and James A. Swartz, "Drugs and Violence in the Age of Crack Cocaine," in Ralph Weisheit, ed., *Drugs, Crime and the Criminal Justice System* (Cincinnati: Anderson, 1990), pp. 141–169.

16. See, e.g., Paul Eddy, Hugo Sabogal, and Sara Walden, *The Cocaine Wars* (New York: W. W. Norton, 1988).

17. See, e.g., Malin Akerstrom, *Crooks and Squares* (New Brunswick, NJ: Transaction Books, 1985); Marsha Rosenbaum, *Women on Heroin* (New Brunswick, NJ: Rutgers University Press, 1981); Richard C. Stephens, *The Street Addict Role: A Theory of Heroin Addiction* (Albany: State University of New York Press, 1991).

18. Norman E. Zinberg, *Drug, Set, and Setting: The Basis for Controlled Intoxicant Use* (New Haven, CT: Yale University Press, 1984); see also Dan Waldorf, Craig Reinarman, and Sheigla Murphy, *Cocaine Changes: The Experience of Using and Quitting* (Philadelphia: Temple University Press, 1991).

19. See Rosenbaum; Stephens.

20. See, e.g., Eric D. Wish and Joyce O'Neill, "Cocaine Use in Arrestees: Refining Measures of National Trends by Sampling the Criminal Population," in Susan Schober and Charles Schade, eds., *The Epidemiology of Cocaine Use and Abuse* (Rockville, MD: National Institute on Drug Abuse, 1991), pp. 57–70.

21. The seven drug types counted were alcohol, marijuana, cocaine, heroin, prescription depressants, speed, and hallucinogens or inhalants. See Inciardi, Horowitz, and Pottieger, pp. 78–81.

22. James A. Inciardi and Anne E. Pottieger, "Drug Use and Crime Among Two Cohorts of Women Narcotics Users: An Empirical Assessment," *Journal of Drug Issues* 16 (1986), pp. 91–106.

23. See, e.g., Rosenbaum, Silverman, James A. Inciardi, and Carl D. Chambers, "Unreported Criminal Involvement of Narcotic Addicts," *Journal of Drug Issues* 2 (1972), pp. 57–64; Jennifer James, "Prostitution and Addiction: An Interdisciplinary Approach," *Addictive Diseases* 2 (1976), pp. 601–618.

24. See, e.g., Waldorf, Reinarman, and Murphy; Jan M. Chaiken and Marcia R. Chaiken, "Drugs and Predatory Crime," in Michael Tonry and James Q. Wilson, eds., *Drugs and Crime*, pp. 203–239; James V. Spotts and Franklin C. Shontz, *The Lifestyles of Nine American Cocaine Users* (Rockville, MD: National Institute on Drug Abuse, 1976).

25. Dana Hunt, "Stealing and Dealing: Cocaine and Property Crimes," in Susan Schober and Charles Schade, eds., *The Epidemiology of Cocaine Use and Abuse* (Rockville, MD: National Institute on Drug Abuse, 1991), pp. 139–150.

26. See, e.g., Hunt; James J. Collins, Robert L. Hubbard, and J. Valley Rachal, "Expensive Drug Use and Illegal Income: A Test of Explanatory Hypotheses," *Criminology* 23 (1985), pp. 743–764.

27. See, e.g., Inciardi, Horowitz, and Pottieger, pp. 56–60; Paul J. Goldstein, Patricia A. Belluci, Barry J. Spunt, and Thomas Miller, "Frequency of Cocaine Use and Violence: A Comparison Between Men and Women," in Susan Schober and Charles Schade, eds., *The Epidemiology of Cocaine Use and Abuse* (Rockville, MD: National Institute on Drug Abuse, 1991), pp. 113–138.

28. "Crack Abuse Patterns and Crime Linkages," funded by the National Institute on Drug Abuse (Grant Number R01 DAO 4862); James A. Inciardi, Principal Investigator; Anne E. Pottieger, Co-Principal Investigator and Project Director.

29. This supposition implies that most treatment entries were voluntary—which is in fact what we found. Of the 73 women interviewed in treatment programs, 68% entered the program voluntarily. This held for 64% of the 42 Heavy crack users in treatment, as well as 63% of the 19 Moderate users and 92% of the 12 Typical users.

30. See Inciardi and Chambers; Inciardi and Pottieger.

31. Goldstein, Belluci, Spunt, and Miller, "Frequency of Cocaine Use and Violence"; Paul J. Goldstein, Patricia A. Belluci, Barry J. Spunt, and Thomas Miller, "Volume of Cocaine Use and Violence: A Comparison Between Men and Women," *Journal of Drug Issues* 21 (1991), pp. 345–367.

32. This study is described in detail in Inciardi, Horowitz, and Pottieger.

33. For analysis of the crack-business involvement of the total 254 youths in the supplementary crack subsample, see James A. Inciardi and Anne E. Pottieger, "Kids, Crack, and Crime," *Journal of Drug Issues* 21 (1991), pp. 257–270.

34. David N. Nurco, John C. Ball, John W. Schaffer, and Thomas E. Hanlon, "The Criminality of Narcotic Addicts," *Journal of Nervous and Mental Disease* 173 (1985), p. 98.

35. John C. Ball, Lawrence Rosen, John A. Flueck, and David N. Nurco, "The Lifetime Criminality of Heroin Addicts in the United States, *Journal of Drug Issues* 12 (1982), pp. 225–239; James A. Inciardi, *The War on Drugs: Heroin, Cocaine, Crime, and Public Policy* (Palo Alto, CA: Mayfield, 1986), p. 140.

Treatment and Policy Issues for Crack-Dependent Women

"Women who feel like garbage tend to treat themselves as such."
— *Naya Arbiter, Amity, Inc., 1991[1]*

"If the only ways of escape people have are through drugs and sex — which offer a rare chance to feel like a real human being — and both of these are closely linked with AIDS, then what hope is there of addressing the issue of AIDS prevention without addressing the underlying issue of what people are trying to escape from?"
— *Marie St. Cyr, 1990[2]*

Crack-cocaine has provided the media with many lurid, shocking, and sensational stories. As already detailed in Chapter 1, television and press coverage of the crack "epidemic" has focused heavily on the high addiction liability of the drug, the street violence associated with crack distribution, and the tendency of many inner city youths to view crack sales as a mechanism for upward mobility. Some of this "hype" had positive effects: It made the general population aware of the problems associated with crack use, and at the same time, it most likely kept many people away from even experimenting with the drug. But on the negative side, media coverage of crack use by women displayed serious problems of stereotyping and myth-making. As Marsha Rosenbaum and her colleagues at the Institute for Scientific Analysis in San Francisco satirically put it:

> In sum, we "know" from reading the paper and watching TV that after one hit of crack, women take off their clothes and have sex with anyone, including the family pet. Subsequently, they beat their children, add crack to their babies' formulas; and for those children who are not already using it, they blow crack smoke in their faces. To make a long story short, women crack users are amoral animals, lacking a conscience.[3]

Their message is clear. Media stories have indeed distorted fact by suggesting that crack makes women so sexually excitable that they will do

137

anything. Undeniably, however, as this study has clearly documented, many crack-dependent persons (both women and men) do indeed engage in a variety of behaviors (sexual and otherwise) that they would otherwise avoid. Some crack-dependent women—and their actual numbers are unknown—have been reported and observed to take off their clothes in crack houses and to engage in any variety of sexual behaviors with dozens, hundreds, and perhaps even thousands of male and female partners. But all of this must be kept in perspective. What the media and many "expert" observers tend to be either unaware of, or just plain insensitive to, are the problems and levels of hopelessness, crisis, misery, distress, and general despair that characterize many of those to be found in crack houses.

It could be argued that women who exchange sex for drugs are members of a special culture. Naya Arbiter of Amity, Inc., a therapeutic community in Tucson, Arizona, has outlined the boundaries of the more general culture of the drug-dependent woman. According to Arbiter, the drug-dependent woman is one:

☐ who has sold herself a thousand times;

☐ who has never paid a taxi driver with money, but with sex;

☐ who has left her child as collateral at the dope house;

☐ whose probation or parole officer represents the most predictable relationship in her life;

☐ whose grandmother was an alcoholic, mother a prostitute, and who started using drugs at 12 and began prostituting with her mother at 14;

☐ who was raised in foster care and can no longer remember the names of her younger siblings because they were all in separate homes;

☐ who watches TV and sees a life she knows she will never participate in; sees health plans she will never achieve, and families she will never belong to;

☐ who works in the sex trade, lives in a storefront, and eats out of a broken dog dish;

☐ whose child has been in 14 placements by age 9;

☐ who is homeless, and feeds her child out of dumpsters.[4]

To these can be added the women who as children were beaten by alcoholic parents, sexually abused on a regular basis beginning at age 6; and forced to steal in order to eat. Although these circumstances and conditions may appear rather extreme and severe, they are not unfamiliar to the crack-dependent women interviewed during the course of this study (as illustrated in the case studies in Appendix B of this book), or to drug-addicted women encountered in criminal justice and treatment settings. As such, it would appear that the activities, struggles, and choices of women who exchange sex for crack are in large part a consequence of the culture of despair and terror in which they are nurtured and socialized, and which they must tolerate and survive.

Given this, are there answers and resolutions? Rather than entertaining such solutions as restructuring society, redistributing capital resources, and legalizing drugs, more realistic endeavors can be addressed, in such areas as HIV/AIDS prevention/intervention, drug abuse treatment, and health care for drug-dependent women.

HIV/AIDS Prevention/Intervention

> If I pulled out a condom in a crack house, I'd be laughed at. If I
> started to take it out of the wrapper, it would be slapped out of my
> hand. If I tried to put it on a man's prick, I'd be slapped across the
> face, or worse. If I get AIDS, who cares anyway, really?
> —*A Miami crack user, 1991*

Attempts to reduce high-risk behaviors among injection-drug users have demonstrated some success. Prevention and education efforts have been institutionalized in many populations and locales once considered impossible to access. Not only are injection-drug users being reached but so, too, are many of their sex partners.[5] Innovative techniques for contacting, educating, and reducing the high-risk behaviors of prostitutes have also been developed and implemented with some success.[6]

Prevention/intervention efforts that have targeted public health clinics and treatment populations, or have used indigenous outreach workers to recruit street populations of drug users and their sex partners may be inappropriate or impractical, however, when it comes to contacting and educating those who spend much of their time in crack houses. Public health agencies and privately funded street intervention teams in a number of communities have experienced a measure of success in needle-exchange efforts and distributing needle cleaning kits to injection-drug users, and in dispensing condoms to the members of *all* high-risk groups. But it is highly unlikely that the owners and operators of crack houses would be receptive to such initiatives. Aside from the paranoia that exists in crack houses, it just wouldn't be good for business. Furthermore, condom use is rare in the crack house. Although the majority of drug users are aware that condoms can reduce the risk of HIV transmission, male customers in bartered sex/drug exchanges are unwilling to use them, and female sexual providers are rarely in a position to insist. As such, condoms are neither discussed nor seen, let alone used.

Yet as crack use endures and the AIDS epidemic continues to spread, it becomes increasingly important to inform women in general and drug-dependent women in particular about effective prevention methods.[7] Effective intervention, however, is another matter. The dilemma is this. The idea of risk is one of the most difficult concepts to address in health education. AIDS prevention initiatives that advise women to insist on condoms or "just say no" fail to recognize that women often lack any bargaining power. For crack-dependent women in particular, insisting on the use of condoms during crack-house sex would not only compromise their access to drugs, but also put them at risk of severe physical abuse.

Conversely, distributing condoms and risk-reduction information in crack houses is not a workable solution. The involvement of women who exchange sex for crack in street-based AIDS prevention/intervention programs is similarly problematic. A more useful approach would involve getting women out of the crack houses by every available means, followed by long-term residential drug treatment, AIDS education, and instruction and guidance in empowerment, assertiveness, and sexual self-determination.

Treatment Issues

> Traditional models of drug treatment and aftercare remain primarily male-oriented, which are not appropriate to the needs and problems of female addicts.
> —*Deborah McMillan and Rose Cheney, 1992*[8]

If treatment is to be a workable answer, then the *barriers to treatment* must be breached. Drug abuse treatment has made great progress in recent decades, but many barriers to treatment remain that are specific to drug-dependent women. These can be summarized into three broad areas — those preventing women from seeking and entering treatment, those that are likely to be problematic in the early stages of treatment, and those inhibiting long-term recovery.[9] Specifics of each include:

Barriers to Treatment Entry

□ lack of economic resources
□ child-related responsibilities
□ lack of women-oriented services
□ lack of appropriate referral networks

Barriers to Engagement in Treatment

□ low self-esteem
□ too many other responsibilities
□ sexism in treatment settings
□ lack of sensitivity to gender issues

Barriers to Long-Term Recovery

□ underemployment and economic difficulties

□ lack of assertiveness and empowerment skills

□ unresolved psychiatric disorders

□ unresolved intimacy/sexuality/self-image issues

Women in general, and drug-dependent women in particular, experience a range of economic disadvantages. Their employment histories are typically shorter and more sporadic than those of men. Their incomes are lower and they are less likely to have company-supported treatment/sick leave benefits. Many women with histories of street-drug abuse have been dependent on illegal sources of income, particularly prostitution. Entering treatment means the termination of all income. People who cannot pay for treatment must rely totally on publicly supported programs, where treatment slots are scarce.

Then there is the matter of their children. Despite the emancipation of women, the women's movement, and the greater involvement of men in child rearing over the last two decades, it appears that with few exceptions women still carry the primary responsibility for their children. Furthermore, many drug-dependent women have been untouched by the advances mentioned above. For the most part, they are single mothers with little or no income. Finding an appropriate place for children while in treatment is at least difficult, and often impossible. Fear of losing their children to state custody frequently prevents women from seeking treatment, and drug treatment programs which allow women to bring their children to treatment are scarce.

Few women are encouraged to enter treatment. Whereas men may seek drug abuse treatment as the result of persuasion or even outright coercion from parents, wives, girlfriends, coworkers, or employers, drug-dependent women infrequently have similar support networks. Many are either the heads of single-parent households, are living alone or on the streets, or are dependent on drug-addicted men. In any of these scenarios, the necessary support for seeking treatment entry is absent.

Once in treatment, barriers tend to persist. Most programs were designed *for men* and *by men*. Moreover, those that do admit women are generally staffed by men and focus on men's issues. Thus, there is a serious gap in the availability of services that address the social, psychological, and medical problems specific to women. These include such matters as low self-esteem, lack of parenting skills, unemployability, anxiety and depression, and the medical complications associated with substance abuse and poor hygiene. Moreover, programs need to provide treatment environments in which women feel safe from stereotyping, insensitivity, and sexual harassment.

Health Care Issues

When you find yourself fucking for money, fucking for drugs, and sometimes fucking or sucking a hairy prick for something to eat or a place to sleep, you're not too careful about avoiding the cruds. What's more, since you're stoned most of the time you don't feel much in the way of pain, or either that your whole body hurts and you can't tell where the trouble is. . . . When some kind of mess starts leakin' out of my crotch like toothpaste from a tube I know it's time to get my ass off to the clinic.

—A Miami prostitute, 1984[10]

It should be clear at this juncture that crack-dependent women likely suffer an inordinate number of medical problems. Physical abuse and outright violence seem to be recurring aspects of crack-house life. In addition, the lifestyle associated with crack dependence includes poor hygiene and diet, exposure to sexually transmitted diseases, and general self-neglect, resulting in a spectrum of health problems ranging from dental to gynecological. Medical complications go undetected and untreated, and can be far more severe and complex for women in the sex industry than for any other group.[11] Prostitutes are at high risk for cervical cancer as the result of initiating intercourse at an early age, having frequent and multiple sex partners, and having a history of sexually transmitted diseases. Since they become accustomed to irregular menstrual cycles and frequent vaginal discharges, they often fail to recognize that something may be wrong.

A related issue here is the debate involving matters of cocaine use, fetal rights, and the prosecution of pregnant addicts. In 1988, Brenda Vaughan of Washington, D.C., spent nearly four months in jail—an unusually long time for a first offender convicted of check forgery. However, the presiding judge felt he had to protect her fetus from cocaine. Pamela Stewart of San Diego, after defying her physician's advice to stop using street drugs during pregnancy, was arrested and incarcerated on a charge of failing to provide for her baby. Her child was subsequently born brain-damaged and died after only six weeks. Bianca Green of Rockford, Illinois, was born in February 1989 suffering from severe oxygen deprivation and died two days later. After cocaine was found in the baby's urine, as well as in the bloodstream of her mother Melanie, the mother was arrested and charged with child abuse, supplying drugs to a minor, and involuntary manslaughter.[12]

With almost 400,000 drug-exposed infants being born each year in the United States, state and county attorneys across the nation have become more inclined to prosecute mothers-to-be who abuse their fetuses by taking illegal drugs. Charges have included child abuse, child neglect, assault, manslaughter, and drug delivery. At issue is whether pregnant women who use drugs should be considered a public health problem, or a problem for the criminal justice system. Without question, cocaine babies are at risk. Crack and cocaine-abusing women are more likely to miscarry, give birth prematurely, and have low-weight babies.[13] In addition, infants born to cocaine users tend to have abnormally small heads and brains, suffer deformities of the genital organs and urinary tract, and experience higher rates of sudden infant death syndrome, also known as SIDS or crib death.[14] They can also suffer subtle neurological damage leading to extraordinary irritability during infancy, as well as learning disorders in later years. Furthermore, a number of these problems may be exacerbated during the early months of life, since intoxicating levels of cocaine can be ingested through breastfeeding.[15]

Prosecutors argue that the threat of criminal charges will help deter pregnant women from using drugs, saving babies from the wide spectrum of ill-effects that prenatal drug use can cause.[16] Similarly, "fetal rights" and "pro-life" advocates insist that the state must intervene to ensure the safety of the fetus. There is also the not-so-hidden pro-life agenda to chip away at the 1972 decision in *Roe* v. *Wade*,[17] which granted women the right to choose abortion as an option, and hence, gave no rights to fetuses.

By contrast, public health officials and women's advocates claim that the threat of prosecution will instead scare women away from the medical help they need. Along with many drug abuse clinicians and researchers, they further argue that drug use during pregnancy is a community health problem that is more properly addressed through the expansion of drug treatment services designed specifically for pregnant women.

How this controversy will ultimately be settled is difficult to predict. On one hand, the growing number of cocaine-babies (or "tox babies" as they are often called, for the toxicological examinations they undergo) has become a major public health problem in some locales. On the other hand, court decisions that would grant legal rights to fetuses could unleash a torrent of fetal protection cases that would have pregnant women (drug-using or not) seeing more of their lawyers then their physicians. The more humane compromise position is drug treatment in lieu of prosecution for those pregnant women who come to the attention of the criminal justice system for drug-related crimes, and the greater availability of treatment services for those who do not.

Postscript

In 1933, attorney Jerome Michael and philosopher Mortimer J. Adler startled segments of the criminological and social science communities with the following comment:

> If crime is merely an instance of conduct which is proscribed by the criminal code, it follows that the criminal law is the formal cause of crime. That does not mean that the law produces the behavior which it

prohibits . . . it means only that the criminal law gives behavior its quality of criminality.[18]

What was so startling about this and other comments in their treatise *Crime, Law, and Social Science* was that it forced criminologists and other social scientists to appreciate the importance of the criminal law in setting the boundaries of its concern. What Michael and Adler were saying was that *there would be no crime if there were no criminal law*, and in so doing they began to call into question the intellectual prestige of the existing body of theoretical criminology.

This anecdote from the annals of crime and law is recalled here because it would appear that the makers of contemporary state and federal drug policies may have borrowed from Michael and Adler. That is, whereas the Michael/Adler treatise asserted that "there would be no crime if there were no criminal law," drug policies seem to be structured around the belief that "there would be no drug problem if there were no drugs of abuse, no drug traffickers, and no drug dealers." This seems to be at the foundation of the 1980s and early 1990s war on drugs.

Historically, American drug policy has included strategies for reducing both the supply of and the demand for illicit drugs.[19] Much of the *supply reduction strategy* is grounded in the classic deterrence model: through legislation and criminal penalties, individuals will be discouraged from using drugs; by setting an example of dealers and traffickers, potential drug sellers will seek other economic pursuits. Supply reduction also includes vigorous enforcement of the drug laws on the domestic front; federal interdiction activities aimed at preventing the smuggling of drugs into the United States; and foreign assistance initiatives designed to eliminate drug-yielding crops at their source. The *demand reduction strategy* consists of treatment for those who are drug-dependent, education and prevention programs for would-be drug users, and research to determine how to best develop and implement plans for treatment, education, and prevention.

In the abstract, American drug policy is not unreasonable, for it is eminently sensible to try to reduce both supply and demand. However, the "no drug problem if there were no drugs/traffickers/dealers" paradigm has resulted in an overemphasis on supply-side policies with only lip service to the demand-side. Further, the supply-reduction strategy has had only limited effectiveness, for just so many drug shipments can be intercepted, and just so many drug dealers and drug-addicted offenders can be arrested. When crack arrived in the mid-1980s and drugs, users, and dealers seemed to multiply and take over entire neighborhoods, supply-side schemes were further enhanced. Policy makers attempted to legislate America out of its drug problem by passing more restrictive drug laws and mandatory sentencing statutes for drug dealers, and by creating elite drug enforcement units in the police sector and specialized drug courts in the judicial sector. At the same time, with the growing number of drug offenders coming to the attention of the criminal justice system, policy makers also tried to build America out of its drug problem by increasing prison space and capacity. All of this has had only limited effectiveness.

What all of this suggests is that American drug policy is in need of a paradigm shift — a shift of emphasis from supply-reduction to demand-reduction. The lessons of Michael and Adler could be restated to read "if there were no drug *users* there would be no drug problem." The logic behind the paradigm shift is this: There is a whole literature that suggests that drug abuse is *overdetermined behavior*.[20] That is, physical dependence is secondary to the wide range of influences that instigate and regulate drug-taking and drug-seeking behaviors. Drug abuse is a disorder of the whole person: the problem is the *person* and not the drug, and *addiction* is but a *symptom* and not the essence of the disorder. As such, drug dependence affects most if not all areas of functioning. In the vast majority of drug users, there are cognitive problems, psychological dysfunction is common, thinking may be unrealistic or disorganized, values are misshapen, and frequently there are deficiencies in educational, employment, parenting, and other social skills. These characteristics are certainly evident in the crack-dependent women encountered in this study.

Within this context, hard-core drug abuse is a response to a series of social and psychological disturbances that a supply-reduction/drug enforcement strategy could not even begin to ameliorate. On the demand-reduction side of the equation, the goal of treatment should be "habilitation" rather than "rehabilitation." Whereas *rehabilitation* emphasizes the return to a way of life previously known and perhaps forgotten or rejected, *habilitation* involves the building of a positive self-image, and a person's socialization into a productive and responsible way of life. This would seem to be the more positive and humane approach to the growing population of crack-dependent women who have been tossed aside by life — without money, influence, or hope.

Endnotes

1. Naya Arbiter, "Women and Children in the Therapeutic Community: Where Hope Started — Betty D." *International Conference on Drugs and Society*, Montreal, September 25, 1991.

2. Panos Institute, "Triple Jeopardy: Women and AIDS," *WorldAIDS*, January 1991, p. 8.

3. Marsha Rosenbaum, Sheigla Murphy, Jeanette Irwin, and Lynne Watson, "Women and Crack: What's the Real Story?" *The Drug Policy Letter* 2 (March/April 1990), pp. 2–4.

4. Naya Arbiter, "Women, Children and Drugs: Against Indifference," *Project Recovery National Training Workshop*, Forsyth, Georgia, January 8–11, 1992.

5. Robert Power, Richard Hartnoll, and Emmanuelle Daviaud, "Drug Injection, AIDS, and Risk Behavior: Potential for Change and Intervention Strategies," *British Journal of Addiction* 83 (June 1988), pp. 649–654; John C. Ball, Robert W. Lange, Patrick C. Myer, Samual R. Friedman, "Reducing the Risk of AIDS through Methadone Mainte-

nance Treatment," *Journal of Health and Social Behavior* 29 (September 1988), pp. 214–226; Richard C. Stephens, Thomas E. Feucht, and Shadi W. Roman, "Effects of an Intervention Program on AIDS-Related Drug and Needle Behavior Among Intravenous Drug Users," *American Journal of Public Health* 81 (May 1991), pp. 568–571; Dale D. Chitwood, James A. Inciardi, Duane C. McBride, Clyde B. McCoy, H. Virginia McCoy, and Edward Trapido, *A Community Approach to AIDS Intervention: Exploring the Miami Outreach Project for Injecting Drug Users and Other High Risk Groups* (Westport, CT: Greenwood Press, 1991); James L. Sorensen, Laurie A. Wermuth, David R. Gibson, Kyung-Hee Choi, Joseph R. Guydish, and Steven L. Batki, *Preventing AIDS in Drug Users and Their Sexual Partners* (New York: Guilford Press, 1991).

6. For a discussion of AIDS and prostitution, including the range of associated prevention efforts, see Martin Plant, *AIDS, Drugs and Prostitution* (London: Tavistock/Routledge, 1990); National Research Council, *AIDS: The Second Decade* (Washington, DC: National Academy Press, 1990).

7. Mary E. Guinan, and Ann Hardy, "Epidemiology of AIDS in Women in the United States," *Journal of the American Medical Association* 257 (April 17, 1987), pp. 2039–2042; Susan Y. Chu, James W. Buehler, and Ruth L. Berkelman, "Impact of the Human Immunodeficiency Virus Epidemic on Mortality in Women of Reproductive Age, United States," *Journal of the American Medical Association* 264 (July 11, 1990), pp. 225–229.

8. Deborah McMillan and Rose Cheney, "Aftercare for Formerly Homeless, Recovering Women: Issues for Case Management," *National Institute on Drug Abuse Technical Review on Case Management*, Rockville, Maryland, February 4–5, 1992.

9. See Josette Mondanaro, *Chemically Dependent Women: Assessment and Treatment* (Lexington, MA: Lexington Books, 1989); George M. Beschner, Beth Glover Reed, and Josette Mondanaro, eds., *Treatment Services for Drug Dependent Women* (Rockville, MD: National Institute on Drug Abuse, 1981).

10. Cited in James A. Inciardi, *The War on Drugs: Heroin, Concaine, Crime, and Public Policy* (Palo Alto, CA: Mayfield, 1986), p. 65.

11. Josette Mondanaro, "Medical Services for Drug Dependent Women," in George M. Beschner, Beth Glover Reed, and Josette Mondanaro, eds., *Treatment Services for Drug Dependent Women*, pp. 208–257.

12. *U.S. News & World Report*, February 6, 1989, p. 50; *New York Times*, April 20, 1991, p. 6; *Newsweek*, April 29, 1991, pp. 52–53.

13. Anne Geller, "The Effects of Drug Use During Pregnancy," in Paula Roth, ed., *Alcohol and Drugs are Women's Issues, Vol. 1, A Review of the Issues* (Metuchen, NJ: Women's Action Alliance and The Scarecrow Press, 1991), pp. 101–106; Ira J. Chasnoff and Sidney H. Schnoll, "Consequences of Cocaine and Other Drug Use in Pregnancy," in Arnold M. Washton and Mark S. Gold, eds., *Cocaine: A Clinician's Handbook* (New York: Guilford Press, 1987), pp. 241–251; Andrew C. Revkin, "Crack in the Cradle," *Discover*, September 1989, pp. 63–69.

14. Beatrix Lutiger, Karen Graham, Thomas R. Einarson, and Gideon Koren, "The Relationship Between Gestational Cocaine Use and Pregnancy Outcome: A Meta-Analysis," *Teratology* 44 (1991), pp. 405–414.

15. Ira J. Chasnoff, Douglas E. Lewis, and Liza Squires, "Cocaine Intoxication in a Breast-Fed Infant," *Pediatrics* 80 (December 1987), pp. 836–838.

16. Rorie Sherman, "Keeping Baby Safe From Mom," *National Law Journal*, October 2, 1988, pp. 1, 24–25.

17. *Roe v. Wade*, 410 U.S. 13 (1972).

18. Jerome Michael and Mortimer J. Adler, *Crime, Law, and Social Science* (New York: Harcourt, Brace, 1933), p. 5.

19. See James A. Inciardi, *The War on Drugs II: The Continuing Epic of Heroin, Cocaine, Crack, Crime, AIDS, and Public Policy* (Mountain View, CA: Mayfield, 1992), p. 233.

20. See, e.g., George De Leon, "The Therapeutic Community for Substance Abuse: Perspective and Approach," in George De Leon and James T. Ziegenfuss, eds., *Therapeutic Communities for Addictions: Readings in Theory, Research and Practice* (Springfield, IL: Charles C. Thomas, 1986), pp. 5–18.

APPENDIX A

Some Considerations on the Methods, Dangers, and Ethics of Crack-House Research

by James A. Inciardi

On the basis of comments in both the preface and the analyses of crack use and street crime in Chapter 6, it is likely clear to most readers by now that the material for this book came from a variety of studies and sources. For those who have never been involved in street research, without a doubt many questions have come to mind. How is all of this done? How does someone from the "straight" world get to know drug dealers and traffickers? How do researchers and "professors" get into crack houses? Why would they even be let in? Once inside the door, what do they do? Is it safe? What are the dangers?

Even for those who have conducted drug studies or similar work, street and crack house research also raises questions of ethics. What do you do if you witness a crime? A rape? Should it be reported to the police? How are informants and subjects protected? Should researchers intervene when they see people being harmed or exploited? To what extent should a researcher "go native" so to speak? Exactly how far should "participant observation" go? All of these are important questions that need to be addressed.

Methods

The analyses, descriptions, portraits, and case studies that make up this book are drawn primarily from three projects, all funded by the National Institute on Drug Abuse (NIDA) during the years 1985 through 1991 to examine drug-taking and drug-seeking behaviors in a variety of Miami (Dade County), Florida populations. These were supplemented, furthermore, with my own independent inquiries. Before going further, let me describe a few of the studies and methods.

1. Street Kids and Street Drugs.[1]   As an extension of other Miami street

studies reported elsewhere,[2] the data were gathered through the traditional "snowball sampling" technique. Briefly, the peculiar life style, illegal drug-taking and drug-seeking activities, and mobility characteristics of active drug users preclude any examination of this group through standard survey methods. As such, the samples were derived through the use of a sociometrically-oriented model.

In the field sites, extensive contacts had been developed and maintained within Miami's networks of drug users through the street work I've been doing since 1971. These represented "starting points" for interviewing. During and after each interview, at a time when the rapport between interviewer and informant was judged to be at its highest level, each respondent was requested to identify other current users with whom he or she was acquainted. These persons, in turn, were located and interviewed, and the process was repeated until the social network surrounding each respondent was exhausted. This method restricted the pool of users contacted to those who were currently active in the street community. In addition, it eliminated former users as well as those who were only peripheral to the mainstream of the street-drug cultures. Although I personally did a portion of the street interviews for this delinquency study, most were accomplished by professional interviewers familiar with the local drug scene.[3] More than 600 structured interviews were completed — 511 males and 100 females. Data on the crack-using females were used in the analyses presented in Chapter 6. Informants were paid a $10 fee for participation in the 45-minute interview.

2. Cocaine and Street Crime.[4]   This study was done in much the same way as the delinquency project just described. The samples and drug-user networks targeted were different, however, since the research interests were limited to persons who were primary *crack*-cocaine and/or *powder*-cocaine users. Moreover, the study design required that half the subjects be drawn from the street and half from treatment.[5] All subjects, whether in treatment or on the street, received a $20 payment for participating in the study. A total of 699 interviews were completed. Data descriptive of the 237 females were used in the Chapter 6 analyses. It was during the course of this study that I began to visit crack houses.

3. "Sex-for-Crack" Ethnography.[6]   The crack-house ethnography was the product of the Miami component of an eight-city study of sex-for-crack exchanges. The research was initiated and funded by the National Institute on Drug Abuse for the purposes of developing some preliminary insights into the attributes and patterns of "sex-for-crack" exchanges, particularly those that were occurring in crack houses; determining the general characteristics of individuals who exchanged sex for crack, or sex for money to purchase crack; assessing the potential impact of sex-for-crack exchange behaviors on the spread of HIV infection; and targeting significant areas for further study.

The other cities in the project were Philadelphia, Newark, San Francisco, New York, Los Angeles, Chicago, and Denver.[7] Although I have never had any formal training in ethnography, I was chosen for the Miami part of the study because of my many years of street research and the contacts I had developed in the local drug community. As with any occupation or profession, when you are doing a specific kind of work in the same locale for a long period of time you get to know a lot of people — not only those in your own business, but others connected with it in one way or another. Physicians, for example, get to know other physicians, as well as nurses, phlebotomists, orderlies, and other members of the health professions; they meet patients, patients' relatives and close family members, and perhaps even patients' priests, rabbis, or ministers. Physicians also get to know pharmacists, ambulance drivers, representatives from medical equipment and pharmaceutical companies, medical and malpractice insurance people, and attorneys. There are likely many, many more. The same thing happens when you study deviant populations. You meet others who study deviants, you meet the deviants themselves, and you come to know those who work with deviants and attempt to control them.

With street research in the drug field, the cast of characters that you run into is quite colorful and extensive. It includes drug users, dealers, and traffickers; drug program directors, counselors, and other treatment personnel; and police and other criminal justice authorities. Moreover, now and then you also run into a sampling of arms merchants, insurgents, mercenaries, assassins, as well as the many groupies and hangers-on that populate the street worlds of heroin, cocaine, and crime. It is through these associations that you communicate with the members of the various drug organizations and subcultures and gain entry into crack houses.

To accomplish the goals of the sex-for-crack project, systematic interviews were conducted with 17 males and 35 females who were regular users of crack and who had exchanged sex for crack or money to buy crack during the 30-day period prior to study recruitment. These interviews were accomplished with the use of an interview guide that focused on current and past drug use and sexual behaviors, crack use, crack-house activities, HIV risk behaviors, and knowledge and concerns about AIDS. The interviews were conducted during the period from November 1989 through June 1990, on a part-time basis, by two employees of an AIDS outreach project who had extensive experience in interviewing on such sensitive topics as drug-using and criminal activities, sexual practices, and HIV risk behaviors.[8] The cases selected for interview were either drawn from the street by seasoned outreach workers, or from a pool of recent admissions (within the previous 48 hours) to local drug treatment programs. The information gathered from the 35 women in this sample represent the foundation of the qualitative data presented in this book.

In addition, from January 1988 through February 1992, I personally visited 11 different crack houses in the Miami area, several more than once, and conducted scores of unstructured interviews with numerous others who served as key informants, including crack users (contacted either in crack houses or on the street), crack and/or cocaine dealers, and police officers familiar with the greater Miami drug scene. Additional insights were obtained from numerous contacts with other players in the local street cultures. The systematic interviews were recorded and transcribed, yielding more than four thousand pages of material. As often as the opportunity presented itself and my memory permitted, my own observations and interviews resulted in a collection of hastily scribbled field notes.

Dangers

The dangers of street and crack-house research fall into four general areas: dangers from grand juries, prosecutors, and police; dangers associated with legitimate law enforcement activity; dangers linked to gaining entry to crack houses; and dangers from the denizens of crack houses.

1. Dangers from Grand Juries, Prosecutors, and Police. When doing research with deviant and criminal populations, there is always the possibility that the criminal justice community will get wind of what you are doing, view your research as a potential source of information or "intelligence," and compel disclosure. Although this may be a problem for journalists now and then, it is not something that drug researchers generally face. There are several reasons for this.

First, research data isn't "intelligence" information. Although street researchers know the locations of crack houses and shooting galleries, and the places where crack users and crack dealers hang out, any efficient drug enforcement group has that same information, and much more. It's their business to know it, and their sources likely have far better "intelligence" than a federally funded researcher.

Second, whenever I send interviewers out onto the street, or conduct interviews myself, I never want to know the names and addresses of my informants. Some will volunteer such information, and you even get to know a few of your informants fairly well. But in most cases, all you really need to know are first names and the general areas in which you can find them when you need to. This keeps them at ease, and makes for more willing cooperation.

Third, I design my interview instruments and ask my questions in such a way that the data collected would be considered as no more than hearsay in a court of law. To cite an extreme but nevertheless clear example, I would never ask a drug dealer such specific questions as: Murder anyone lately? What was the person's name? Where and when did the killing occur? What was your motive? What did you do with the weapon? What did you do with the body? Not only would such queries be of little research value, but just asking them could get a person killed. More realistically, one would pose general and less intrusive questions about the *kinds* of violence that occur in the drug scene, the *frequency* with which they happen, the *reasons* why they occur, the *nature* of victim/offender relationships, and the like.

Fourth, and finally, for studies funded by the National Institute on Drug Abuse, a "Certificate of Confidentiality" can be obtained. What this certificate amounts to is a written guarantee from the federal government that no member of the project team can be compelled by any law enforcement or judicial body in the nation to divulge any of the information collected during the course of the study. Although almost every drug researcher obtains this certificate, I am not aware of any instances when it had to be used.

To make a long and complex discussion simple, the criminal justice community generally leaves researchers alone to do their work.

2. Dangers From Police.   This heading might be more appropriately titled "being in the wrong place at the wrong time." It can happen when you are doing street research. It has happened to me, more than once. During the course of a project in the early 1970s, for example, I was riding in an open convertible with three drug users. Manny and Mo were in the front seat, and Jack was in the back with me. We were on our way to a local shooting gallery. I was getting the $5 tour of the local drug scene, they were my guides, and it was to be my very first "get-off" house. On the way, they stopped at a convenience store so Jack could get some cigarettes. So be it. The rest of us sat in the car and waited. Almost immediately, however, Jack came running out of the store. With money in one hand and a gun in the other, he jumped back into the car, into the back seat right next to me. The car sped off.

Now, I've always been a pretty laid-back person, but there I was, sitting in an automobile, probably a stolen one at that, speeding away from the scene of a violent crime with the perpetrator at my side. Needless to say I got a bit irritated. After threatening Manny (or was it Mo?) and his family and progeny for the next three centuries with all manner of ill-will, ill-fortune, calamity, tribulation, and catastrophe, Mo pulled over and let me off at the curb. As it turned out, they ended up in a high-speed chase — "hot pursuit" as the police like to call it. Manny, Mo, and Jack were arrested about fifteen minutes after we had gone our separate ways, and the stick-up man was identified by a convenience store employee.

In that incident, things fortunately went my way. However, I wasn't quite as lucky late one morning in 1989. It was in a crack house I had visited often, located just off 103rd Street in the Hialeah section of Miami. As I was entering through the *front* door of the house, the police were breaking in through the *rear* door. I was never quite sure exactly *which* police they were — DEA, state or county police, the "Jump Out Gang" (a special drug task force), "Miami Vice," Crockett and Tubbs, or all of the above. Whatever and whomever, they burst through the door and into the room like renegades from some warrior-cop hell. *Mad Max*, *Road Warrior*, and *Terminator* (1 and 2) all flashed before my eyes. In seconds, everyone in the place, including me, was spread-eagled (face down) on the floor, searched, cuffed, and put into what was once called a "paddy wagon."

As it turned out, the police were doing a sweep of the area, with warrants to enter certain premises where they had "probable cause" to believe that crack was being manufactured or sold. In all, 100 or more souls were taken into custody that morning and placed in several detention cells. Since our "processing" wasn't all that speedy, I spent the next several hours in jail with a fairly large gathering of paranoid drug users who were beginning to "crash" (that post-drug-euphoria letdown). A few fights broke out every so often, and sometimes I didn't get out of the way fast enough.

Eventually, I was taken out of the cell for "processing." Since I had had neither drugs nor weapons in my possession when the police searched me, and since my identification suggested that I was indeed the drug researcher I claimed to be, about the only thing they could have officially charged me with was something like "being in a disorderly place." But the police were interested only in drug arrests, so along with a few others, I walked.

These are the kinds of dangers that police can pose for drug researchers.

3. Dangers in Gaining Entry to Crack Houses. There are no specific dangers associated with gaining entry to crack houses — not usually, at any rate. You either get in or you don't. The dangers exist inside, not necessarily at the door. However, getting in can be a bit knotty and ticklish at times.

The best protection for a researcher in circumstances such as these is to be himself (or herself, although my observations suggest that female researchers would be in even more danger than I was, in crack houses that have public sex and an ever-present potential for rape). In other words, don't go undercover. Find a "protector" who will take you to the crack house, who will vouch for you, and introduce you around. Most of the time my protector was a small-time cocaine dealer that I had known for years. He would introduce me as a researcher, a university health worker, and the like. In this kind of a situation, a medical school I.D. doesn't hurt (I had one, through my association with the University of Miami School of Medicine).

Next, the crack-house owner or bouncer will want to know *why* you are there. "Curiosity" is one answer, but something a bit more pragmatic works better. Wanting to know something about the lifestyles of drug users — who they are, how they cope with the problems of family and addiction, their health needs — these are believable interests, and can get you in the door. It should be added, however, that the "house man" has absolutely no interest in research or public health. There is no altruism associated with letting *anyone* inside. Rather, it's the protector's word, and how believable a person you are. If he doesn't believe you, or doesn't like your looks, or is just having his usual bad day, there could be trouble — *big* trouble if he thinks you're a cop. However, if you do manage to pass muster, then like everyone else you have to pay a fee to get in — usually $10 to $15 for researchers and $2 to $5 for everyone else. Once inside, there will be a weapons search.

I have used a number of protectors over the years, and all expect to be paid for their time and service. There is one protector that I use more often than the others, and if I am going someplace I have visited many times before, I don't use any at all. On one recent occasion, my adventure involved a new crack house and a new protector, and he didn't like the "honest" approach for gaining entry. His reaction was as follows:

> How do you suppose we explain this? For Christ sakes, I'm not gonna tell them you're planning to write a fucking book . . . [extended pause] Give me $15 to give to the man at the door an' I'll just tell him that you're with me and you're a pervert that likes to watch people have sex. That should do it.

Well, that did it all right, but I got a few strange looks.

4. Dangers From the Denizens of Crack Houses. Crack houses are not among my favorite spots to visit. Most that I've been to are dirty, depressing, smoke-filled, sometimes violent, and always just on the verge of chaos. A house man will offer to sell you some crack, and you must say no. Women, and sometimes men, will offer you sex, and you must say no. Truly, "*participant* observation" is absolutely out of the question. Aside from such pragmatic issues and concerns as the potential for overdose, HIV and other sexually transmitted diseases, and morality and fidelity if applicable, "going native" destroys one's credibility and integrity as a researcher. Should that occur, any special protections a researcher might have quickly evaporate, and suddenly you become just another john and crackhead. Under any of these circumstances, research becomes impossible.

If one is not selling crack, using crack, engaging in sex, or bartering sex for drugs, then someone in the crack house might ask the question: "Why are you here?" A truthful answer should be given, with no moralizing. Also, no staring, and no interfering in other people's business or arguments. Sometimes fights break out. On one such occasion in 1990 my protector suggested: "don't interfere, just disappear." Once there were gunshots in the next room. Everyone hit the floor; no one was hurt.

The only potentially serious difficulty I ever faced occurred in the aftermath of the crack-house roust described earlier. Because of all of my research in Miami, I maintain a home in the area. During a return visit from the North some weeks after my "arrest," I found a message on my answering machine. It was from my favorite protector. He said to stay away from 103rd Street. I called him, and he told me that the owner of the crack house that had been raided was willing to pay money to have me brought there to explain why the police showed up at the same time I did.

I had a price on my head. I asked him how much. He said $200. I was insulted, but I never went back to that crack house.

Ethics

My first direct exposure to the "sex-for-crack" market came in 1988, during an initial visit to a North Miami crack house. I had gained entry through a local drug dealer who had been a key informant of mine for almost a decade. He introduced me to the crack-house "door man" as someone "straight but OK." Stationed inside the main door of the crack house, the "door man" is the person who lets people in, checks for weapons, and watches for police. After he checked us out, my guide and protector proceeded to show me around.

Upon entering a room in the rear of the crack house (what I later learned was called a freak room), I observed what appeared to be the gang-rape of an unconscious child. Emaciated, seemingly comatose, and likely no older than 14 or 15 years of age, she was lying spread-eagled on a filthy mattress while four men in succession had vaginal intercourse with her. After they had finished and left the room, however, it became clear that, because of her age, it was indeed rape, but it had not been "forcible" rape in the legal sense of the term. She opened her eyes and looked about to see if anyone was waiting. When she realized that our purpose there was not for sex, she wiped her groin with a ragged beach towel, covered herself with half of a tattered sheet (affecting a somewhat peculiar sense of modesty), and rolled over in an attempt to sleep. Almost immediately, however, she was disturbed by the door man, who brought a customer to her for oral sex. He just walked up to her with an erect penis in his hand, said nothing to her, and she proceeded to oblige him.

When leaving the crack house a few minutes later, the dealer/informant explained that she was a "house girl" — a person in the employ of the crack-house owner. He gave her food, a place to sleep, and all the crack she wanted; in return, she provided sex — any type and amount of sex — to his crack-house customers.

What does a researcher do in a situation like this? Interfere in the rape episode? Distract the rapists and get the child out of the house? Reprimand the crack-house owner for the sordid activities he promoted? Leave and call the police? Try to talk the child into leaving? File complaints of child abuse? What? What would you do?

When I first walked into that room — and I can still vividly picture the scene — my reaction was one of highly repressed outrage. My thought was to somehow get between the men and the child, provide a distraction, play it by ear. But as I made a move toward the group, my protector took me by the arm, quite firmly I might add, and said in a very matter-of-fact way:

You can't do anything. Just let it be. If you do *anything*, I'll have to kill you. It's as simple as that. I brought you here, I vouched for you. You interfere, and if *they* [pointing to the men with the child] don't do you in, I will.

He went on to point out that since it was *he* who had brought me into the crack house, anything I did was a reflection on him; that if I made trouble, *he* would be the one who would suffer for it; that he had witnessed trouble in crack houses before, with some people having their throats cut for far less; and that in all likelihood the child would suffer too, with a beating and possibly a vicious rape. It was for these reasons that he had threatened me.

Before long I realized that making contacts with police or child protection agencies would have served little purpose. After several visits to the crack house I got to know the child in the freak room somewhat. Her name was Leona, she was 15 years old—almost 16—and had been addicted to crack for almost a year. It was clear that although she was indeed being exploited, she had no intention of leaving the crack house, for it was the only place she had to live. She was ashamed of what she was doing, and it was for that reason that she had covered herself when I first saw her in the freak room. But she also stated that the crack-house owner took care of her, and that she would never testify against her keepers.

With repeated visits and some subtle pressure, I convinced Leona to enter a residential drug treatment program. She did, but split after only nine weeks, and then dropped out of sight for well over a year. As it turned out, she was living in a crack house just down the street from the place where I had first met her.

I've run into other situations in crack houses. I saw a woman badly beaten, the result of her attempt to steal crack from another user. I saw another woman come into a crack house with her baby. The child was so dirty and neglected that she had maggots in her diaper. Repeated visits to crack houses made it clear that there is little or nothing I could do while in the confines of the house. Being on the outside, however, is another matter. For the woman who was beaten for trying to steal crack, I managed to get her to an emergency room and a crisis counselor. For the child, a clean diaper and a little soap and water worked wonders. It was the first time I had changed a diaper in more than a decade. (It's like riding a bicycle.) I also brought two cases of Pampers to where the mother and child lived.

The point is this. There is degradation, brutality, despair, injustice, and exploitation in the crack business. There is little or nothing an observer can do to change the course of on-going events in smoking rooms and freak rooms. To do so would likely instigate serious violence. But there are many other things that can be done—later, subtly, and however temporarily. Moreover, by maintaining access to crack houses by a policy of noninterference, the doors to the crack houses remain open to researchers. Through open doors one can do outreach for prevention and recruitment into treatment.

Postscript

In 1991 I ran into Leona on the steps of the Dade County Court House. She had just been arraigned on a petty larceny charge, and released on bail. She was 18 years old, living on her own, supporting herself through street prostitution and petty theft, and claimed to have her crack use "under control." She admitted that the nine-week stay in the treatment program had been a turning point in her life. After leaving, she was taken in by a prostitute friend of her sisters, and taught the "tricks of the trade." Now she had a place of her own. She felt that things were looking up for her. She looked healthy, and she was talking about finishing high school.

In early 1992 I spotted Leona once again, this time soliciting on Miami's Biscayne Boulevard. When I pulled over to talk to her, she thought I was a trick. She was embarrassed when she realized who it was. She didn't look well, and she told me that she was HIV-positive. That was the last time I saw her.

Endnotes

1. Grant No. RO1-DAO1827, "Drug Use and Serious Delinquency," from the National Institute on Drug Abuse; James A. Inciardi, Principal Investigator, Anne E. Pottieger, Co-Principal Investigator and Project Director; project period, September 1985 through August 1988.
2. See James A. Inciardi, "Heroin Use and Street Crime," *Crime and Delinquency* 25 (July 1979), pp. 335–346; Susan K. Datesman and James A. Inciardi, "Female Heroin Use, Criminality, and Prostitution," *Contemporary Drug Problems* 8 (1979), pp. 455–473; James A. Inciardi, "Women, Heroin, and Property Crime," in Susan K. Datesman and Frank R. Scarpitti, eds., *Women, Crime, and Justice* (New York: Oxford, 1980, pp. 214–222; James A. Inciardi, "The Impact of Drug Use on Street Crime," *Paper Presented at the 33rd Annual Meeting of the American Society of Criminology*, Washington, D.C., November 11–14, 1981; Susan K. Datesman, "Women, Crime, and Drugs," in James A. Inciardi, ed., *The Drugs-Crime Connection* (Beverly Hills: Sage, 1980), pp. 85–105; James A. Inciardi, Anne E. Pottieger, and Charles E. Faupel, "Black Women, Heroin and Crime: Some Empirical Notes," *Journal of Drug Issues* 12 (Summer 1982), pp. 241–250; James A. Inciardi and Anne E. Pottieger, "Drug Use and Crime Among Two Cohorts of Women Narcotics Users: An Empirical Assessment," *Journal of Drug Issues* 16 (1986), pp. 91–106.
3. Our thanks must go here to Brian R. Russe, Jody Rosen, and Paul Nemeth for their help with the many hundreds of street interviews.
4. Grant No. RO1-DAO4862, "Crack Abuse Patterns and Crime Linkages," from the National Institute on Drug Abuse; James A. Inciardi, Principal Investigator, Anne E. Pottieger, Co-Principal Investigator and Project Director; project period, September 1988 through August 1991.
5. Our thanks must go here to Brian R. Russe, Rose Anderson, Jim Scaringi, and Joseph Fishwick for their help with the treatment and street interviews, and to Bruce Hayden of Spectrum Programs for his cooperation with the project.

6. This research was supported, in part, by Contract No. 271888248/Task Order #1 from the National Institute on Drug Abuse to Birch & Davis International, Inc; Mitchell S. Ratner, Project Director; James A. Inciardi, subcontractor.
7. For the results of the eight-city effort, see Mitchell S. Ratner, ed., *Crack Pipe as Pimp* (Lexington, MA: Lexington Press, 1993).
8. Our thanks go to Rose Anderson and Mary Comerford for their help during the interview phase of the project, and to Brian R. Russe and Elizabeth Partin for their important outreach efforts.

APPENDIX B

Case Studies

Ever since the publication of William Healy's *The Individual Delinquent* in 1915 and W. I. Thomas and Florian Znaniecki's *The Polish Peasant in Europe and America* in 1918,[1] the case study method has earned widespread recognition as a distinctive and independent approach to the study of social phenomena. The advantage of the case study lies in its potential to discover most, if not all, of the variables relevant to the particular issue, phenomenon, or individual under scrutiny. In its detailed description of a particular case, it attempts to convey an understanding of similar cases. Most importantly, the case study can provide insights that cannot be provided through statistical analyses.

Within this context, included here are seven case histories of persons who traded sex for crack in Miami. The cases selected represent a wide diversity of individuals. Collectively, however, they reflect the backgrounds and experiences that appear to be most common in the sex-for-crack industry. Specifically, there is:

☐ Lucy T., a 35-year-old black woman who was introduced to prostitution by her mother;

☐ LaTisha D., a 38-year-old black woman whose husband introduced her to drugs and whose addiction to crack led her into prostitution and crack-house sex;

☐ Susan S., a 40-year-old white woman, highly paid as a streetwalker, who lost her husband, children, home, and business as the result of crack addiction;

☐ Lisa F., a 25-year-old white woman and mother of three who grew up in poverty and began a career in prostitution at age 13;

☐ Sylvia M., a 21-year-old white woman who has been "on the streets" since age 12, a drug user and a prostitute;

☐ Sybil P., a 26-year-old black woman who became a prisoner in a crack house; and,

☐ Robyn R., a 31-year-old white male transvestite with a female gender-role orientation.

Together, these case histories provide additional insights into the dynamics of initiation to drugs, prostitution, crack use, crack addiction, and crack-house sex.

Lucy T.

Lucy T., 35 years old when interviewed for this study, was born and raised in Miami. Her mother was a barmaid and she never knew her father. She grew up with two brothers and four sisters, all of whom have different fathers. Her mother used pills during Lucy's childhood, particularly Valium.*

Lucy took her first alcoholic drink when she was 12, introduced to her by her mother. However, she didn't drink regularly until she was 17, although she started sniffing glue at age 13. Lucy's mother often brought men home from the bar to have sex with them for money. At 14, Lucy's mother "turned her out" (introduced her to prostitution) by setting her up with "dates" from the bar. Lucy was not aware until years later that the men had been paying her mother. Lucy also recalls being sexually abused by one of her mother's male friends when she was about 8.

When Lucy was 16, her older brother returned from the army. He and his friends would smoke marijuana. In an attempt to "be with the crowd," Lucy also began smoking marijuana. At a party, her brother introduced her to "downers" — prescription sedatives and tranquilizers. Lucy began taking pills regularly, eventually taking as many as 15 a day for about a year and a half. She was most often using both Valium and Quaalude.†

By 17, Lucy's brother had introduced her to heroin. Almost immediately, she began speedballing — injecting as well as snorting heroin, cocaine, and various amphetamines. During all the phases of Lucy's injection-drug use, sharing needles was common. Lucy's drug of choice was heroin, but she would use cocaine to pick her up when the heroin made her too "mellow."

Lucy quit school at 16. Her drug use made it impossible for her to get to school, much less stay there and learn anything. She ran away from home several times, engaging in prostitution to support her drug habit. On one occasion when she left, she got herself a pimp, but her mother found her and brought her back home. However, Lucy ran away shortly thereafter, and, still 16, began a relationship with a man 30 years her

---

*Valium is a minor tranquilizer used for the treatment of tension and anxiety. Once among the most widely prescribed drugs in the United States, it has a significant abuse potential and addiction liability, particularly when taken in conjunction with alcohol or other central nervous system depressants.

†Quaalude is a potent central nervous system depressant similar to the barbiturates and once prescribed for sedation and sleep. Because of the widespread abuse of this drug during the 1970s and early 1980s, it is no longer legally available in the United States.

senior. He supplied her with money for drugs in exchange for sex. Eventually, she returned home again.

By the time Lucy was 18, she was heavily addicted to heroin. Her mother took her to the Youth Authority, where a counselor tried to enroll her in a methadone program. But the treatment staff felt that she was too young to be on methadone. Instead, they put Lucy into a detoxification program. After the 21-day regimen Lucy was released, but immediately relapsed to heroin use. About a year later she tried to get methadone, but was rejected once more because of her age. She decided not to go through detoxification again.

By age 24, Lucy was mainlining heroin and turning tricks regularly to support both her and a boyfriend's drug habits. Lucy's boyfriend admitted himself to a drug rehabilitation program. When he completed his treatment stay, they both stopped their heroin use. However, they began snorting cocaine. Lucy left this boyfriend not too long afterwards. She went to work in a massage parlor, and the other women there introduced her to crack. This was 1984 and Lucy was 30 years old, a veteran drug addict and prostitute.

Lucy left the massage parlor and began working on the streets. Her crack use increased continually until 1986, when she tried to stop. In her opinion, crack was worse than heroin, so she started injecting narcotics again. But she never stopped using crack.

Because of her crack use, Lucy began doing things she had never even contemplated before, even while on heroin. For instance, she had sex with other women; she had anal sex; she sold herself for less money than ever before. She even began trading sex for drugs rather than money. Lucy also regularly worked in crack houses. She described them as "disgusting" and crowded. People would smoke and have sex in the same room in front of other people. Lucy insisted that her crack-house tricks rent a room for sex, refusing to have sex in front of others. After having sex, Lucy would return to the stroll. She rarely stayed in the crack house to smoke after finishing with a customer. Lucy would have five to seven customers a night, and most of the sex was oral. During this time, Lucy either stayed with her sister or slept in cars.

Lucy experienced numerous rapes and assaults while working on the streets. On one occasion, after a customer paid her for sex, he asked for his money back. She refused. The customer and two of his friends beat her. She was hospitalized for several weeks and still needs reconstructive surgery of her jaw.

Just before Lucy was interviewed for this study, she had entered treatment voluntarily because she was tired of living life on the streets addicted to crack. While in the program, she was diagnosed as HIV-positive. She tries to understand the virus as best she can so she can remain healthy as long as possible. She has no particular post-treatment plans.

LaTisha D.

LaTisha D., 38 years old at the time of interview, is the second oldest of four children. She has a sister and two brothers, one of whom is epileptic. All of her siblings were raised in the same house. LaTisha's mother was a moderate drinker, but her father was an alcoholic who fought continuously with her mother.

At age 15, LaTisha quit school to have her first child. The pregnancy was the outcome of her first sexual experience. She married the father of her child when she was 18 and he was 22. Her husband supported them, and they lived with her mother. Over the next 13 years, they had seven more children. LaTisha was 28 when her last child was born.

LaTisha's first drug use was at 18, and involved marijuana and alcohol. She began using for "recreational" reasons and does not recall any problems at the time. She smoked marijuana once or twice on weekends. Her older brother and her husband, both of whom had been smoking for a few years, introduced her to marijuana. All of her siblings, except the epileptic brother, used marijuana, alcohol, cocaine, and crack. LaTisha's older brother eventually moved to Washington, D.C., to get away from his drug-using friends. He is no longer using drugs of any kind.

She recalls that her husband was pressured by his friends to try different drugs. He experimented with Quaaludes and "black beauties" (amphetamines), but never used any of them regularly. When he was 25 he began injecting cocaine with LaTisha's older brother. LaTisha tried shooting cocaine once, years later, just to see what it was like. She reports not feeling any effect from it. LaTisha's drug use remained infrequent and limited to marijuana and alcohol until she was about 26. Then she began snorting cocaine, having been introduced to it by friends she had met at bars.

She used cocaine about three times a week at first, and never used at home. Eventually, both LaTisha and her husband increased their use. About four years later, when LaTisha was 30, she started using crack. Her husband had stopped using intravenous drugs and they moved to a different neighborhood. By this time, they had eight children. The people in the apartment downstairs were selling marijuana and crack. LaTisha's husband began working for them, selling drugs. Frequently, customers from downstairs would come to their apartment to buy drugs and to have LaTisha's husband hook up their "rigs" (drug paraphernalia) for them. These customers would also use LaTisha's bathroom as a place to smoke. Her husband was rarely paid in cash, but rather in drugs, which he used. She says that he would often go on seven- and eight-day smoking binges during which he neither slept nor ate. LaTisha tried to confront him about his drug use, which led to verbal arguments that sometimes ended in violence. She recalls that he had never struck her prior to his smoking crack.

Eventually, LaTisha became involved in her husband's drug-selling and crack use. After all the children were asleep, LaTisha would join her husband in the crack house downstairs. She was shocked at the behavior of people on crack. She was particularly astounded to see women taking off their clothes in front of everyone, participating in all types of sexual activities. Her husband was adamantly opposed to LaTisha smoking crack and refused to let her try. After several months, the other customers in the crack house convinced him to let her try. She got sick and threw up the first time. But she tried again, and found it quite pleasurable.

For a few months, LaTisha only smoked a few times a week. Slowly, her crack use began to increase until it got out of hand. She also began drinking three or four beers while smoking. Occasionally, LaTisha would smoke marijuana with crack in it, a *"lace joint."* She also smoked marijuana in order to regain her appetite; when she smoked crack LaTisha would not eat. At this time, LaTisha's husband began locking her in the apartment so she wouldn't go to the crack house. After the children were asleep, LaTisha would jump out the bathroom window and go to another crack house a few blocks away.

LaTisha's husband had been on probation for selling marijuana. However, he went to prison for 18 months for violation of probation. While he was there, LaTisha's crack use increased drastically. Her welfare check and food stamps were turned over to her daughter. LaTisha would be gone for a week or two at a time, smoking and prostituting. Her eldest daughter would take care of the other children. Occasionally, LaTisha would baby-sit children in the neighborhood or clean the apartment building for extra income. Some of this money was spent on food and clothing for her children; most of it was spent on crack.

She began having sex for crack while her husband was in prison, because she had no money with which to buy crack. At first, she was very hesitant to have sex with anyone else in the crack houses she frequented. However, as her crack habit increased, her inhibitions decreased and she began having sex regularly. She had between five and ten different customers a night. She had vaginal intercourse more often than oral sex. Once she had sex with a female — freaking. She used condoms regularly; her customers were cooperative.

LaTisha describes two kinds of crack houses; clean ones with a few regular customers and dirty ones with a lot of customers. She says the dirty ones are chaotic and make her paranoid. She preferred the clean ones, but often frequented, and had sex in, the dirty ones. LaTisha witnessed and experienced numerous violent acts during her eight years of smoking. In one crack house, a customer tried to steal several rocks. The owner pushed him into the street and in front of about 25 people shot him in the head. The "house man" (crack house owner) put the body in a dumpster. No one called the police.

One time while smoking, LaTisha met a friend from school, a man with whom she had smoked crack on several other occasions. He asked her to have sex with him and she agreed. When they were in the room, she asked for her money first, a common request. He refused to give her money and began pushing the bed and dresser and other furniture in front of the door so she could not leave. The man began smoking crack and refused to share any with LaTisha. After he was high, he began threatening to throw her out the window. He eventually did. People in a nearby crack house saw her fall and called 911. The police never found the man, but the paramedics patched her up. A few months later, LaTisha saw the same man in another crack house. He apologized and asked her to smoke with him. She turned down the offer.

On another occasion, LaTisha was in a car with a customer. He drove her to a remote spot and asked her to undress. When she did, he began calling her names and threatening to shoot her. Terrified, she jumped from the car and ran with her dress in her hand. The trip home was 10 miles, all on foot, but at least she still had her dress.

LaTisha has seen three murders in crack houses and more fights than she can either remember or count. She's been raped three times by customers. Once a customer held a knife to her throat and was about to rape her when another man walked by. LaTisha screamed and the rapist ran, taking her clothes with him. The other man walked her back to the crack house, got her some clothes, and had sex and smoked crack with her.

After serving his prison sentence, LaTisha's husband returned to their home. He immediately pressured her to stop using drugs. Both LaTisha and her husband are HIV-positive. He is asymptomatic and is taking AZT. She is currently in a drug rehabilitation program. At program completion, she plans on returning home to care for her husband, her children, and her grandchildren. LaTisha is a certified nurse's aide and hopes to find a job in the field.

Susan S.

Susan S., 40 years old at the time of interview, grew up with a sister and two brothers. Neither her mother nor her father used drugs. Susan's father was a singer in a night club. He did drink heavily, but Susan did not consider him an alcoholic. Since he worked at night and slept during the day, Susan and her siblings couldn't bring friends home or make noise in the house. Her father was quite strict.

At 15, Susan married a 28-year-old man in an effort to get away from her father. She continued to go to school, and managed to graduate from high school. Her first sexual experience was with her husband the day they were married. During this marriage, Susan had one miscarriage. Her husband had three children from a previous marriage. The eldest son lived with them.

Susan's husband introduced her to beer. He drank every day, although Susan never considered this a drinking problem. She drank about two beers a week. After six months, Susan divorced him and immediately married again. Her stepson from the first marriage introduced her and her second husband to marijuana. At the time he was 16 and Susan was 20. She smoked daily, about 20 joints a day for about three years; then she reduced her smoking to weekends. At 32, Susan began feeling paranoid when she smoked so she stopped completely and has not smoked marijuana since.

About three years later, the same stepson gave Susan some Quaaludes. She and her husband both enjoyed the drug's effects. Her husband obtained a prescription for 100 pills every three months. Susan supplemented these with Quaaludes bought on the streets. She was taking about 15 pills a day. She used Quaaludes for a year and a half or two years when she heard that if you stopped using them, cold turkey, you would go into convulsions. Scared of the effects of withdrawal, Susan admitted herself into a 28-day drug rehabilitation program. After six days her fears diminished and she left the program. Although Susan never used Quaaludes again, she did start using Valium.

About this time, she separated from her second husband and leased a bar/lounge in Miami Springs. One of her employees introduced her to "uppers" (amphetamines). She enjoyed the energy and stimulation they engendered and continued to use them. She used "speed" daily, as much as she could get her hands on. Susan also began to drink, about a fifth of Scotch daily.

She divorced her second husband and immediately married for a third time. She and her new husband owned a mirror and window shop. She worked in the business, keeping the books. They had two sons, one when Susan was 23 and one when she was 30. She had one abortion after the first son and another abortion when she was 33.

It is with this husband that she began smoking crack. Beforehand, Susan had tried snorting cocaine. Several of her friends would get together to play cards and one man would bring the cocaine. She disliked it because it left a burning sensation in her nose. During a visit to Las Vegas, she tried crack. She was 38 at the time. When she returned to Miami, she showed her husband how to make crack and they both began using it daily. Susan's crack use increased dramatically, until she was smoking about 20 rocks a day. She spent 10 months in prison for writing bad checks. She and her husband lost their business, and eventually separated when she refused to give up crack. That was when she got into prostitution.

Susan had used crack about 45 minutes prior to participating in this interview, and had not been to sleep in three days. She rents a hotel room with a boyfriend. If either of them have any money, they spend it on crack. Neither Susan nor her boyfriend smoke in crack houses. They buy their crack and leave.

Susan pays her rent and purchases her crack with money she earns through prostitution. She gets up every morning at about 9 A.M. in order to get enough customers to pay for the hotel room by 11 A.M. She charges $20 to $40 for oral sex. She takes most of her dates to a park close to her hotel so her boyfriend can provide protection. Susan has about 20 regular customers that she sees weekly. Two of these take her to hotels for sex. Infrequently, Susan can make $100 from a single customer. She has been prostituting for about one and a half years. When she is unable to work, her boyfriend will make money by selling drugs. Susan has been incarcerated about a dozen times for prostitution. Each of these times she spent from 3 to 25 days in jail.

Susan's sons are ages 17 and 10. The eldest one lives with her mother and the younger one lives with his father. Susan is still married to her third husband, the father of her children. She goes home to see them fairly frequently.

Susan is unsure of her future. She is becoming more afraid of the streets and is contemplating getting a "straight" job. However, she is unwilling to give up the income she earns through prostitution, about $5,600 a month. She realizes she cannot go back to her husband, but also knows that she has no intentions of staying with her boyfriend. Susan says that when the situation gets bad enough she will quit crack and the streets.

Lisa F.

Lisa F., 25 years old at the time of interview, was raised by an alcoholic mother and a father who was rarely home. They lived with her mother's stepfather, who molested Lisa continually while she was a child. Her step-grandfather used alcohol and pills—Valium and Darvon.* Her mother was neither aware nor concerned if Lisa did not come home.

She began smoking cigarettes when she was 13. She had just entered junior high school and smoked to be "in." The same group pressured her into smoking marijuana. Lisa describes herself as being promiscuous at that time. Her first vaginal intercourse was when she was 13, and she began having sex with boys and men in her neighborhood at 14, mostly oral sex. It was at this time that her career in prostitution began.

Lisa had a friend, a prostitute, who introduced her to her "main john," George. He liked Lisa, and would make dates for her with his friends who would pay her $25 to $50 for sex. She would give George $5 after each date. George also paid her for posing for photographs. He introduced her to Valium as a way to relax. Since Lisa and the rest of her family lived in poverty, she enjoyed having all the extra money to buy things that "the

---

*Darvon is a prescription painkiller, considered to be not much more effective than common aspirin. However, the drug can be injected, providing an effect similar to heroin, but with less potency.

other girls at school were wearing." At 14, Lisa also became involved in her first "threesome." With a male and a girlfriend, she would use Quaaludes and then have sex. The male paid both girls with money and drugs.

Lisa dropped out of school after the ninth grade. Although she did well academically, she did not get along with the other students. Her drug use also made it difficult to stay in school. At 15, Lisa's boyfriend, whom she eventually married, introduced her to cocaine. She tried freebasing, but preferred snorting. She liked the cocaine "high" and the energy it gave her. At 16, she started drinking alcohol, but never drank either regularly or excessively.

Lisa married at 17 and had her first child at 18. Three months before her child was born, her father died from a massive stroke. Six months later her mother died from cirrhosis of the liver. Lisa was a waitress at the time, and her husband convinced her to start nude dancing at the neighborhood bars for the extra cash it would provide them. She would drink before she danced, and she danced only when they needed extra money. When she was 18, Lisa tried crack. She seemed to be hooked immediately. Within six months of initiation, Lisa was smoking daily; within a year, she was smoking all day, everyday.

At 18 Lisa was arrested for grand theft. Her husband was a purse snatcher, and Lisa would sometimes use the stolen credit cards, forging the owner's signature. One time she became "greedy" and used the cards for several days. She was arrested and spent two nights in jail. The state dropped the case so she was never convicted.

When she was four months pregnant with her second child, her husband went to prison. At the time of the interview, he was still incarcerated. She had her second child when she was 22 and her third child when she was 23. Her husband is the father of only the first two. When her husband went to prison, Lisa sent her eldest child to live with his uncle. The second child has been raised by very good friends. Neither of these children is in Miami. A crack dealer is the father of her third child, who was put up for adoption at birth. Lisa smoked crack during her second and third pregnancies, but she claims that neither of the babies were affected.

Before her husband went to prison, he paid for almost all their drugs. They would get crack at a local crack house, but smoke at home. When her husband's money would run out, Lisa would turn to prostitution. But she was never a streetwalker. Rather, she would call on acquaintances who would pay her for sex. Eventually, she started smoking in crack houses. There was one in particular she used, which she described as quite organized, with the owner providing pipes, lighters, screens, and crack. Customers paid extra to stay and smoke and use the house pipes.

Lisa considered the owner of this crack house to be her friend. She would clean his place after everybody had finished smoking, and he would frequently let her stay there. She had sex with him on several occasions, but it was never in exchange for crack. Eventually, her crack habit got out of hand, her behavior became offensive and disruptive, and she was told to leave and never return. However, the owner had another crack house about four blocks away. There, rather than paying to stay and smoke, customers shared their crack with the people running the place. Moreover, the women smoking there didn't have to *buy* crack, but could obtain it in exchange for sex. Most of the customers knew each other, but occasionally strangers would use the house. These new faces insisted that the women give them sex before they shared their crack, whereas the regulars were more laid back, understanding that they would always receive sex for the hits and rocks they gave the women.

When Lisa first started frequenting this crack house she was pregnant with her third child. The owner refused to sell her crack and told her to come back after she had had her baby. After the child was born, Lisa would stay in this house for days at a time, sometimes going for three or four days without cleaning herself. Two weeks before entering treatment, a man with whom she was having sex put her up in a hotel room, provided her with food, and kept her off the street and away from crack. She was receiving public assistance and food stamps at this time, half of which she gave to the woman who was taking care of her second child. The rest she kept for herself. Prior to these last two weeks, Lisa would spend all of her money on crack.

Lisa is currently in drug treatment. She decided that after more than a decade of drug use, the last two years of which involved crack, enough was enough. She is working on her GED and wishes to take care of her second child after she completes treatment. Her eldest is with an uncle and is happy there, and she is not permitted to see her youngest, the child she put up for adoption. She is HIV-negative, and considers herself lucky.

Sylvia M.

Sylvia M., 21 years old at the time of interview, was raised in St. Louis, Missouri, with her four brothers. Her father, a security guard, was an alcoholic and a marijuana smoker. He physically abused Sylvia and her brothers. Sylvia remembers her mother working all the time, but she can not recall exactly what she did. Her mother was often not home.

Sylvia didn't get along with her parents and began running away at age nine, primarily because her father was sexually abusing her—a trauma that continued as long as she was home. She disliked school and skipped several days a week. A truant officer tried to intervene, but Sylvia ended up in juvenile detention centers and in and out of foster homes. She also spent a lot of time on the streets as a runaway.

Her drinking began when she was nine. She and her brother, who was 11, stole liquor from their father's liquor cabinet. They would drink four or five times a week, whenever they felt they could get away with it. A year later Sylvia started stealing money from her parents to buy marijuana. She was smoking about four times a week. At 10 she started using speed — "black beauties."

By the time Sylvia was 12 she was no longer returning home. Occasionally she would spend time in a group home. She had also begun prostituting to support her drug habit. She was on the streets trying to prostitute when a pimp offered to teach her how. She would give him all the money she made and in return he would give her drugs, clothes, food, and a place to live. He had four other girls and they all lived in the same place. During this time she had four to five customers each week, and was the victim of considerable violence by both her pimp and customers. Once a customer stabbed her four times in an attempt to get money from her. She was hospitalized and had her lungs drained. Sylvia stayed with this pimp for a year until she moved to Chicago at age 15.

In Chicago, Sylvia and a female friend began stealing cars and boats and selling them. They would hot wire the cars and then hitch up trailered boats and drive off. They stole 30 cars and 7 boats, and were never caught. At about the same time Sylvia began to inject cocaine. She was staying with a prostitute who was about 21 years old. She watched this woman shoot cocaine and she then tried it on her own. Sylvia immediately began the daily use of intravenous cocaine and used for about a year and a half. When she stopped, it was to shift to crack.

Sylvia had seen other people smoking crack — other prostitutes and customers. One of her dates offered her crack and she tried it. From initiation, at age 16, Sylvia was addicted.

At 18, Sylvia became pregnant. Her child died in his sleep when he was three months old. The father of the baby was a boyfriend Sylvia had been living with for about three years.

Sylvia moved to Miami about two years ago and continues to prostitute on the streets. She worked as a dancer for a few months, but her crack habit caused her to miss work, and she lost her job.

Currently, she is smoking about $300 worth of crack a day. The more money she makes the more crack she uses. She drinks alcohol while she is smoking, but doesn't use any other drugs. She feels that alcohol helps to decrease her craving for crack, and she prefers to smoke alone. Previously she smoked in crack houses, but now considers them unsafe. She has not been in a crack house in about six months. Sylvia buys her crack on the streets. She has oral sex in cars, for which she charges $20. She insists that her dates use condoms during vaginal intercourse, and because of this she doubts that she is HIV-positive. She uses crack and other drugs with her customers, and accepts drugs as payment for sex.

Frequently, Sylvia will start work at 3 A.M. She turns enough tricks to be able to buy crack. She smokes, at home or in an alley, and returns to the streets when she has no more crack or money. Sylvia will prostitute and smoke for three- and four-day binges before returning home to sleep and bathe.

Sylvia checked herself into a six-month outpatient drug program while in Miami. She only attended a few appointments and then stopped going. She spent 60 days in jail recently for shoplifting. She stole shoes because she did not have any to wear. Sylvia has been arrested and jailed for prostitution about 30 times. She has also been arrested for armed robbery.

Sylvia would like to stop using drugs, get her life together, and get a nice apartment. She also would like to get a job working with children. She took a nurse's aide test about six months ago, but did not pass. She is currently wearing braces to hold her teeth in from when a customer hit her and rammed her chin into the dashboard of the car. She is waiting to have oral surgery, but cannot find a surgeon who will treat her. She considers crack a big problem and realizes that no one can make her stop using it until she's ready.

Sybil D.

Sybil D., 26 years old at the time of interview, was born in Cincinnati. Her mother was a prostitute, and she never knew her father. Her most vivid childhood memories revolve around her mother's prostitution — customers in their apartment, drinking and arguments, drug use, and sex. She witnessed her mother being beaten and raped several times, and at age 9 she was raped by one of her mother's tricks.

Sybil's mother was a heroin addict, and when Sybil was 10 her mother "turned her out" to prostitute for her. She started drinking then, and smoking marijuana. By the age of 11 she was soliciting on the streets of Cincinnati, but was arrested and placed in a group home. After only a month there, her mother died of a heroin overdose. Sybil ran away, and went back to the streets.

On her 12th birthday she met William, a pimp who promised her money and clothing if she would pose for pornographic films. They drove to Miami where the filming was to be done, staying at motels along the way, posing as father and daughter. Every night they would have sex, and William would instruct her in the "fine arts of good sexing" as he would call it. She didn't like it, but William was gentle, and he would always make her climax. She was ambivalent about this, because she enjoyed the pleasurable sensations but felt dirty at the same time. She reconciled her ambivalence through alcohol and marijuana — mostly marijuana, which William supplied for her.

She was used in three films during the first two weeks she was in Miami. Although she had had sex with dozens of people by the time she got into films, she hated the experience. She found it degrading, or as she put it:

> Twelve years old and makin' a living by bein' photographed with men jerkin' off and comin' on your face, suckin' a guy's cock at the same time, or havin' to lick a girl's pussy. It was awful.

She went on to state that it was a job and she needed to live, and that William was good to her. All of this time she lived in a small house that William owned in North Miami. William and his 16-year-old daughter Lilly also lived there. Lilly was also in the films, and was a prostitute as well.

For almost two years, Sybil lived with William and Lilly, doing a few films, soliciting on the streets, and having "special dates" that William would arrange with South American men who liked "young black American girls." During these years, Lilly introduced Sybil to cocaine. By the time Sybil was 16, she was heavily addicted to cocaine. William would argue with her about it, and one day he beat her and locked her in the house so she couldn't get her drugs. She eventually escaped through a window, ran away, and never went back. She hasn't seen William or Lilly since, but she heard that he was arrested on an assault charge.

Sybil lived in abandoned buildings, solicited customers, and continued using cocaine, but moderately. She got herself a job as a topless dancer in a Miami Beach club, and she felt that it was the best time of her life. She recalled:

> Men would be lookin' at me, fingerin' me a little when they put tips in my panties after each dance, an' always feelin' me, but I still felt good about myself. It was a real job, my first *real* job. I had a Social Security card that I got with a fake birth certificate, an' I was legitimate. I'd get good tips, I'd get a check each week, and I had a checking account at a bank. I got my own place, a TV and a microwave, and I had some dignity.

Sybil continued her dancing, prostitution, and cocaine use. She was arrested for soliciting several times, but never served more than a few days. She had a few boyfriends, but never anything serious. Her cocaine use escalated dramatically, and by the time she was 20 she considered herself a hardened street addict. By 21 prostitution and drug sales were her main sources of income, supplemented by shoplifting and stealing from johns. In 1986, at age 22, she was introduced to crack. She spent a lot of time in crack houses, smoking and exchanging sex for drugs and money.

In 1990, a local crack dealer brought her to a special kind of crack house, a "brothel house" as she called it. The owner was a crack dealer/ pimp she had known for some time, and the sex/drugs exchange system was somewhat unique. Sybil was to be a "house girl," and not directly involved in the payment or sex/crack bartering process. For the sexual services she would provide to customers who paid the "house man" (the house owner) for either sex or crack, she would be paid with crack, other drugs, and room and board. The primary purpose of the house seemed to be sex, not crack. She recalled in 1990:

> Bein' that I been workin' the streets since I was eleven and don't really mind sexin' a lot of different guys, I thought it would be a real easy deal for gettin' all the "cracks" [more than one rock] that I needed. So

this bond man [drug dealer] that I'd know'd real well takes me in. He says all it is is givin' a lot a brains [oral sex]. Well man, I know'd a lot a brains. I probably done more *fellatio* [her emphasis] than any lady on the street. . . .

I really got myself into somethin' bad. It wasn't just brains like he said. It was everything. There was guys pushin' their natures [genitals] everywhere — in my mouth, in my guts [vagina], up my ass; guys gettin' off in my face; one guy goin' down on me with five others watchin' and jerkin' off. Most of the time I just didn't care, 'cause I was gettin' all the rock I wanted. But times I just wanted to be left alone, but I couldn't. One time they raped me, man, they raped me, 'cause I wouldn't fuck 'em just that minute. They held me down and beat me and did all kinds of terrible things. . . . And I tried to leave but I was a prisoner there. After the rape I tried to leave, but the man at the door says he's got his orders and I can't go. So when I try to get out he slapped me around and they rape me again. They raped me again real bad this time . . . one fuck pissed on me after he was done. An' then to teach me another lesson they hold back on the pipe. . . .

After a while I got sick, and I was all bruised and looked so bad, that they threw me out. They just threw me out like I was just some piece of shit.

Shortly after this incident Sybil was arrested for armed robbery and was placed into drug treatment as a condition of probation. At the time, she was HIV-positive and already symptomatic for AIDS. In 1992, Sybil died of *P. carinii* pneumonia.

Robyn R.

Robyn R., 31 years old at the time of interview, is included in this analysis because of his female gender-role orientation. He grew up in a small town in Ohio. His mother and father divorced when he was six. Robyn saw his father on weekends and during the summer. He describes his relationship with his father as "OK, when he wasn't drinking." His mother was a barmaid and his stepfather was a carpenter. They married when Robyn was nine. He had a twin sister, and an older sister and brother, neither of whom were living at home when he was growing up. His older brother committed suicide when Robyn was an adult. Robyn describes his step-father as "alright," although he does recall being hit by him.

Robyn's first sexual experience occurred when he was 12. While his older sister was in the hospital having a baby, his brother-in-law Tom was babysitting him and his twin sister. His sister was asleep, and he and Tom were watching TV. Robyn asked Tom if he could "suck" him, and Tom said yes. Robyn had heard people at school talk about "giving head" and was curious about it. He enjoyed the experience but it never occurred again with Tom.

Two years passed before he had another sexual experience. Robyn was at his grandmother's house with one of his male cousins. They had oral sex with each other, and Robyn considered it to be no more than adolescent experimentation. At 16, however, he began frequenting gay bars every weekend. There, he would "pick up" men and have oral sex, as well as both receptive and insertive anal sex. At this time, Robyn was not using any drugs. He was drinking, however, having started at age 15 with straight bourbon to be "part of my stepfather's family." He enjoyed drinking and getting drunk.

When Robyn was 17 he spent the summer at the home of his older brother in Sanford, Florida. He got a summer job at a local restaurant, where his coworkers introduced him to Quaaludes and Valium. During this time he continued to drink and began smoking marijuana. It was routine to mix Quaaludes and rum to "lude out" (enhance the euphoria) as the expression went. Most of Robyn's drug use was limited to weekends. However, by the end of his summer stay in Florida he was using Quaaludes three or four times a week.

Robyn attributes much of his teenage drug use to his early struggles with being gay. As he put it:

> At that time I had just started becoming more open with being gay,
> and looking back now, I probably drank and used drugs because of that.

He also began having sex with men he met in both gay and straight bars and in the restaurant where he worked. Except for marijuana smoking, his drug use came to a halt when he returned to Ohio at the end of the summer. Back home, he went to straight bars, but would frequent the gay clubs in a neighboring town. After graduating from high school, Robyn worked as a welder in a car factory. Several months later he began moving around, ending up in a gay resort near Orlando, Florida. He worked in a restaurant, and was drinking heavily, smoking marijuana, and experimenting with LSD.

At age 22, Robyn's drug use increased at the same time that he began cross-dressing and impersonating women. He also began taking hormones and started looking more like a woman. Robyn then moved to Fort Lauderdale, Florida, with a gay friend who also wished to be a woman. He reduced his alcohol intake, drinking primarily as a response to his boyfriend's alcoholism. However, Robyn continued to smoke marijuana occasionally, and began snorting cocaine on a daily basis.

It was just after his move to Fort Lauderdale that he began his career in prostitution. He would solicit as a female and would frequently snort cocaine with his customers. All his customers were male, half assumed he was female, but the rest knew he was a man. He commented that getting male johns who knew he was not a woman was easy, or as he put it:

> I'd just stand on a street corner until someone came along and said:
> "Can I pop you in the ass?"

Robyn continually maintained the female role in all of his relationships. He moved in with a male lover who did not want anyone to know

Robyn was male. Both Robyn and his lover snorted cocaine three or four times a week. After about a year of living together they both quit drinking completely. However, they began to inject cocaine. It took Robyn about three months to learn to inject himself properly. Most of the time he would shoot drugs at the homes of other prostitutes. Although Robyn was injecting cocaine daily, he stayed away from heroin, fearing both addiction and withdrawal. He supported his drug habit (as well as his boyfriend's) through prostitution. Both "booted" and shared needles regularly.

After about a year, both stopped their intravenous cocaine use, shifting exclusively to daily marijuana smoking, averaging fifteen joints (cigarettes) a day. Robyn's sole source of income continued to be prostitution. His lover was a construction worker, and Robyn's prostitution caused friction in their relationship; his lover preferred that he find another kind of work. However, the money was good and Robyn had no desire to quit. He always worked on his own and never had a pimp. However, he was raped on many occasions.

Robyn and his boyfriend considered their lives to be fairly routine until Robyn acquired some crack and brought it home. One of his customers had introduced him to it. Robyn insisted that his boyfriend be included. The customer would bring crack by once a month and the three of them would smoke together. They used glass pipes because they liked to watch the smoke swirl out the stem. After several months of smoking crack only occasionally, Robyn began weekending. When business picked up during the winter, the "tourist months," he started smoking crack daily. On average, he smoked 15 rocks and drank a quart of wine every day. Eventually he got to know the local crack dealers personally. Most of his contacts were made on the streets while he was hustling. He would buy crack on the streets and smoke anywhere that was convenient.

Robyn frequented only one crack house. It had many more women than men, and it was ethnically mixed with whites, blacks, and Hispanics. Robyn assumed all the females were prostitutes and that the males were local residents. He described this crack house as very well organized, with an owner, a door man, and a lookout, as well as prostitutes provided by the crack-house owner. Occasionally he would take his customers to the crack house. They would smoke and rent a room for sex. Although a few would run away when they realized they were in a crack house, most stayed. Robyn usually knew which crack houses were being watched by the police and which ones would be raided. He stressed that the police let the prostitutes know what was going on in an attempt to get information from them.

For about one year Robyn and his boyfriend sold drugs from their apartment. His boyfriend would control the crack and Robyn would be in charge of the money. He felt this would protect them if the police raided their place. According to Robyn, they could not be arrested for selling because the person giving the crack to the customers was not collecting any money. Frequently, customers would give them jewelry, which they would pawn. Because of their success, they were burglarized by both customers and friends.

Robyn admitted that he would do anything while high on crack. He and his boyfriend often had sex in front of their crack-house customers. Many times another male customer would join them. Robyn would be the receptive partner in anal intercourse while giving oral sex to a third party. He considers these episodes as fantasies fulfilled that need not be repeated.

Eventually, Robyn and his boyfriend gave up their crack house, but they continued to use crack regularly. Robyn solicited more and more customers and as a result was constantly in and out of jail. They lost their apartment and were both living on the streets. Robyn's boyfriend blamed him for their predicament and left him. Robyn's crack use escalated; he was charging $40 and $50 for oral sex on the 10 to 15 customers he had every night, and most of that money went to crack.

When soliciting on the streets, Robyn refused to get involved with pimps, and his comments about pimps are identical to those often heard from female prostitutes. For example:

> I can't see working and giving all my money to somebody else, and getting treated like shit when they are supposed to be taking care of you. It's not true, pimps do not take care of you. They take your money and might buy you clothes every now and then, but they do nothing for you. The only time they protect you is if someone is trying to get you to leave them and they make it sound like they'll protect you but it's only because they want to keep you to work for them. And they beat you up all the time, especially if you don't make enough money for them. And I had one that was after me last week and as a matter of fact he was going to kill me because I would not give him money.

It was at about this time that Robyn found out he was HIV-positive, a condition he attributed to his increased crack use. He solicited fewer customers, and limited his activities to oral sex. However, he never told any of his clients that he was HIV-positive. Too, he became careless about choosing customers. One night he sensed that a man he was about to approach might be a police officer. Ignoring his instincts, thinking only about getting money to get more crack, he made the approach anyway. He had been correct. Robyn was arrested and spent three months in jail. While there, Robyn participated in a drug rehabilitation program. He also had anal intercourse on numerous occasions. In prison, condoms are never used because there are none available. Some inmates would improvise with rubber gloves taken from the kitchen, but this was rare.

After his release, Robyn entered a drug treatment program, where he was contacted for this study. At the time, he was 31 years old. His ambitions are to remain drug-free, attend school, and eventually become a drug counselor. He also looks forward to taking hormones again and dressing as a woman, neither of which he was permitted to do while in jail and treatment.

Endnote

1. William Healy, *The Individual Delinquent* (Boston: Little, Brown, 1915); W. I. Thomas and Florian Znaniecki, *The Polish Peasant in Europe and America* (Chicago: University of Chicago Press, 1918).

APPENDIX C

A Glossary of Crack-House Lingo

Groups that are devoted to specialized activities or purposes peripheral to the mainstream of society have a unique and artificial language. Moreover, every trade, occupation, and profession has its distinctive vocabulary. Physicians, attorneys, probations officers, sociologists, and cooks and secretaries all have a jargon of their own, designed to fit their special interests. Slang, jargon, argot, lingo, cant, or whatever other designation is preferred, is a verbal camouflage with its own symbolism that serves many purposes. It may reflect both isolation and in-group solidarity; it may emphasize the attitudes and values of the group while down-grading those of the rest of society; and is typically a shorthand referencing for artifacts, activities, and technical processes that are not easily communicated through conventional language.

Crack-house lingo seems to be most of these things. Furthermore, it reflects much of the content of the culture of crack users and dealers. The terms and usages which follow were recorded in Miami from crack users, dealers, and others in contact with crack-house life.

backs A single "hit" on a crack pipe.

back up The second "hit" on a pipe, generally described as far less potent than the first.

bake, baking Crack, or the process of making crack.

base Any form of cocaine base, including crack and freebase.

base baby A child conceived and gestated by a crack-using mother.

base, butter, cents, or head A soliciting slogan used in the crack house to negotiate the sex-for-crack exchange. Translation: "For some crack, cocaine, or money, I will give oral sex."

base gangs People in crack houses who beg for drugs or otherwise attempt to obtain crack from other customers by devious means.

base car An abandoned car used as a place to smoke crack.

base heads People who exchange sex for crack in crack houses.

base house A crack house.

base whores Women who exchange sex for crack in crack houses.

basing Making crack.

beam A single "hit" of crack, as in "Beam me up Scotty," from TV's "Star Trek." See *Scotty.*

beejay or BJ Oral sex, short for "blow job."

bitch A woman; a prostitute.

black beauties Amphetamines.

bloodsucker A woman who performs oral sex on a menstruating woman.

blowing bubbles Blowing crack smoke into the vagina.

blow job Oral sex by either a man or woman.

blow up Chemical additives used to increase the size of crack rocks. "With some blow up you can make a nickel rock look like a dime rock."

blueberry A lesbian who will exchange sex for crack with a man or woman.

board The table or board in a crack house where the crack is displayed.

board man The person in the crack house who maintains the board. It is generally a man, and he rarely handles the money.

bomb bag A large white plastic bag in which drugs are delivered to a crack house.

bond man A drug dealer.

booting A process involving the use of a syringe to draw blood from the user's arm, mixing the drawn blood with the drug already taken into the syringe, and then injecting it back into the vein.

boulder A large piece of crack.

boy Heroin. See *girl.*

boys and girls Heroin and cocaine.

brains Oral sex.

brick A large slab of crack.

bubb A "hit" of crack or a snort of cocaine.

bugging out Behaving in a paranoid manner, as the result of crack or cocaine use.

bum rush Oral sex to a woman, by a man or another woman.

butter *Powder*-cocaine.

caine Cocaine or crack.

cap A vial in which crack is packaged for sale.

change purse A vagina.

chickenhead A woman in a crack house who will do anything, usually sexual in nature, for a "hit" or piece of crack.

clocking Selling crack in a street drug market.

cocaine coma The prolonged period of sleep that follows several days of binging on crack without sleeping.

coke Cocaine or crack.

coke house A crack house.

combolo A Spanish term for crack.

come To climax.

comeback Chemical additives used to increase the size of crack rocks. See *blow up*.

cooker 1) A person in a crack house who makes crack; 2) For injecting drug use, a small container—bottle cap, baby food jar, etc.—used to mix heroin or cocaine with water prior to putting it into a syringe.

cookie A large quantity of crack, approximately 90 rocks.

cop To purchase drugs. "You watch while I cop."

cop man A drug dealer.

copping area A place where drugs are bought and sold.

crack Crack has a variety of meanings: 1) *crack*-cocaine; 2) a vagina; 3) vaginal intercourse; 4) a prostitute; 5) a woman who exchanges sex-for-crack in crack houses.

crack for crack Exchanging sex for crack. "Let me give you some *brains*, or some *crack for crack*." See *brains*.

crack house A place where crack is bought, sold, and/or smoked.

crackie A woman who exchanges sex for crack in crack houses.

cracks More than one crack rock.

crack spot A crack house.

crack whore A woman who exchanges sex for crack in crack houses.

creeping Stealing pocketbooks from cars in gas stations while the customer is inside paying for gas.

crib A crack house.

crucial An especially long or good hit of crack. "I needed a *crucial* to get myself right."

date The male customer of a prostitute, or a person who purchases sex in a crack house. Same as *trick* and *john*.

dealer 1) a drug seller; 2) the owner of a crack house.

devil's dick A crack pipe. "It seems like all I do is suck men's dicks so I can suck the *devil's dick*."

dime, dime rock, dime vial A $10 piece of crack.

D.O.A. Heroin.

doctor A person who injects drugs into someone else's arm for a small fee. "I can never hit the vein, so I get a *doctor* to hit it for me."

doo-doo The residue left in a pipe after the crack has been smoked.

doo-wap Two crack rocks.

dope man A person who sells crack.

drug hounds Regulars in a crack house. Same as *rock hounds*.

door man The person at the door of a crack house who lets people in, checks for weapons, and watches for police.

downers Depressant drugs, such as tranquilizers and barbiturates.

eightball A large quantity of crack, generally an eighth of an ounce, and sold in a block form.

fast head Oral sex during which the penis is sucked very rapidly. See *slow neck*.

fire A lighter, match, or torch used to vaporize crack.

flavor Crack.

freak, freaking A *freak* was originally a *crack whore* who would engage in oral sex with another woman. However, it now refers to anyone who trades any type of sex for crack. It also refers to a male giving oral sex to a woman. "He wanted both of us in the bed so we got into bed. We laid side by side. He wanted us to *freak* with each other but we did not . . . . But still we both laid there and he *freaked* both of us . . . oral sex, he did it all to her."

freak room A separate room in a crack house where sexual activity occurs. "I would lock people up in the *freak room* so they were alone. I would give them a key for the inside to let themselves out, but I would lock them up so no one could get into where they were at. I'd give them thirty minutes for $10 in the *freak room*, it was nice."

freebase Cocaine in its base form after all the impurities have been removed.

freebasing Smoking any form of cocaine base (*crack* or *freebase*).

fuck the dog To waste time. "When he's all done [climaxing] I don't *fuck the dog*, I get rid of it quick. Spit it out."

geek cigarette A marijuana or tobacco cigarette laced with crack. See *geek joint* and *lace joint*.

geek joint A marijuana cigarette laced with crack.

get-off house A crack house, or a *shooting gallery*.

girl Cocaine. See *boy*.

girls Street prostitutes.

G-man The bouncer or security man in a crack house.

G-rock A piece of crack weighing one gram.

gorilla, gorilla pimp Crack or cocaine.

gram rock A piece of crack weighing one gram.

graveyard An abandoned building used as a crack house.

guard dog A man, woman, or child working in or for a crack house who watches for the police. Same as a *look-out man* or *watch back*.

gut bucket A woman who exchanges sex for crack in a crack house.

guts, gut A vagina.

half house Oral and vaginal sex sold as a package deal. "How 'bout *half house* for that rock there?"

handball Crack.

hand job Masturbation, done for one person by another.

hard white Crack.

head, heads Oral sex.

head, bully, or cock A soliciting slogan used in the crack house to negotiate the sex-for-crack exchange. Translation: "For some crack, cocaine, or money, I will give oral, anal, or vaginal sex."

head hunter A woman who trades sex for crack in a crack house.

head job Oral sex.

high   Euphoria.

hit house   A crack house.

hole   1) a bad neighborhood; 2) a vagina; 3) a prostitute.

house girl   A woman who literally lives in a crack house, and who provides sex to the customers smoking in the crack house.

house lady   Same as *house girl*.

house man   The owner of a crack house.

hut   A crack house.

jizz   Semen.

john   The male customer of a prostitute, or a person who purchases sex in a crack house. Same as *trick* and *date*.

joint   A crack or marijuana cigarette.

juggling   Selling crack, or any drug, for double what it is worth.

jungle   A crack house.

kibbles and bits   Small pieces of crack.

kingrat   A crack-house owner.

lace joint   A marijuana cigarette laced with crack. Same as a *geek joint*.

look-out man   A man, woman, or child working in or for a crack house who watches for the police. Same as a *guard dog* or *watch back*.

mainlining   Injecting drugs into the vein.

mastercharge   A crack pipe. "Don't leave home without your mastercharge."

Miami device   A crack smoking device, usually made from a small liquor bottle, pill bottle, soda can, or baby food jar. Same as *ouzie*.

mission   A crack smoking binge, lasting several days, during which users do not eat or sleep.

Mr. Windows   A crack user who has become so paranoid from smoking cocaine that he or she thinks the police are everywhere. Same as *window watcher*.

natures   Male or female genitals.

nickel, nickel rock, nickel vial   A $5 piece of crack.

nine!   A warning that police are in the area.

nut   An orgasm, usually from oral sex. "Stoney was real happy, because he was just a green kid and was happy to have me *get off his nut* (make him climax)."

off the stroll   Having retired from prostitution. See *stroll*.

on the stem   Smoking crack.

outlaw   A prostitute who works without a pimp.

ouzie   A crack smoking device, usually made from a small liquor bottle, pill bottle, soda can, or baby food jar. Same as *Miami device*.

pee   Pure cocaine.

paymaster   A man who purchases sex in a crack house.

penny, penny rock   A single hit of crack given to a woman in exchange for oral sex.

peter A penis, but sometimes used to reference a vagina.

pimp A man who solicits for a prostitute and receives all or part of the money she earns in return for giving her protection and shelter.

pimp stick A can opener or other jagged object used to damage the vagina or face of a prostitute.

pin baby A woman who provides sex for small amounts of crack.

pin bride Same as a *pin baby.*

ping ting ting A Spanish term for *geek joint.*

pin joint A small *geek joint.*

piper A crack smoker.

player A pimp.

product Crack or cocaine. "When he runs out of *product,* he does anything for more, even fist-fuck a man in the ass."

puff Bogus or imitation crack. Same as *wax.*

pussy 1) a vagina; 2) a prostitute.

pussy power Using sexual leverage to obtain crack. "If I want to use my pussy I can always get as much as I want. The pussy works. It's called *pussy power.*"

pussy sex Vaginal intercourse.

raspberry A male who exchanges sex for crack in a crack house.

ready rock Crack.

regulars A prostitute's regular customers.

resort A crack house in which crack is prepared, bought, sold, and smoked, and in which sex is traded for crack.

rez The residue in the pipe after a rock is smoked. It is scraped off the pipe and either sold or resmoked.

rim job To lick the anus. Same as *rimming.*

rimming To lick the anus. Same as *rim job.*

road dog A street companion. Same as *running buddy.* "It is the man who watches out for you. The guy who watches your back when you do crimes, he watch out for AIDS, he took care of my insecurity and I provided him with dope and stuff like that."

rock Crack.

rock castle A fortified drug house where crack is manufactured.

rock master A crack dealer or owner of a crack house.

rock monster Any person who trades sex for crack in a crack house.

rock star A woman who trades sex for crack in a crack house.

roxanne Same as an *ouzie.*

rubber A condom.

rubber man A person who either sells condoms to prostitutes or distributes them free as part of an AIDS prevention project.

running buddy A street companion. Same as *road dog.*

rush The intense flood of pleasure that is felt soon after drug intake.

safe house A *shooting gallery.*

Scotty Crack, from "Beam me up Scotty," of TV's "Star Trek."

scrug Any person who attempts to get sex for free in a crack house.

sex To have sex. "After I *sexed* him, he gave me a 'hit.'"

shake The shavings from crack rocks when they are broken to be sold in smaller quantities. *Shake* is often smoked in *geek joints*.

shit Drugs or money.

shooters Drug injectors.

shoot up. To inject drugs.

shotgun The smoke inhaled from a crack pipe and blown into someone else's mouth so they can get high from the same "hit."

shooting gallery A place where injection equipment is rented and drugs are injected.

skeeter head A women who trades sex for crack in a crack house.

skeezer A women who trades sex for crack in a crack house.

skillet A pipe used to smoke crack.

skin-popping The intramuscular (into the muscle) or subcutaneous (under the skin) injection of cocaine, narcotics, and other drugs.

slaying Paying a prostitute before receiving sex, and then stealing the money back or taking it by force after the sex.

sleigh Vaginal intercourse.

slobbing on Bob Providing oral sex.

slow neck Oral sex during which the penis is sucked very slowly, as compared to a *fast head* where the intent is to bring the customer to a climax as quickly as possible. *Slow necks* typically cost more than *fast heads*.

smack Heroin.

smoke house A crack house.

space base A mixture of crack and PCP. Same as *space rock*.

space rock A mixture of crack and PCP. Same as *space base*.

speed Amphetamine or methamphetamine.

speedball A mixture of heroin and cocaine, or heroin and amphetamine, typically injected.

splitting Rolling marijuana and crack into a single "joint."

stem A pipe used to smoke crack.

straight shooter A long metal or glass stem about eight inches long used to smoke crack.

strawberry A young girl who exchanges sex for crack in a crack house.

streetwalker A prostitute.

street worker A prostitute.

stroll The major streets where prostitutes solicit customers.

taste A sample of someone else's drugs. "This lady was so crazy for the drug that she'd suck me just for a *taste*."

technician A person who makes crack-smoking paraphernalia, or shows people how to smoke crack.

tool Any type of crack-smoking paraphernalia.

toss-up A woman who exchanges sex for crack in a crack house.

trick The male customer of a prostitute, or a person who purchases sex in a crack house. Same as *date* and *john*.

trick baby A prostitute's baby fathered by a *john*.

turning out Becoming a prostitute; a prostitute having his or her first customer.

turn-out Someone who recently became a prostitute.

turning tricks Prostitutes providing sex to customers.

tweaking While high on crack, imagining that every speck of dirt on the floor is a piece of crack, and hence, picking up and examining these specks. "They was all *tweaking*, down on their hands and knees on the floors, crawling around, picking up every little thing they saw."

uppers Stimulant drugs, such as amphetamines.

v-up A term used by crack-house owners to tell customers that they must either buy more crack or leave the house.

watch back A man, woman, or child working in or for a crack house who watches for the police. Same as a *guard dog* or *look out man*.

wax Bogus or imitation crack. Same as *puff*.

white Crack.

white cloud Crack.

window watcher A crack user who has become so paranoid from smoking cocaine that he or she thinks the police are everywhere. Same as *Mr. Windows*.

works Drug paraphernalia, usually drug injectors.

Name Index

Subject Index

About the Authors

James A. Inciardi (Ph.D. in Sociology, New York University, 1973) is the director of the Center for Drug and Alcohol Studies at the University of Delaware and a professor in the University's Department of Sociology and Criminal Justice (and formerly the director of the Division of Criminal Justice from 1976 through mid-1991). Dr. Inciardi has an appointment in the Comprehensive Drug Research Center at the University of Miami School of Medicine and is a member of the South Florida AIDS Research Consortium. Before coming to Delaware, Dr. Inciardi was director of the National Center for the Study of Acute Drug Reactions at the University of Miami, vice-president of the Washington, D.C. – based Resource Planning Corporation, and associate director of research for the New York State Narcotic Addiction Control Commission. With almost 30 years of experience in the drug field, he has done extensive consulting work both nationally and internationally and has published more than 150 articles, chapters, books, and monographs in the areas of substance abuse, criminology, criminal justice, history, folklore, social policy, AIDS, medicine, and law.

Dorothy Lockwood (M.A. in Sociology, University of Delaware, 1987) is an associate scientist with the Center for Drug and Alcohol Studies at the University of Delaware. She is the co-principal investigator and project director of a major drug-abuse treatment demonstration grant funded by the National Institute on Drug Abuse. Prior to joining the Center, Ms. Lockwood was a research specialist at the Delaware Council on Crime and Justice where she conducted policy-oriented research on both the adult and juvenile justice systems and evaluations of state-operated offender programs. She has numerous publications and presentations on drug abuse treatment for offenders, therapeutic communities, women and drug use, and substance abuse.

Anne E. Pottieger (Ph.D. in Sociology, University of Delaware, 1977) is a scientist at the Center for Drug and Alcohol Studies at the University of Delaware. Dr. Pottieger has been the project director and co-principal investigator for several grants funded by the National Institute on Drug Abuse, including studies of self-reported crime among heroin users, criminal patterns among women drug users, and the role of drug use in serious delinquency. Her publications include numerous articles, chapters, and books on drug/crime relationships, criminological theory, drug research methodology, drug emergencies, and juvenile delinquency.